In the Chinese city

Perspectives on the transmutations of an empire

Table of contents

Collection edited by Frédéric Edelmann, editorial coordination by Yves Kirchner, scientific oversight by Francoise Ged, Head of the Research Observatory of Architecture in Contemporary China.

Prefaces

In the Chinese city
François de Mazières

Ideology and transformation
Josep Ramoneda

The fascination with the grand scale
Francis Rambert

Introductions

Questions on the transformations of an empire
Frédéric Edelmann

Cities and filmmakers
Jordi Balló

Note: on occasion we have been obliged to retain the traditional written form or the form provided by the authors, rather than unifying the Chinese terms in pinyin.

In the Chinese city

With *In the Chinese city* and *Positions*, in the summer of 2008 at Palais de Chaillot, the Cité de l'architecture & du patrimoine is seeking to cast new light on architecture and the city in China. Co-produced with the Centre de Cultura Contemporània de Barcelona, this exhibition will be shown in Spain in the autumn of 2008.

In the Chinese City: the task is not without ambition, an exhibition on Chinese cities, which have been changing at such a rate in the last two decades that we don't know which to focus on—apprehension, jubilation at the powers of transformation, the quality of the innovations, sadness at the scale of the destruction, of the pollution... In this, our ambition resembles that of the knife grinder. It is about looking: presenting multiple viewpoints, slowly deciphering things and describing contradictory situations where they exist, to elicit questions and analyses. Because of this, we are convinced, as are all those we have interest in China, that we share common questions regardless of borders: what should be our attitude to the city for the inhabitants of today and of the decades to come, what capacity does architecture have to give life to yesterday's heritage and a heritage that will bring pride tomorrow, and in so doing, what tools, what practices, what experiences can we share, with regard to the ever more densely populated metropolis? Do not relations of urbanity begin, in Chinese, with the ideogram that combines the figure "two" (the plural), with the character for "man"?

Presenting a plurality of perspectives and impressions obviously calls upon cinema and photography. In this respect, we are particularly happy to share this adventure with the Barcelona Centre for Contemporary

Culture, an expert in transverse approaches and multimedia, with which we express our common wish to go beyond the frontiers of Europe and to combine talents. It is first of all the filmmakers, photographers and writers of China who encourage us to speak of the city by and with cinema, all those artists whose stories arouse the anxieties, the passions and the hopes of those millions of citizens confronted with the changes of a particularly bloody 20th century, actors and witnesses to the sought-after integration into international currents of this early 21st century.

For the first time, remarkable objects from China are to be presented in Europe—a 100m^2 model of the city of Beijing at the end of the 20th century, ancient models of traditional timber architecture, a historic rubbing of the Suzhou stele, then called Pingjiang—are displayed alongside classical works preserved in our museums, combined with contemporary models of ambitious architectural projects, the new emblems of the cities.

These images, models and films of China cannot be shown without China, and this is the outcome of a long effort, headed by Frédéric Edelmann, general curator of the exhibition, with the support of Françoise Ged, head of the Observatory of Contemporary Chinese Architecture, which is part of the Cité de l'architecture & du patrimoine. The Observatory, created in 2001, is now recognized by architecture and urban planning professionals of both our countries.

May these proofs of friendship and trust from all the personalities involved, creators, professionals and institutions in China, close partners such as Tongji University and new lenders, help us advance further in our mutual need for sharing and knowledge.

François de Mazières
President of the Cité de l'architecture & du patrimoine

Ideology and transformation

One day, economists and historians may be able to explain the brutal transformation currently underway in China, a country where almost everything is only two or three years old, and the oldest things you see are ten years old. There are divergences between those who see the Chinese process as a large-scale repetition of other processes that have taken place in the past in connection with the rise of capitalism, and those who think that a different model may be emerging, one that obeys laws with which we are not yet fully familiar. No one, however, dares to pronounce on the future of this model, which has changed the physiognomy of the country in 15 years, applying the principle of creative destruction at a dizzying rate, vastly outpacing Marx's most visionary predictions.

It all begins with demographics. One billion three hundred million people constitute an immeasurable force, particularly if they are ready for anything, raised in an age-old culture of submission and respect for hierarchy. Hundreds of millions of people have already abandoned the countryside to seek work in the city, bringing about unprecedented levels of internal migration. And there remains a reserve army of millions more who, when they leave their place of residence, become displaced persons in their own country, ready to go anywhere to find work. And all this under the authority of a Communist party that has spawned a new dominant elite made up of a modern breed of party cadres, the new business leaders and the strong men of science and technology. Subjected to tremendous political, economic and social pressure, the landscape of the cities is changing at fantastic speed. Everything old falls before the bulldozers and diggers. With the failure of the socialist utopia, citizens must now join in a new dream: China, the great power, capable once again of being the world's leading nation. The nationalism of Greater China is the ideological merchandise that the government peddles, to the cost of minorities such as the Tibetans.

China's cities are unrecognizable to anyone who saw them fifteen or twenty years ago. Whilst the unstoppable transformation continues, we thought it would be interesting to focus on Chinese urban culture. To excavate the cultural and historical roots of the Chinese city as the basis for an archaeology of the modern city. And to show the modern Chinese city as a way of understanding the scope of the great rupture currently in progress, whilst at the same time pointing out the slender lines of continuity between the two of them. The aim, therefore, is to consider a few myths of Chinese urban culture and see how they might develop in the future. From Chongqing (China's biggest city), which feels like another planet, to Beijing, with its signs and trappings of power, via Shanghai, which still has something of the bourgeois city, samples taken from the Chinese urban world will bring the visitor closer to this apparently limitless emerging power, which fascinates and worries the western world in equal measure.

The urban role of the two institutions organising this exhibition—Cité de l'architecture & du patrimoine in Paris and the Centre de Cultura Contemporània de Barcelona—fully justifies this joint gamble. China today is still a big unknown in the West, which perceives it with prejudices— favourable and unfavourable—that do not aid understanding. The fascination that China arouses in sectors of the business world suggests that their rejection of the Soviet Union was not because it was Communist, but because it was inefficient in its exploitation of labour. Western political leaders contemplate it with a mixture of fear and hesitation, but are very afraid to arouse the ire of the Beijing government. In either case, the words change depending whether the emphasis is placed on macroeconomic data, the treatment of citizens or neo-imperial great power pretensions. In the face of such confusion, the exhibition claims only to present a series of references and icons of the past and realities of the present. A grain of sand so that European citizens can begin to penetrate that particular phenomenon which is the great urban transformation of China.

Josep Ramoneda
Director of the CCCB

The fascination
with the grand scale

Megacities, metropolises, satellite cities, themed cities, "gated communities", "eco-cities", *lilong, hutong*... The city is a plurality. Hence the multiplicity of "Perspectives on the transmutations of an empire" afforded by the exhibition *In the Chinese city* curated by Frédéric Edelmann.

The scope is wide. Extra-wide. Mounting an exhibition on the contemporary city implies immersing oneself in the immensity of the Chinese landscape and its history. Without assumptions, far from the beaten track and ready-made images on the modernisation of China, the exhibition subtly establishes the links between Chinese culture and the present-day city. Formerly a place of hierarchy, now hyper-globalised. Let us take a second look at the word *Chengshi*, the Chinese for city, a combination of two words—*cheng*—meaning rampart—and *shi*—meaning market. Few ramparts remain, but shopping centres are countless...

The six city portraits filmed specially for the exhibition by young Chinese filmmakers directed by Jia Zhang Ke, author of *Still Life*, record the upheavals that fascinate so many of us.

Yes, in a country of ever present rurality, the Chinese city is undergoing a profound transformation, a transformation as much about explosion as composition. Density is at the heart of this great urban adventure. And mobility is a major factor to be integrated into the contemporary landscape. The shift from the bicycle to the car has also contributed to the city's changing physiognomy. Hence the proliferation of urban highways, creating a new layer 7m up, the locus of all the city's traffic jams and travelling shots. And, whilst the undersides of these powerful infrastructures provide a backdrop for light shows reminiscent of Miami, photographers enjoy the giant spaghetti of the city centre interchanges.

Economic growth and urbanisation go together. Over fifty years, China's transformation has been driven by urban demographics. In 2007, more than 45% of the Chinese population (i.e. 600 million people) was living in cities, compared with only 13.6% in 1954. And China now has 37 cities with more than a million inhabitants, as well as several megacities like Shanghai, a mushrooming city of more than 15 million, Beijing, as big as Île de France, or Chongqing municipality, equivalent in size to Benelux. And it would be interesting to compare the area of Shenzhen with that of Los Angeles... Seeing these figures, it is tempting to think that construction in China is about mastering the grand scale, like the 3000 km of the Great Wall. Only 3000! And the immense and famous Three Gorges Dam project, which displaced some 4 million people, would only confirm the impression. This is a country where transformation means migration.

Exclusive to China, we also see a sort of "museification" of this great, all-encompassing transformation. Proud of its development, each big city has set up its own "urban planning museum", whose focus is not the past (the destruction of the old districts is scarcely mentioned) but resolutely the future.

In Shanghai, for example, the building stands beside the city hall, in counterpoint with the Grand Theatre and opposite the Arts Museum. Is this a sign that urban planning is one of the fine arts? In fact, urban planning is a new concept for the Middle Kingdom. It appears for the first time in 1930, in connection with a premonitory "Greater Shanghai". It was not until 1952, the year of Le Corbusier's Living Unit in Marseille, that an *ad hoc* department was created at Tongji University, again in Shanghai.

The aim of this first exhibition on the Chinese city is precisely to look at the scope of these urban phenomena, and at new typologies of districts and other urban fragments.

One is reminded of Rem Koolhaas and his pioneering Harvard research project on the emergence of the Pearl River Delta. Noteworthy too is the sustained interest shown by French architecture schools (in particular the Nantes, Malaquais, Versailles trio) in the laboratory of the Chinese city. The Beijing Olympic Games, with their significant icons and other major buildings, and soon the 2010 Universal Exhibition in Shanghai, both contributory factors in accelerating urban transformation, will serve only to whet the appetite for this urban substance.

Francis Rambert
Director of the French Institute of Architecture

Xihuangsi Buddhist Temple, 7 July 1912. Stéphane Passet
© Albert Kahn Museum

Questions on the transformations of an empire

Frédéric Edelmann

Never in human history has a country experienced so great a transformation in so short a time. It is legitimate in fact to speak of an explosion, a paroxysmal version of a collection of changes on a scale—that of China or the Middle Empire (*Zhongguo*)—to which simplistic responses, not to say a single perspective, would be inappropriate. As will be seen later, we began this task with a number of initial assumptions. These assumptions were born of the clash of multiple and contradictory feelings and observations that China arouses. They are also partly attributable to Chinese poetry, or even Western poetry, both of which are capable of fine moments of complicity. And finally, they contain a certainty: there is no single truth, whatever the perspective from which we regard the country, be it philosophical, urban, economic, cultural, etc.

Dream China, real China

Sometimes, we have to accept the coexistence of opposing points of view, without seeking to solve equations whose solution, if there is one, lies in the future. On the other hand, we can make a simple observation: the image that China conveys, like the image—however pluralistic—that external observers have of it, is incomplete and false, like those postcards which, by focusing attention on a fragment of reality, miss out the essential. So it is in those photos of Beijing or of the canals of Suzhou, composed to eliminate the tower blocks and skyscrapers that now typify the skylines. Better still, or worse, they let us believe in the permanence of a China which, in essence, no longer exists and, by definition, they give us none of the keys to the understanding of a country isolated by its languages and its writing, which too few people seek to understand.

Otherness is thus posited as an absolute. However, this impression is reinforced by what we are generally allowed to see of the country: its archaeological remains, its painting, fragments of culture defended by the guard dogs of sinology, as Paul Nizan might have written. The China that is delivered to the public is inaccessible, a dream, more than a real China. What we seek to provide here is the vision of a real China, yet with the certainty that the dream can re-emerge at any time, reflecting the fascination that seizes us at the scope and speed of the country's transformations.

The exhibition framework...

To attain this reality, which we well know cannot be captured within the covers of a book or the framework of an exhibition, we have applied the following methods and principles.

Within the Cité de l'Architecture & du Patrimoine, an institution that seeks to link the past and the contemporary, but has no aspirations to universality, we have confined our attention to the cities, entities with multiple embodiments and dimensions in space and time. Then, in this plurality of the city, we have attempted to find common themes, whether historical, geographical or cultural, and to drive the point home we have taken six examples—the most we could aspire to—out of the unlimited inventory of urban examples that the country offers. Since everyone has "their own idea" of China, no one will rediscover in our approach the memories of their most recent trip.

It would have been impossible to leave out Beijing and Shanghai, or likewise Canton, which we chose as the primary focus of the Pearl River Delta. Chongqing, the least well-known of the country's great cities, proved essential for the strategic, urban and human issues that it enabled us to elicit. We could have chosen Hangzhou as the archetypal city of culture, but finally Suzhou won out, because of its richly documented urban history. Xi'an might seem a stereotypical choice but there is such a contradiction between the supposedly ideal image of the first imperial city (Chang'An) and what it has now become, that it seems to us a worthy representative of other cities like Shenyang, Anyang, Kaifeng, Zhengzhou, Chengdu, Taiyuan or even Nanjing. The absence of Lhassa should not be seen as a political statement.

Whilst the political situation of Tibet, a civilisation clearly identifiable by its language, its customs, and its history, cannot be ignored, Lhassa's destiny is neither more nor less enviable in terms of heritage and urban development than that of the great cities within China. For us, the issue of Tibet is primarily indicative of the Chinese government's concern about the growing problem of water reserves. The largest reserves are located in the great lakes on the high plains of Tibet, which are also the source of the country's main rivers, the Yangtze (Blue River) and the Yellow River, as well as the Mekong, also called the Red River. In addition to Tibet's role as a water tower, there is also the less immediately urgent question of its significant mineral reserves, and the quest for "secure" borders for a China which, despite its current might, continues to see itself as surrounded. In this respect, the question of other border regions, such as Xinjiang, and of the rights of the peoples who are their historic occupants, is no less noteworthy than the fate of the Tibetans, nor indeed of the hundreds of millions of Han, the majority ethnic group, whose rights are trammelled by their unfathomable poverty and the geographical dependence imposed on them by the "hukou", a document that combines the demands of a passport and the information content of an identity card.

Similarly, we make no specific allusion to the matter of religions (Buddhism, Taoism) or to that of the dominant philosophical current (Confucianism for more than 2000 years). Our approach is more to seek out the temples behind the walls of the factories that now occupy them, to understand the physical structure of the Confucian schools and their place in the city, or of the *Yamen*, headquarters of the imperial prefectures, or the location of the towers where bells and drums once orchestrated the patterns and rituals of the cities...

... and what underlies that framework

The things we have left out also correspond to the fields best served by historians and sinologists. However, the very choices we have made can give fragmentary life to all the realities left by the wayside. One of these realities, in fact the first, is the Chinese countryside, more than half of a total population of more than 1.3 billion. For no town rat can exist without the country rat. The history of the countryside is that of a peasantry that has always been called upon to build roads, canals and cities. So they are in that respect omnipresent in these pages.

Nor have we alluded to the rich diversity still, for the present, to be found in the towns and villages. It is here that the legacy, the immense variety and diversity of Chinese architecture, still survives. Although damaged by the instability of the ground, by floods, wars and the cruelties of the Maoist period, many have remained, if not intact, at least sufficiently uniform to give us a true picture of what China was, to maintain the link between past and present, to make the country's culture readable. The rural exodus and overpopulation are helping to create the conditions of their demise. Tourism has been recruited to save some of the most prestigious of these sites. But tourism is what, most radically, deprives them of their authenticity, into the remotest reaches of Yunnan, of Hunan or of Xinjian, which are also the regions of the great cultures, the Zhuangs, the Uyghurs, the Miaos, the Yi... This phenomenon also threatens certain Han "minorities" like the Hakka (or Kejia), whose formerly indestructible fortress villages (*tulou*) in the Fujian region are beginning to dissolve beneath the rains.

Mao again, where the Chinas meet

This multiple universe somehow continues to coexist with the explosion of the megacities, with the uncontrollable—if not uncontrolled—transformations of the Middle Kingdom.

Contrary to popular western belief, this explosion which—in a supposedly communist country—is engendering a nation marked by a paroxysmal form of economic liberalism, is a recent phenomenon: less than two decades in its urban and architectural dimension.

The prevailing sense is that of a sort of continuity, of which Mao Zedong remains the emblematic symbol. But if there is no clearly stated historical (or at least political) discontinuity in the recent period, how do we explain these transformations which are dramatically apparent in the scope and image of the cities, so clearly advantaged compared with the rural populations? How do we connect them with the major ruptures that have marked the 20th century, paradoxically less well-known, it is true, than the historical upheavals of Imperial China. The absence of clear information, or rather the occupation of the "terrain" by propaganda of all kinds, helps to confuse the issues. Just one example: the comparison of the metamorphosis of Beijing (or in reality of all the cities) with that of Paris under Napoleon III certainly reveals a misunderstanding of the work of Haussmann and his team, but also an abysmal blindness to the mechanisms operating in the Chinese capital and in the megacities inspired by it, in a spirit of emulation. Likenesses are not similarities. The fact that we have forgotten the sufferings of poor Parisians in the 1850s and 1860s does not legitimise an acceptance of the sterilisation of China's cities to the almost exclusive benefit of the rich or well-off, a minority in today's People's Republic of China.

There is no shortage of talented sinologists. But they are scattered, probably too few in number given the multiplicity of the issues, and often specialised in fields which—because they upset no one—are the only ones to receive financial resources. In China itself, an intellectual elite is reemerging, but analysis, a critical or simply sociological attitude, remains much less important than the obligation to act that arises out of their observations. The freedom of the individual, the survival of the families of academics and researchers is threatened the moment the yellow line of political correctness is crossed. It therefore demands great self-sacrifice of contemporary historians, even historians of architecture or heritage, to speak freely and to survive in what has become the empire both of poverty and of a sometimes unbridled luxury.

The weight of the past

Twentieth-century China grew out of successive ruptures in which foreign powers played a major role, either as importers or instigators of violence, or as inspirers of theory or suppliers of dogmas for the two pivotal moments that were the revolution of 1911 and the birth of the People's Republic in 1949.

One of the difficulties of the exhibition plan and of this work is to differentiate between the history of events, social history and individual history. In a country of such size, and in the historical murk that continues to surround it, how do you separate the major historical events, the life of a population that follows, independently if not docilely, its own patterns, and finally the specific timeframe of the cities, the processes that drive their silent or sudden transformations. As everywhere else, the transformations of urban landscapes, the changes in mentalities and behaviours, the publication of decrees, the shifts of power, all belong to different registers. But in China, all these things follow laws completely different from those of nations more familiar to us.

In the 19th century, "unequal treaties" opened the way to the physical metamorphosis of urban landscapes and infrastructures. The photographers of the time brought back images of China which seem to show a profound uprooting of the country. The structures of the cities and buildings are damaged. Outside the cities, the archaeological features revealed by Victor Segalen or Édouard Chavannes and of course the visual record preserved by Albert Kahn, suggest a state of deterioration, a lack of maintenance, sometimes ruins, the type of ruins that speak of abandonment. We think that there was greater continuity with the past than in Europe perhaps out of ignorance and undoubtedly also because of the "delay" in industrialisation. Nonetheless, each feature has the appearance of fragility due to neglect, as if the country were held in a sort of limbo, like a sleeping kingdom.

It is not just the weeds growing from the roofs or the temple courtyards that alert us. All these photos seem to suggest that after the Opium Wars, as imperial power unravelled, rituals and the value of the objects or monuments through which they operate, have lost part of their meaning. China is weighed down by too heavy a legacy, whose ubiquitous magnificence has become impossible to maintain. This feeling is perhaps an illusion fostered by the relatively short period over which these pictures were taken. That might be true for each individual collection, but the accumulation of evidence is troubling. It could also arise from the fact that these photographers are themselves trailing the progress and construction of the railways, and therefore see only a linear slice of the country, a modern version of the silk route. But can one genuinely only see these images as false testimony, partial in both senses of the word, a generalised aestheticism of a decaying legacy? How then should we see China? Do we have enough facts to imagine the empire already fragmented, to re-establish a continuous geography between its pockets of wealth and poverty, its cities and its deserts? How should we see early 20th-century China other than as a tangle like the Great Wall, that dragon monument born of a succession of uncompleted and useless bastions, whose defensive folds sometimes confront each other like enemy fortresses?

The petrified empire

However, at the same time, the country manifests a frenetic life, even in the expressions of its greatest destitution, at least once the photographers turn their lenses on the street, on life, rather than on the eternity of petrified camels or stone horses. Then the gap between the lives of peasants and of the poor inhabitants of the cities or city margins, becomes smaller. Even if we confine ourselves to the country's urban dimension, the rural populations of the interior—all those peasants (*nongmin*) who flocked to the construction sites of emergent modernity, to become, by a sort of strange phonetic inversion, the famous *mingong* (migrant workers)— have long been a presence in China's human landscape.

The urban streets in the photographs reveal impressive gaps in wealth, but the activities, the human density, the encounters, the commerce, the markets, the strolling players, the funeral processions, the crowds, all create a sense of permanence at least as tenacious and lasting as the most stable of the buildings.

The urban images of today suggest that, at least in the lower classes, preoccupations and activities have changed scarcely more than the structure of the characters. The sleep of the worker stretched out in his wheelbarrow is the same in the 19th century as now at the start of the 3rd millennium. The patience is the same, the sufferings, the manifestations of extreme poverty, retain a magnificent consistency. In this respect, of course, China could be our twin, distanced by the "alien" manifestation of its culture, but beyond that, there is an embeddedness in time, a permanence of the soul, an impassivity in the face of change, however slow or however sudden, a capacity to laugh and to accept, which could make the Chinese peoples the guardians of a city of peace... If history had not so often sought to undermine that serenity.

A succession of misunderstandings

To most Westerners, however, what was important in the 19th and 20th centuries, was not Man, nor life, but some degree of control over the economic or maritime infrastructures, and perhaps the conversion of souls. This period ushered in a series of ever faster physical transformations. The arrival of the train in Tiananmen Square in 1902 causes as much fright and astonishment as the development of the railways in 19th-century Europe. This was also the time of the first non-trade contacts, and the China in which the aspiration towards a specifically Chinese republic emerged was one still marked by Confucianism and obedience to the figure of the emperor.

Is this a rupture or a threshold? One of those periods of change whose real significance can only be judged in the light of history?

At the end of the 19th century, and more systematically in the first half of the 20th, the first western-style legations, churches, stores and brands appear in Beijing. The disparity in clothing and appearance would not look out of place in the Paris of Zola or of Vallès. The social contrast is matched by a juxtaposition of civilisations, a process clearly reflected in the history of dress fashions. Above the long robes of the mandarins appear the cocked hats and huge round spectacles with non-corrective lenses which give the figures in certain portraits the appearance of deep sea fish. The son of the mandarin flexibly matches the elegance of the cassocked priest who accompanied the return of the western powers.

Our perception of modern China is no more reliable than that of those photographers. There is no reason why our ideas about the country and its cities should be more credible than those of most past observers. At least we have the benefit of rigorous observers like Simon Leys (although his view of urban realities seems to have been clouded by the distance from Hong-Kong), Jean-François Billeter or, contrastingly, François Jullien, who have taught us not to take at face value the images that the country offers us and that so many intellectuals have been quick to seize upon or appropriate. The big round spectacles served no corrective function, and the glasses through which we see the country continue to have excellent distorting effects.

Was the 20th century the century of night or of light, of unceasing oppression or of a tangible break with the real structures inherited from the Emperors?

First contact

In 1998, Françoise Ged and I spent a few days together in Beijing before attending the first colloquium organised in China, at Suzhou, by UNESCO's World Heritage Committee. During the brief interlude in Beijing, we spent sleepless nights and days travelling round a city without light, where restaurants and hotels were still rare and almost all dependent on State structures. The old city, inside the second orbital road, had changed little since Deng Xiaoping's arrival in power in 1978. It is shown in the drawings, but in particular in a large relief drawing measuring almost 150 square metres, produced by the Beijing Institute of Urban Planning in 1999, which thus reveals conditions at a slightly earlier stage. The disappearance of the city walls, the opening up of Dhang'an Avenue, the creation of Tian'anmen Square, a few buildings to the East and West, do not fundamentally alter the urban and architectural structure, at least in the heart of the city, an area not much smaller than central Paris.

However, a new transformation—slow and powerful—was already in progress. Its primary manifestation was the appearance of the special economic zones in the south and the emergence of Shanghai as a financial metropolis, made partially autonomous through its distance from the capital. Interminable train journeys remained the norm, with their obsolete but appealing military trappings—trains were a place of laughter and conversation. Airline companies were in their infancy but the foundations were being laid for a brutal shift in the burning sun of the third millennium and for the ever-changing image we have of some supposed ideal of modernity.

Little time remained as the 20th century came to a close and the 21st opened to live at the pace of the cities like Beijing, whose form had remained unchanged for seven centuries, or of Shanghai, whose physiognomy had become frozen in the immutable outline of the Bund. True, the Huangpu River now flowed through the financial metropolis and, since Jiang Zemin and the Shanghai Gang succeeded Deng in 1989, the ambitious skyline of Pudong was emerging like the faintest of Chinese shadows.

In Beijing, in 1998, the eastern and western financial districts fringing the second orbital road, had begun to establish a strange competitive relationship. The city now extended to the fourth orbital road. The fifth was under construction and the space between them active as a spillway both for the populations who—willingly or reluctantly—were leaving the centre, and for those who, in time-honoured fashion, came in from the country each season to work on the great State infrastructure projects.

Neon signs and advertising were still a rare sight in the Beijing and Shanghai nights. Propaganda was less in evidence. Its symbols had aged. Slogans and loudspeakers seemed briefly less omnipresent. It was still difficult to obtain reliable city maps. In the first years of this new China, the outline of the streets where it had almost become easy to walk without an authorised guide, itself became a set of signs and tracks.

Our common destiny, and what we miss

One day, in France, a friend introduced us to a mysterious text by the Austrian writer Peter Handke, *Der Chinese des Schmerzes.* It has nothing to do with China. The writer remains within the confines of Salzburg. The reference to the Chinese is more as a metaphor of distant faces which suddenly reveal the authenticity of their features. The book is primarily a fictional approach to the question of thresholds and transformations, two notions that are constants of space and time in the Middle Kingdom.

Handke wonders what happens at the moment the threshold is crossed, an instant that can be long enough for a metamorphosis to occur. A notion that we encounter time and time again in Chinese philosophical thought but also in the concrete realities of the city. Doors—thresholds—were partly erased during the revolutionary period. Just as the potential for changes in thought and the free development of the individual were erased. At the same time, the melodramatic monologue of Mao and his little red book replaced the inexhaustible reservoir of signs that was and has partly re-become the Chinese language.

Handke's book begins with this first metaphorical sentence, a sentence with no immediately comprehensible origin: *in the night the black of the characters painted the lights of the city.*

Today in China, the lights of the city, and more generally the realities of the country, seem to evade the large majority of outside observers. Some refrain from observation or comment of any kind, pleading a label that no longer exists and, in many cases, with the simple aim of doing business in the world's most populous country. Others tour the country with their eyes glued to the pictures in tourist brochures and postcards, all the more blind to the terrible lies for the fact that the true history of the country seems taboo in China, and almost as much so outside.

Although information is hard to come by, not least because of the difficulties of the language, China is nevertheless much less opaque than many like to believe. Both within and without it is multiple, blessed with lucid observers, scrupulous historians, however few in number. All in all, if there is one thing that we can all do, it is simply to open our eyes, or else to close them, as Handke advises, in order to look more deeply into the soul of the heirs of this most durable of civilisations.

Have we opened them, have we closed them, in offering this reading or re-reading of the city for the exhibition at the Cité de l'architecture & du patrimoine in Paris and the Centre de Cultura Contemporània de Barcelona?

The act of writing

The first hypothesis we formulated, which subsequently led to the symbolic encounter with Handke's text, is that of a certain continuity between the page layout of traditional writing (originally vertical) and the layout of the steles with their plans of the cities, or at least of the imperial cities. This hypothesis perplexed western specialists (although we have found an explicit trace in an interview with Jean-Pierre Angrémy [1]), whereas it easily found an echo with architects and urban planners, as if it were an innate truth.

We have kept it as a working hypothesis, without seeking to prove it. This allows us to make a link between culture and the development of the cities, as we do in the West when we look for the sources of our civilisations in the archaeology of signs.

In China, writing is always a trace, an imprint, beginning with tortoise shells and carrying on through the long sequence of steles engraved with thoughts, sometimes inseparable from the calligraphy of the thinkers. Writing and its codes, like the liberties taken with those codes, reflect the layout of the avenues and streets, of the *hutong* and the courtyards, of each of the houses, just as they reflect the organisation of the original society.

The hierarchies of thought, of the society, of the cities, though not strictly superimposable, can help us to read this world without ten years of arid study and comparative linguistics. And what strikes us at the other end of the journey, not the spatial journey we have just taken through the cities and the streets, but the temporal journey through the last century, are the upheavals brought about by the pressure of economic changes.

Few languages are resistant to change. The simplification of writing imposed by Mao was furiously rejected by the Chinese outside China and at least by those sinologists not in thrall to the thoughts of the Great Leader.

1—"Ideally, I think that Beijing should be discovered from the air. You need to fly over Beijing to perceive that sort of immense quadrilateral or double quadrilateral, in which you can see a swarm of right angles, of regular intersections, of streets and avenues that all intersect at impeccable right angles, forming a sort of immense chessboard, a game of go, or a starting point for an adventure... a chessboard on which every street outline constitutes a mystery, a question mark, an ideogram, a forbidden place to be explored."
Interview with Pierre-Jean Rémy in Pierre Sipriot's programme "Titre courant" broadcast on Channel 1 on January 23, 1977.

Did the change to a horizontal layout, which may have pleased graphic designers and newspaper typesetters, really arouse no sense of vertigo in a society that saw man as a creature of the middle, between earth and sky?

Through a similar process, the very structure of society was reversed: ancestor worship, the unfailing respect owed to grandparents and parents, was turned upside down with the single child policy in a population that had grown from 600 million to 1.3 billion in less than half a century. The cult of the single child—of the only son in small towns—places a little emperor, a willing despot, at the centre of the home.

The overturning of landmarks

This theme is ubiquitous in contemporary artistic production, which is the only place where this kind of metaphor can be used to refer to possible social, and therefore political, dysfunctions. Photography, painting, cinema, poetry... in fact, any form of expression, provided that it is confined to the realm of the image, of the symbol, and does not threaten the established order and the powers that be, is able (almost) freely to reflect reality. No doubt, censorship and self-censorship are not new. But the reality must be particularly cruel for violence, barbarity, orgy and derision, pushed to the extreme, to have become the ordinary motifs of front-line artists. Since the crude exposure of day-to-day life has become a grammar in its own right, the filmmakers of what is called the "sixth generation" have rediscovered the immense expressive power of cinema.

Photography sometimes follows a different path. It is prepared to travel to the final thresholds of imagination, thresholds of terror or light which give us little access to the photographers" real thought processes. The best painting or sculpture takes the same approach, making the cruellest of western or Japanese practitioners look like choirboys. All this reflects part of the country's realities. A reality all the more appalling in that—while the State seeks to control self-expression, to hold back protests against the new forms of injustice—it has withdrawn from its role as evenhanded judge. The drama of contaminated blood, of AIDS, of orphans, of organ grafts, of executions with or without trial, seems out of control, and all this inevitably delights the manufacturers of stereotypes about a country in which most of the population wishes only for justice and to be left in peace.

Would such a situation have been possible before the two major changes that the society has undergone: the reversal of family hierarchy and the huge widening of the wealth gap?

What future for China?

Although the countryside pours ever greater numbers of peasants into the cities" factories and building sites, it remains apart from this effervescence. For the moment, this duality protects its architectural heritage and what remains of its cultural heritage. Despite the visual and moral pressure of the innumerable television channels, and despite the temptations of breezeblock, the old towns, the old villages partially abandoned by their youngest inhabitants, retain the knowledge of the old rules of architecture and in some cases the memory of the layout of the city.

In the cities, on the other hand, finding signs of the past is becoming an impossible quest. Most of the great cities that were the pride of China—Beijing of course, but even more so the old capitals like Xi'an, Luoyang, Kaifeng, or more modest cities like Chengdu, Qufu or Kunming—have been practically destroyed or are nothing more than heritage industry caricatures of themselves, reduced to pastiche to attract the gaze of postcard lovers. At the same time, however, i.e. over the last ten to fifteen years, a gradually growing awareness, not of the historic value of the ancient city centres but of their tourist appeal, has led to the manufacture of a composite past, formed partly of caricatures (as is the case for several UNESCO classified cities like Lijiang) and partly, on the outskirts, of an archaeological hyperactivity that can itself be perplexing.

This is particularly true of Xi'an which, apart from the famous emperor Qin Shi Huangdi (259-210 BCE), honoured beyond his merits by cinema and television, boasts a thousand and one museums containing remains that are as comprehensible to a lay public as the first characters of Chinese writing. This does not prevent the coaches arriving, and millions of Chinese, followed by a small cohort of foreigners, now travel every year to visit a past whose essence is lost.

All this of course reflects the pessimistic aspect of our vision of China. We could further exacerbate this pessimism by reference to the country's ecological, hydrological or epidemiological problems, but these aspects contain the potential for such disasters that we can let them speak for themselves.

However, we need to explain the fascination that China exercises over us. We know that we find its faults all the easier to see in that the combination of its nationalism and its imperious rejection of any real form of democracy tend to encourage a one-sided reading. However, the China that we describe lucidly, we believe, or unjustly as they would say, is also like a second homeland to us. It is the country which for a while carries the future of the world, but it is also a plurality of nations, a collection of territories and multiple peoples, each of which is still capable of offering us the richness of its culture.

A——Li Lang 黎朗. Intersection in Chongqing, 2005. © Li Lang

Cities and filmmakers

Jordi Balló

Cinema for an exhibition

Can an exhibition generate a movie? We knew from our own experience (at the CCCB) with the exhibition *Erice/Kiarostami. Correspondences* that this objective was possible if the proposal was ambitious and open enough to interest the most talented filmmakers. And that the concept of a film for an exhibition was not an end in itself, but rather the possibility of opening the way for future encounters of the resulting film with its viewers. In this context we tried to respond to the need to get a filmmaker's perspective on five cities along the China itinerary, the exploited city. Five Chinese filmmakers united by a shared vision of cinema, a critical attitude towards reality, who in getting together also proposed a generational message.

The choice of Jia Zhangke

We immediately thought of Jia Zhangke as the right director for this project. His vision matched perfectly our concept of the general tone of the exhibition, with that very stimulating nature of his films that capture the essential elements of reality without renouncing incursions into the territories of fiction. The films of Jia Zhangke always move between different levels, between reality and fiction, between the individual and the collective, between randomness and planning in shooting, and thus he is a model for other directors from around the world we also engage in this same creative quest. But also, given his personality and his role in new Chinese cinema, Jia Zhangke was the one director who had the ability to attract other directors, perhaps the only one with such indisputable authority. We knew his work very well though we had not dealt with him personally. I contacted Marie Pierre Muller, director of the Cinema du Réel Festival, who had probably done more than anyone else in Europe to promote the leading Chinese directors, especially Jia Zhangke. There was also another concurrence that says a lot about Jia Zhangke's interest in the international community of filmmakers: He had been a major champion, when he was on the jury at Rotterdam, of the film *El cielo gira* by Mercedes Álvarez, which also won at the Cinema du Réel

Festival that year. Jia admired the film, which drew a natural link between his cinema and the documentary school emerging at that time in Catalonia. These were some of the reasons we thought Jia might be interested in the type of project we were proposing.

The other filmmakers

The contact took place at the Venice Festival 2007, a festival that, under the direction of Marco Muller, had been the scene of Jia Zhangke's big international debut, when his film *Still Life* won the Golden Lion in 2006. The film was also a popular hit in Europe when it opened in cinemas, becoming one of the film events of the year. The first contact was almost collective, on the terrace of the Excelsior, along with other Chinese producers and filmmakers who had a collective film at the festival. Jia Zhangke joined us and I explained the idea to him and we agreed to meet the next morning to hash out the details. At our second meeting, at which Marie Pierre Muller was also present, the filmmaker told us of his interest in the idea of the portraits of the five cities based on specific stories, as well as the personal challenge that it meant for him to assume the supervision of project, including the choice of other filmmakers and overseeing each project. He also thought that he should do one of the pieces, as he did. He added that we should include an industrial town from the north, and that we did. Finally, the five cities were going to be Shanghai, Guangzhou, Chongqing, Xi'an and Suzhou. The process had thus begun.

After a few weeks we received proposals from the five directors associated with the five cities. These were not rookies, but rather directors whose works had appeared at festivals and others who had worked in other areas. They were: Han Jie (Shanghai), awarded in the Rotterdam Festival for his film *Walking on the Wild Side (Lai xiao zi)* (2006) ; Li Hongqi (Guangzhou), winner of the Prize Netpac at the festival in Locarno for his film *So Much Rice (Hao duo da mi)* (2007), an award he shares with Peng Tao (Chongqing) for his film *Little Moth (Xue Chan)* (2007), and finally Chen Tao (Xi'an), winner of the Cinéfondation award at the Cannes Festival for his short film *Way Out (Ru Dao)* (2006). Jia Zhangke (Suzhou) had added to his international prize list a new award in Venice for his documentary *Useless (Wu Yong)* (2007).

Chronicle of a Film

The Bed — Shanghai

Shanghai, the excess of desires becomes the very body of life of the city. Here, too many young people live far from their homes, drawn by its charm, trying to figure out what they want from this sexy, high-priced metropolis.

The city becomes a hotbed of these people's dreams.
The bed is a practical and essential element in our lives.
The bed travels with people, witnessing the many choices of the world.
Is the bed alive? If we believe that we are alive, then the bed is too.
—Han Jie

L'Être et le Néant (*Being and Nothingless*), Han Jie.
© X-Stream/CCCB/Cité de l'architecture et du patrimoine

The story of a bed in a city in transformation: this is the plot thread of the film by Han Jie. But this bed has no symbolic dimension; this is not a conceptual film. On the contrary: in the first images of the dead man and his family in mourning, we feel the sorrow that underlies the film from then on, as we visit, in the company of the dead man's bed, intimate settings of the city. And we understand that the object will be a circumstantial detail but under no circumstances will it diminish the strength of the characters.

In its central fragment, the film conveys the feeling of Shanghai as a device of seduction. Young Amy works in a sales office and suffers, and tolerates, the harassment of a customer who fêtes her. Her boyfriend Xiao Cui tries to contact her by mobile phone but does not succeed. This communicative silence enables Han Jie to achieve a powerful sonorous effect by introducing the music of the ringing phone into Amy's world, as an evocative and disturbing means of making Xiao Cui present in his absence. The uncertainty and sadness of the young woman vis-à-vis the two men speak volumes about the moral demands of a modern-day boom town, where social differences intervene in the disorder of love. In the encounter between Amy and Xiao Cui on the bed that has led us there, there is an embrace that is at once separation and discomfort, culminating in the tear of the actress, sincere, like a point of light on her sad face.

The wide shot of the towering city provides (as Jacques Tati did in *Playtime*) only a glimpse of its skyscrapers by reflecting them in the glass façade of a new building. An image that contrasts with that of a desolate urban space, amidst a process of destruction and change, where the bed will be placed as another castoff of a city that has decided to rid itself of its urban memory. The final sequence, at the Shanghai Centre of Modern Art, with the bed on exhibit, expresses the moral ambiguity of the whole film, with a group of silent youths occupying the stands and gazing into camera, nonplussed like spectators in their own future.

On the Outskirts of Xi'an (Xi'an)

Xi'an is a relatively closed-minded industrial city, but its people are beginning to change under the impetus of China's economic growth. The film presents us with a young man run aground in love, family and work, underscoring his innermost feelings, his reactions and choices in the face of the changes in the outside world.
—Chen Tao

Xi'an, dans la banlieue (Outside Xi'an), Chen Tao.
© X-Stream/CCCB/Cité de l'architecture et du patrimoine

Zhang Jian is a young man of 26 who lives in Xi'an, and works in the admissions offices of a school. Shao Ping, also 26, is his ex-girlfriend. Sadness and loneliness seize the young man from the first frame, where he wanders through his workday, his bedroom, his sitting room, sharing the noise of the television with his mother. His relationship with peers does not bring him out of his emotional state, disturbed by the constant recurrence of missed calls on his mobile, rendered a veritable open road to nothingness, to communicative solitude. We sense in a sequence in which he spies on the girl that this must be the reason for his melancholy, expressed in these interior spaces and in fleeting images of the city, as he pedals along on his bicycle. Finally comes the encounter between the two, which we understand from the outset as a farewell, and which Chen Tao resolves, unlike the other scenes of dialogue, with shot/reverse-angle, with which the gestures of both, although subtle, acquire their full meaning: arranging one's hair, smoking, not answering a phone call... Shao Ping expresses concern about the future of her former boyfriend, before telling him of her intention to marry another man. A gentle caress from her marks the end of the sequence, in a gesture that seems to say that he will not forget her.

In the final scene, Zhang Jian goes out on the roof of his building and looks out over the city. A slight but significant crane movement lets us see what he sees while maintaining the composition of the shot: the loneliness of the protagonist confronting the city's contemporary skyline, which speaks to us precisely of this ambivalent sentimental relationship, in which the city seems a distant witness to this infinite sorrow, presented to the viewer as a cold place, of neither hope nor despair.

A Constant Flow — Chongqing

Under the dark sky of Chongqing, noise and chaotic crowds fill the city. Adverts for mobile operators China Mobile and China Unicom, signs for all types of banks, everywhere attractive, dazzling women in new clothes, giving people an intense desire for the material and an oppressive feeling of suffocation.

In this place, the biggest exporter of manpower in China and the economic capital of the upper Yangtze, people moving endlessly from one place to another. These people are moved from Chongqing to points all over China, to become the silent executors of urban construction.

They gather in unknown cities, surviving in every corner of the concrete constructions in this age of vicissitudes with contradictions, alienation and powerlessness. Nobody cares where they come from or where they will go next... All they have left is their faith and hope.
—Peng Tao

Attente (Wait), Peng Tao.
© X-Stream/CCCB/Cité de l'architecture et du patrimoine

In China, Chongqing is perhaps the city that has provided the richest vein of imagery for film-makers in recent years, because it is one of the most extreme examples of the tensions underlying the enormous processes of transformation of the land and city. This is due to the symbolic nature of the erection of the gigantic Three Gorges Dam, considered at once a vast engineering work that reveals the secular power of construction in the country, and a disaster that has brought forced displacement of the inhabitants of the area occupied by land and water, removed by the hundreds of thousands to other parts of the country. This friction between destruction and construction, between emigration and settlement, is present from the first frames of this film by Peng Tao, in which a woman, A Quin, carries her baby on her back as she crosses the city in a cable car, a city we can only sense, covered by a thick layer of fog and smog, making it permanently invisible. The mother and baby go to a post office where the voice of an official informs her once again that no letter has come for her. And she insists, lamenting how she writes letters to her husband and gets no answer. The continuous percussive thud of letters being stamped establishes a subtle sonorous relationship between the fragile woman and child and the relentless cruelty of the system.

Throughout the film one feels the strength of the documenting of the reality in relation to the woman's need to survive. She runs a small food stand, like all else around her, threatened with demolition, as the character painted on her door warns. Customers are scarce; in fact she has only one, a businessman with cash-flow problems speaking agitatedly over the phone. The worst omens soon come true, and the woman is forced to abandon her space and embark on an uncertain path of survival. The businessman gives her a temporary job working in a company kitchen, giving her a brief respite in her hellward slide.

In this woman's wanderings we travel through the spaces of conflict, with bulldozers ripping away at homes and vast areas of consummated devastation, where the floodwaters will soon arrive. In this still life the woman and her baby make a home, confronting a vision of the nocturnal city, with the buildings all alight, announcing a difficult and distant well-being. Because in this area of transformation only desolation reigns, pending an improbable future encounter.

Happy New Year — Guangzhou

Located in a subtropical area, Guangzhou is much livelier than the northern towns. Multitudinous phenomena burst forth rapidly and wither at the same speed as if the city operated like a vast fermenter. Choosing the theme of "Happy New Year" in this context and accompanying it with narration is highly appropriate.
—Li Hongqi

Nouvel an (*New Year*), Li Hongqi.
© X-Stream/CCCB/Cité de l'architecture et du patrimoine

A nearly empty apartment, with two bunk beds. Two men, insurance agents, talk about their dreams, in the New Year's tradition. Through their dialogue we get a glimpse of the underlying economic problems of their lives, threatening even their occupation of this sad room. A third person joins them and reads an advert: he is an insurance agent like them, but does not say so at first. They have nothing to offer him, nothing to buy. Everything is part of a strange ceremony, with no apparent way out.

The tone used by Li Hongqi recalls the theatre of situation, this tedious immobility of the workplace, where competition and boredom reign, where, beneath the conventions of men hungry to make a sale, hide the dramas of disillusionment. The various male characters, all dressed in black suit and tie, as if they were part of an unseen higher entity, parade their desolation on the street, in the supermarket – symbolic spaces in their emptiness, occupied only by these of men in black, like something out of a sci-fi film. The story of competition in the workplace reflects one face of China's burgeoning economy, as seen in this area of the country: a prosperous and vital region where the evils of savage capitalism take root. This film is a parable of the working world, permeated, as one would expect, with apathy, hopelessness, which also affects the latest newcomer, who comes to occupy the space where he started out from, like a never-ending circle.

Love Across the River — Suzhou

An ancient city, through the exquisite botanical garden and branching rivers of which we can see the clues to or traces of its ancient culture. Two couples, two men and two women, once lovers, meet again a year later. The breath of the youth of yesteryear can still be smelt in their conversation.

Does love remain within our realm of possibilities? Is youth really over? Given the nature of the ties that bind the ancient city, what kind of existence ecological does their culture require?
—Jia Zhangke

Cry Me a River, Jia Zhangke.
© X-Stream/CCCB/Cité de l'architecture et du patrimoine

At the time of wrapping up this piece for publication Jia Zhangke's film is in the final edit phase. But we have the script, which tells the story an encounter between two former couples, two men and two women in the city of culture, at a reunion to honour an old university professor of theirs. This new encounter spurs the four young people to evoke lost love and sex, in poetic and vibrant confessions. The river plays a major role in this wall of melancholic silences. The script evidences this fusion, in which the director succeeds brilliantly in so many of his earlier films, between the impossibility of love and the pull of the landscape. It shares with most of the films from this collective work dealt with above certain figures and themes: unrequited love, the barriers to communication, the rise of a new economy that holds youth in its grip and a general attitude of resistance and a glistening of hope, that wields eloquent silence as a weapon, as a way of saying that all is finally understood.

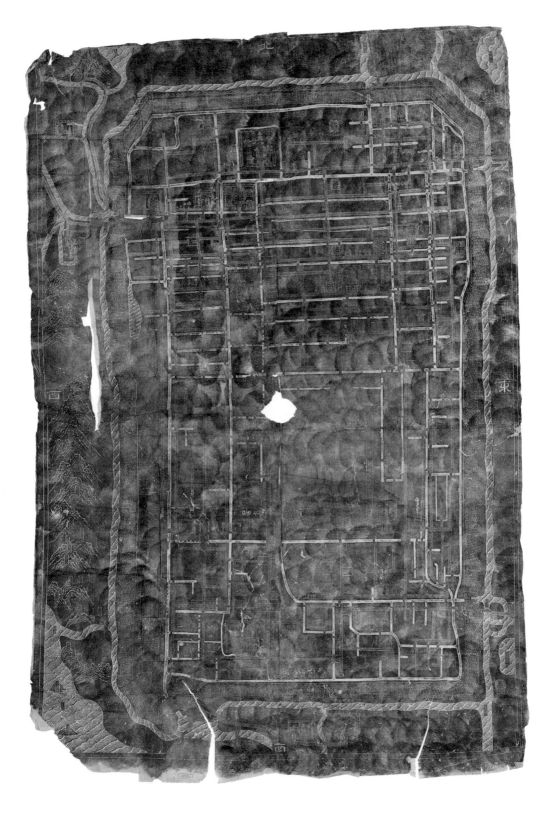

The Suzhou steles

The city of Suzhou, nicknamed the Venice of the Orient, contains an exceptional number of engraved steles recounting the history of the city. They are mostly collected in the Stele Museum, which is itself housed in the Temple of Confucius. The readings and geographical representations are often combined with explanatory commentaries, which makes this collection a unique record of the urban and symbolic history of a city.

The six steles shown in the photographs here complement each other, although they were not made to form a series. In particular, the sky map, engraved in 1247 from a reading of 1191, was brought to Suzhou with a degree of scientific care that enhances the city's reputation as a heaven on earth.

Imprint of the Pingjiang stele produced before the "1917 Restoration"
© Collection Library of Congress, Washington.

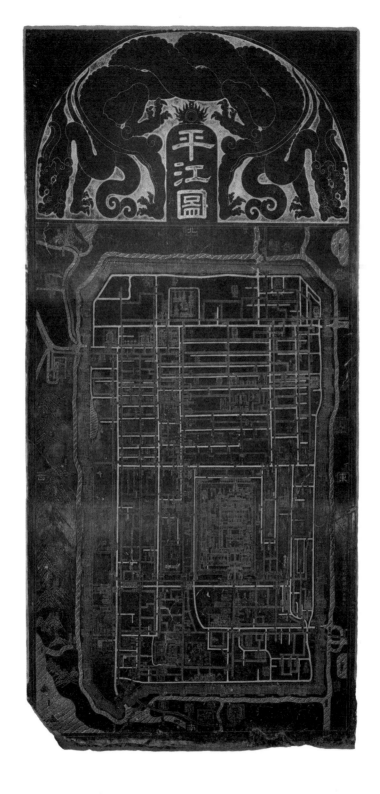

Stele of the Pingjiang map, engraved in 1229. Original dimensions: 276 cm x 141 cm, Temple of Confucius, Suzhou.
© Wang Hao/Suzhou Bureau of Cultural Heritage

Stele of the sky map, engraved in 1247. Original dimensions: 216 cm x 108 cm, Temple of Confucius, Suzhou.
© Wang Hao/Suzhou Bureau of Cultural Heritage

Stele of the imperial genealogy: list of emperors from the beginning to the Song dynasty emperor Lizong (1224-1264), engraved in 1247. Original dimensions: 182 cm x 100 cm, Temple of Confucius, Suzhou.
© Wang Hao/Suzhou Bureau of Cultural Heritage

Stele of the geographical map: map of China, engraved in 1247. Original dimensions: 200 cm x 107 cm, Temple of Confucius, Suzhou. © Wang Hao/Suzhou Bureau of Cultural Heritage

Stele of the Suzhou water management map, engraved in 1797. Original dimensions: 165 cm x 80 cm, Temple of Chenghuang, Suzhou. This stele is a symbolic reminder of the importance of the canals, of the need to maintain them, of the essential respect for their flows, rather than a technical document. Although it only indicates the main canals (four north-south, three east-west), it nevertheless reveals the importance that the Chinese attributed to hydrographic work.
© Wang Hao/Suzhou Bureau of Cultural Heritage

Stele of the Gusu map: map of the city of Suzhou, engraved in 1783.
Original dimensions: 116 cm x 89 cm, Temple of Confucius, Suzhou.
Gusu is the former name of the city founded in 541 BCE, which took the name Suzhou in 581 (Sui Dynasty). This map, the most accurate and detailed of all the old documents, was produced in 1745 during the reign of Qianlong, before being engraved under the city's old name. © Wang Hao/Suzhou Bureau of Cultural Heritage

The finest representation of Suzhou

Danielle Elisseeff

The history of Suzhou dates back to the end of the Spring and Autumn Period, to the 6th century before the common era. The ancient city (historians call it Gusu 姑蘇), established at the location where the city stands today, had its moment of glory at the beginning of the fifth century BCE, when it became capital of the surrounding region: the Wu country 吳, one of the three principalities then in armed competition to dominate the lower Yangtze.

The memory of Gusu—its vast eight-gated wall (24 km in circumference) and its eight ports on the arms of the river—still survives, but any tangible traces of it are long gone since, in 473 BCE, Wu fell to its neighbour, the Yue 越.

It was almost a thousand years before the city again achieved significance, this time economic, when it became one of the stages on the Grand Canal, a vital communication route that the Sui emperors began building in 584. Since that time, it has linked the two halves of China, bringing essential products from the South to the then capital (in the Valley of the Yellow River, at Xi'an), in particular good quality construction timber, used for official buildings, and even more important the rice and rolls of silk used to pay the officials. The city, which at this time took its existing name of Suzhou 蘇州, was coiled and protected in one of the loops of the canal that both encircled and irrigated it.

Five hundred years later, in the middle of the 11th century, the city again experienced rapid growth, when the human and political balances in Central Asia changed. The Chinese no longer had access to overland routes without paying heavy tribute, as they initially did with the Qidan (from 1005) in the North of the country, then with the Tangut, in the North West. The latter had just founded (1038) the kingdom of the Xi Xia (the "western Xia"); they controlled the routes around the Gobi and Taklamakan deserts, whilst the Tibetans held the routes to Southeast Asia. After a failed military attempt, the Chinese chose to sign a treaty (1044) with the Xi Xia, as they had with the Qidan. The consequences were serious, since it obliged the Song to pay heavy annual tribute (in silver, silk and tea). After this, therefore, the Empire's external trade was essentially conducted by sea; cities located near the great ports, and the main staging posts on the North-South section of the Grand Canal, played a major role.

However, this prosperity suffered a terrible setback in 1125. A new people, the Jurchen, moved into Northern China at this point and founded a foreign dynasty, called the Jin 金. The Song emperor was taken prisoner and died in captivity, while his government took refuge in the Yangtze valley where they were pursued by the Jin; in the process, they razed the city (1130), before withdrawing, as the Song armies responded and finally managed to contain the invaders in the Yellow River valley.

However, the city was in ruins, while still facing the influx of refugees fleeing the regime that the Jurchen had introduced in Northern China. Gradually though, the city recovered, eventually reaching its current size. Nonetheless, Suzhou experienced further terrible times a century and a half later (in 1275) at the hands of the Mongols, four years before they conquered the whole Empire and founded the Yuan dynasty (1279).

The map shown here, called the "Pingjiang" map (*Pingjiangtu* 平江圖; Pingjiang, the name that the city was given in 1113 and that remained in use until the end of the Yuan dynasty, is now one of the city's administrative subdivisions), provides a record of the city long after the Jin invasion, in full revival in the first half of the 13th century. This unique document was produced under the authority of Li Shoupeng 李壽朋, then prefect of Suzhou. Despite remaining only ten months in post, this official performed a significant task of organisation and administrative standardisation, of which this map is the most impressive example.

Mapping his region was a prefectural duty, as evidenced by Zhu Changwen 朱長文 who, under the Northern Song, produced an *Illustrated Atlas of the Wu Region* at the request of the government. He added a preface (*Wu jun tu jing xu jixu* 吳郡 圖经續記序) containing a reminder of the official directives: each district must be mapped; regional maps must be checked and updated every three years and a printed copy must be sent to the authorities through the normal channels.

Given its geographical position and its role as a stage on the Grand Canal, it is not surprising that Suzhou was one of the best served cities in this respect, with some 40 maps to its name. It is said that the first dated from the time of the First Emperor (221-210 BCE), then that a second was made in 877 to record the city's new layout: largely destroyed following a serious riot, it was redesigned at this time by the local official, around a set of regular axes laid out in the shape of the character *ya* 亞.

However, Li Shoupeng's work, completed in 1229, is of unique beauty and interest, in particular because it was transposed onto a stone stele. This practice of engraving on steles, which dates back to the beginnings of the Empire (221 BCE), gave official value to the information recorded (texts, drawings): from legal codes to the texts on the civil service examination curriculum, everything important in imperial China, which was to be used as a reference, is "engraved in marble" (a "marble" that can also be sandstone or granite).

The prefect Li Shoupeng assigned the task of making this map (H: 279 cm ; W.: 138 cm) to a team of four people. It was undoubtedly no easy assignment, since they had to go to every part of the city, conduct surveys, then verify in situ that the drawing matched the location (as far as that was possible with the methods of the time). One of these men, a big player in the project, was Li Shouming 李壽明, the magistrate of the prefecture. He had the tricky job of drawing the actual outlines, a task in which he apparently involved every one of his subordinates; then he oversaw the transfer to stone, and the engraving of the map itself and of the texts identifying the sites, buildings and monuments. Three master engravers, Lü Ting 呂挺, Zhang Yuncheng 張允成 and Zhang Yundi 張允迪 worked on it.

The map, which sketches the outline of the main monuments in the form of axonometric views, provides a detailed and very vivid description of the state of the city at this period of relative peace, in the year 1229, when the authorities believed that, after almost four generations of labour, it had finally achieved an unrivalled splendour. The canal network structures the urban space and give the map its very particular appearance: situated on the edge of the Yangtze Delta, the city is inevitably dominated by water; in fact it is because of this that people settled there, to the point that certain maps mention the direction of flow of the water in the canals.

The authors draw what they see by eye: the grid map (each square representing a rectangle measuring one *li* per side, i.e. approximately 500 metres) would not appear until the late 19th century. The plan, on a scale of 1:2000 and oriented north-south (north at the top, south at the bottom, which is in line with modern practice but contrary to that of a certain number of ancient Chinese maps), provides the landmarks needed for orientation and travel: the canals, the 314 bridges, the streets (309 over bridges), but also the 65 workshops, the temples, the monasteries and convents and, slightly apart in the southeastern quarter of the city, the 93 official buildings. The city wall is described with particular care, as is the state of the site outside the walls, in the city's immediate surroundings.

The surrounding hills are thus depicted in three dimensions, whilst "wavy" lines indicate the lakes, the 18 arms of the delta or rivers and the stretches of water. In all, the map mentions 644 sites, 614 of which include toponymic or informative captions. Linguistic analysis reveals their repetitive character, with multiple references to "small bridges", "pure waters", punctuated with addresses referring to the "river behind the street before" or "the house by the water near the small bridge".

Finally, this magnificent map suggests how the city differs from the conceptual model of the capital city described in the "Zhou Ritual", the *Zhouli* (although this work is much more a collection of general principles than the description of a particular reality). Here, the administrative buildings are completely integrated into the urban fabric: the government organs in the north, facing the city which stretches at their feet. Some commentators see this map of Suzhou under the Southern Song as proof of its economic vitality, suggesting that day-to-day practicality took priority over administrative theory, in so far as the city's commercial and economic development altered the theoretical ideal, without causing complaint.

In 1917, it was decided to deepen the engraving of the stele; the work, later declared a protected heritage artefacts (1961), is currently kept at the Suzhou Museum of Steles, in the Temple of Confucius, founded here in 1035 by one of China's most famous scholars and ministers, Fan Zhongyan 范仲淹 (989-1052), a great educational reformer, amongst other things, and an active player in the introduction of a new system of knowledge testing: examinations.

With such a work, the question of accuracy necessarily arises. This map is an administrative document to which its instigator, the prefect, assigned great value, since he took the trouble to have it engraved and to have rubbings made (this was precisely the purpose of steles, a practice that guaranteed the reliability of documents, whereas printing, and especially woodcuts, required frequent reengraving of the wooden boards and the concomitant accumulation of errors, since the carved characters quickly eroded).

However, does this administrative document to which such value is attached actually tell the truth? Does it provide an accurate picture of the city as it was at that time? Or is its primary purpose to legitimise the actions of the prefects and then, as it moves up through the hierarchy, to please the government departments in the capital which, in their turn, will please the emperor by giving him good news from the provinces?

Does not this map, perhaps the most beautiful of all those depicting Suzhou as it was in the past, somehow reflect an ideal order?

The contemplation of this elegant quadrilateral which seems to resonate with peaceful life also suggests another interpretation or association of ideas: its connection with writing. Did Li Shoupeng look at his elegantly drawn city in the same way as he contemplated a piece of calligraphy? Was he aware of it? Was he deliberately seeking to make it a calligraphic character?

Or was the process unconscious, because in China any city that embodied the authority of the State must necessarily appear well ordered? Everything that has meaning—and therefore, above all, the characters used to give plastic form to language and thought—is ordered. In fact, it seems likely that an official city was not organised to resemble an ideogram, even if this observation comes naturally to the mind of any foreign observer. The official city takes the appearance of a character because, like a character, it is used to create links between people, regulated links that must obey the universal order.

So it is no accident that this map of the city matches a scarcely more recent (1247) map of the sky, also kept in the symbolic location of the Temple of Confucius. Mapping the sky is not new: there are examples dating back from the 4th century BCE and they are common in Han tombs; but it is at Suzhou that we find the most fascinating representation, in the form of this enormous stone measuring one metre by two.

Garden

The traditional garden was an enclosed garden, designed by scholars beside their homes as a place of meditation and leisure. They take different forms depending on position and local vegetation. The best-known gardens are those of Jiangnan, a region south of the Yangtze near Shanghai and Suzhou, famous for the number and refinement of all its gardens.

The more magical and mysterious the name of a garden, the greater its fame: Master of Nets Garden, Surging Waves Pavilion Garden, Humble Administrator's Garden, Forest of Lions Garden, Liu Garden, Double Garden... From belvedere to miniature forest, from mountains to lakes, from kiosk to Lake Tai stone table, each was its own journey of discovery. The master of the household invited his friends to listen to concerts on pipa or *guzheng* (古筝 Chinese zither).

Public squares and spaces were not so much a part of the structures of cities as of the extensive grounds of temples or guild headquarters, where people met as now they meet in the public gardens. And alongside the domino players, old and young, rose kites painted with all the shapes of heavenly mythology.

The word for kite is *fengzheng*, which means wind zither. The story goes that it was invented by Lu Ban, the god of carpenters, as a means of flying above the enemy, which tends to prove that kites are indeed living creatures possessing eyes.

In the great cities of today the municipal authorities build great parks, where people like to meet, do *taijiquan* (Tai Chi) exercises, dance, breathe the green and natural air, sing, perform concerts and old plays or fly their kites.

Liu garden in Suzhou. © OACC

The traditional Chinese garden: a world apart

Chiu Che Bing

> "When the heart is far away,
> the place is naturally apart"
>
> Tao Yuanming, "On drinking wine—V "

The Chinese character for garden is *yuan* (園)

Professor Tong Jun,[1] a pioneer in the study of gardens in China, suggests an interpretation of the character: a wall that delineates the space within which the garden is designed, a pond to provide nourishment, rocks to form a framework, buildings to provide places of communication and intimacy, and vegetation as a reminder of of permanence and ephemerality.[2]

Undoubtedly a microcosm, a world apart.

Ji Cheng,[3] a master gardener in the late Ming dynasty, author of the *Yuanye* (" 園冶 "), the first and only surviving Chinese work exclusively dedicated to the art of gardening, begins his treatise with a chapter dealing with the assessment of the site, a sign of the importance of the quality of the place where the garden is to be created. He states his preference for a "site on a mountain covered with woodland", which offers natural relief with "peaks and hollows, meanders and depths, escarpments and overhangs, large flat areas". However, the feeling of apartness is much more a state of mind than a physical location, and if Ji Cheng considered it inappropriate to build gardens "near the market", does not the clamour fade as soon as the door closes? A retreat within tumult, peace and serenity at the heart of the city, is that not a world apart! At the heart of the old city of Shanghai, a sign reading "Mountain covered with woodland at the heart of the city" places it in the Three Ears of Corn Hall.[4]

A——The character *yuan*. Calligraphy by Mr. Chung Wah Nan, *The Art of the Chinese Gardens*.

1——Architect (童寯1900-1983), trained in the Architecture Department of the University of Pennsylvania, a pupil of Paul Cret. On his return to China, he visited the gardens of the Jiangnan, and wrote a *Chronicle of the Gardens to the South of the River* (*Jiangnan yuanlin zhi*, "江南園林志") which, because of the Japanese invasion and the civil war, would only be published in 1963.
2——Tong Jun, *Jiangnan yuanlin zhi*, Beijing, Zhongguo gongye chubanshe, 1963, p. 7.
3——Ji Cheng (计成 1582-ap.1634), *Yuanye. Le Traité du jardin*, translated from Chinese into French by Che Bing Chiu, Besançon, Éditions de l'Imprimeur, 1997.
4——The Garden of Peace and Comfort, Yu yuan 豫園, was built by a mandarin for the "enjoyment" of his parents, in the mid-16th century. The garden was rehabilitated in the reign of the Emperor Qianlong.

But when conditions are no longer right for the practice of urban reclusion, then one must turn one's back on the city. Tao Yuanming,[5] refusing to bow like a servant in return for five bushels of rice, returns to the "fields and gardens"[6] to lead an existence free of the constraints imposed by a society governed by the moral rules and the codes of conduct dictated by Confucian doctrine. The man of culture can then devote himself at leisure to the ineffable sentiment nature arouses in human beings. "In the eastern palace I pick a chrysanthemum, I see the mountains of the South, in detachment and serenity".[7]

It is on seeing a painting by Wang Wei,[8] *Blue Fields in Rain and Mist*, that Su Shi[9] exclaims: "When I taste the poetry of Moji, I find paintings in his poems; when I contemplate the painting of Moji, I find poems in his paintings." Wang Wei, considered the founding father of black and white *shanshui*[10] (山水)and Tao Yuanming's successor in the *tianyuan* (田園) poetic genre, is undoubtedly the man who best embodies the scholarly ideal and achieves an osmosis between painting, poetry and landscape design.[11] At the end of his life, Wang Wei withdrew to his home in Wangchuan (輞川), the Jante Valley. He dedicated a sequence of twenty quatrains, *Along the Jante*, to this country dwelling, together with paintings executed on the walls of a nearby monastery.

B——For a moment, on the lake, I turned round: Around the blue of the mountain rolled the white clouds. Wang Wei, Lake Yi , *The Blue Seasons*, p. 209. Guo Zhongshu (?-977), *Wangchuan tu (Along the Jante)*, horizontal roll, detail Lakeside Pavilion, Taipei, National Palace Museum.

5——Tao Yuanming (陶淵明, 365-427), archetype of the haughty man of culture, a great wine drinker and lover of landscape.
6——*Tianyuan* is the poetic genre dedicated to the reclusive life amongst "fields and gardens". Tao Yuanming is considered the founding father of the genre.
7——Tao Yuanming, *Œuvre complète*, translated into French, introduced and annotated by Paul Jacob, Paris, Gallimard, 1990, p. 191-192.
8——Wang Wei (王维, 701-761), an accomplished scholar, excellent poet and painter, and fervent Buddhist. After his retirement from his career as a mandarin, he devoted himself to the improvement of his home, Wangchuan, in Lantian (蓝田), Blue Fields, 50 km from the capital Changan (长安). Wangchuan became the model for all garden loving scholars. *Les Saisons bleues, l'œuvre de Wang Wei*, French text by Patrick Carré, Paris, Phébus, 1989.
9——A multitalented scholar (苏轼, 1037-1101), a significant figure in the Song dynasty, a great lover of wine and nature, believer in the return to a state of nature.
10——Literally "mountains and waters", *shanshui* is the term for landscape painting.
11——Although the *Yuanye* is the only work on gardening in traditional China, numerous essays were written on the art of *shanshui*, the principles of which can easily be transposed to the disciplines of landscape and garden design. A particularly good example is the "six rules of painting" by the painter and theorist Xie He (谢赫, working around 500). François Cheng, *Souffle-Esprit. Textes théoriques chinois de l'art pictural*, Paris, Seuil, 1989.

Speaking of mountains and water, Confucius, Master of Ten Thousand Generations, said: "The man of intelligence is attracted to water, the man of *ren* [12] to mountains; One seeks movement, the other repose. [13]

According to the *Yijing*, the attributes of the mountains are stability and repose, like the skeleton of the world, and the attributes of water are lightness and communication, lively and active flow, which brings nourishment to the plains and valleys it runs through. By linking man with the pairing of mountain and water, the Master incorporates him into a system of correspondences and puts him into a position to act, opening up the doors of a an eternal universe in perpetual motion. Nearer our time, Professor Chen Congzhou [14] expresses his perception of the relations linking mountains and water, inseparable elements like *yin* and *yang* in the Taiji, the Supreme Pinnacle, as follows: Water unfurls its meanders on contact with the mountain, the mountain comes to life through the water that surrounds it .[15]

C——As you walk, you wonder if there is another universe. And as you raise your head, how deep are the feelings aroused. Ji Cheng, *Yuanye. Treatise on the Garden*, Raising mountains , p. 247. © Chiu Che Bing

12——A not easily translatable cardinal virtue of Confucianism, sometimes rendered as *humanism*.
13——Confucius, *Entretiens*, translated into French by Anne Cheng, Paris, Seuil, 1981, p. 59.
14——Chen Congzhou (陈从周, 1918-2000), a connoisseur of Chinese gardens, was landscape adviser to the Chinese-American architect, in particular for the Bank of China in Hong Kong. His remarkable *On Chinese Gardens* (*Shuoyuan*, "说圈") was published in a bilingual Chinese-English version by Tongji University Press, Shanghai, 1984.
15——*Op.cit.*, p. 3.

In China, the term for creating a garden is *zaoyuan* 造園), "building a garden". Building, because a garden is designed and structured like an architectural construct. Building also, because a Chinese garden is never created without architectural features. Osvald Sirén[16] rightly says that "a Chinese garden is quite simply inconceivable without buildings to divide it, surround it, complete it .[17] The axial symmetry of the layout, the solemn appearance of the halls, is contrasted with the formal whimsy, the sensation of lightness in the kiosks and belvederes. The alternation between areas of fullness and emptiness imprints pattern on the space and prompts the visitor to penetrate to the heart of the place s resonance and to feel the vibration of the primordial breath *qi*. Imagination can then replace the eye, illusion can interfere with the real and the horizon of the everyday can open to the infinite. The openings, the shapes of doors and windows, whether geometrical or irregular, frame carefully staged views. A few characters placed above the resulting pictures and parallel sentences placed here and there, reinforce the reference to a pictorial work. Li Yu[18] invented a device, like a roll of landscape painting in which the central image changes with the seasons and with the moods of the master of the house. On the immaculate whitewashed walls emerge a knotty pine branch, a few long bamboo stems, coloured spots of flowering prunus, fleeting moments that belong to the constantly recurring cycle of days and seasons. This is what Shen Fu,[19] a poor scholar from the city of Suzhou[20] calls giving density to empty spaces by materialising the unreal, opening dense spaces by realising the unreal,[21] the outcome of a clever and ingenious day-to-day application of elegance and distinction.

16——Swedish sinologist (1879-1966), author of numerous works on China, including *Garden of China*, New York, The Ronald Press Company, 1949.

17——*Op.cit.*, p. 5.

18——Li Yu (李漁, 1611-1679?), early Qing dynasty dramatist and garden designer. Some of his *Notes on leisurely moods* are translated by Jacques Dars under the title *Carnets secrets de Li Yu Au grès d'humeurs oisives*, Arles, Philippe Picquier, 2003.

19——Shen Fu (沈復, 1763-?) lived near the Blue Wave Pavilion (沧浪亭), one of the oldest still extant gardens in the city of Suzhou.

20——The city of Suzhou 苏州, nicknamed the Venice of the Orient, had several hundred gardens in the imperial era. A dozen survive today, four of which are on UNESCO's world heritage list. In 1956, Professor Chen Congzhou published a first analysis of the gardens of Suzhou, with some 200 photographs captioned with poetic couplets, combined with surveys by architecture students from Tongji University of the Humble Administrator's Garden (Zhuozheng yuan) and the Lingering Garden (Liu yuan). Professor Liu Dunzhen, from the Department of Architecture at Nanjing Polytechnic (today South-East University of China) has published *Suzhou gudian yuanlin*, the reference work on the traditional garden, which has surveys of fifteen gardens in that city.

21——Shen Fu, *Six Récits au fil inconstant des jours*, translated into French by Pierre Ryckmans, Bruxelles, Larcier, 1966, p. 66-67

The concept of scenery is the fundamental element in garden construction. In the character *jing* (景) which refers to clarity, scenery is the illuminated part of an object. Establishing scenery implies the presence of a human gaze, which takes in the scenery and completes the construct. It is the human being, by his sensibility and aesthetic sense, who gives meaning to the scenery. For Ji Cheng, scenery emerges out of opportunity and although it is a creation of man, [... can] seem to be the product of Heaven. It is the introduction of buildings in appropriate places that creates a sequence of sceneries which form contrasts and oppositions that retain the visitor's interest. A successful garden is one where the scenery changes at each step, providing new viewpoints created by intentional framing processes. The winding route of a path helps to guide the walker s gaze and to frame his view.

The notion of dissimulation and discovery is essential in the creation of a garden. A Chinese garden only reveals itself as the walker advances, through a subtle operation on space and time. The conceptual principles employed entail the notions of separation, quest, suggestion and passage, a sequence that Professor Chung Wah Nan[22] describes as the four tempos of the score.[23]

D——The glimpse of a pagoda through the circular frame of a window: like a folio painting by Li the Young; The rocky shards of a craggy mountain: like part of a half-panel by the Great Fou. Ji Cheng, *Yuanye. Treatise on the Garden*, On the garden, p. 91. *Distinguished Guests Pavilion (Jiabin ting), Humble Administrator s Garden (Zhuozheng yuan), Suzhou (Jiangsu province).* © Chiu Che Bing

E——Whilst the clouds flow to the rhythm of the music, Glasses raised, the mists of twilight linger. Ji Cheng, *Yuanye. Treatise on the Garden*, A site near a river or lake, p. 122. *Waterside pavilion where one can wash one's hat cord (Zhuoyin shuige), Master of Nets Garden (Wangshi yuan), Suzhou (Jiangsu province).* © Chiu Che Bing

F——Feeling responds to purity and withdrawal, The soul rejoices at the mountains and ravines. Suddenly the mind, released from the world of dust, awakens, Seems to penetrate into of a painting and stroll within it. Ji Cheng, *Yuanye. Treatise on the Garden*, Borrowed Scenery, p. 284. *Pavilion of Haitang Flowers Blossoming in Spring (Haitang chunwu), Humble Administrator s Garden (Zhuozheng yuan), Suzhou (Jiangsu province).* © Chiu Che Bing

22——Architect (钟华楠), teacher in the Architecture Department of Hong Kong University, author of *The Art of Chinese Gardens* ("中国园林艺术"), Hong Kong, University Press, 1982.

23——*Jardin du lettré. Synthèse des arts en Chine*, Boulogne-Billancourt, Musée Albert-Kahn, 2004, p. 209-217.

Discovery is behind every rock or every clump of bamboo, at the threshold of every moongate, at the meeting of every path.

"The mountain fades, the spring fails, departure point?
In the shade of the willows, beyond the splendour of the flowers, a new village."

Plants constitute the essential element that animates and reflects the continual transmutation of the garden, whilst emphasising the site's relief or marking the features of the terrain. Certain species are planted for their symbolic value the evergreen pine to symbolise longevity, the bamboo to evoke human sincerity, the prunus *junzi* for renewal, the promise of rebirth and the return of spring others for their evocative power: the chrysanthemum for the emblematic figure of the poet Tao Yuanming, the weeping willow for the pleasure of life in Jiangnan, South China...

Although the garden is designed within the tangible boundaries of an enclosed space, its perception must break free of the encompassing walls and extend to the surrounding splendours. Xie Lingyun,[24] in describing the screen of cliffs pressing at his doorstep and the gleaming billows soaking the window frames, breaks free of the boundaries of the enclosure and includes features from outside the garden. By establishing a link between inside and outside, he creates the illusion of spatial continuity between the foreground and background. This is the principle that Ji Cheng theorises through the term borrowed scenery *jiejing* (借景).

G—Transplanting the bamboo before the window, Planting a few pear trees to redivide the courtyard; The penetrating brightness of the moon gently disturbs the books and zither lying on a couch; The moaning of the wind envelopes and creases a crescent of autumnal water. Ji Cheng, *Yuanye. Treatise on the Garden*, "On the garden", p. 96.
A Branch beyond the bamboos (Zhuwai yizhixuan), Master of Nets Garden (Wangshi yuan), Suzhou (Jiangsu province).
© Chiu Che Bing

24—Xie Lingyun (谢灵运, 385-433), a poet and a great lover of landscape, is considered the founding father of the *shanshui* poetry genre. J. D. Frodsham, *The Murmuring Stream, the Life and the works of Hsieh Ling-yün*, Kuala Lumpur, University of Malaya Press, 1967.

Borrowing a view of real, tangible features—the slim outline of a pagoda against the blue of the sky—but also more abstract, immaterial phenomena—a moonbeam, the glimmering of a lake, morning mist, the glow of twilight... But also borrowing by summoning all the senses, hearing and smell, the singing of washerwomen returning from the stream, the chanting of monks in the nearby monastery, the fragrance of orchids in their secret hidden places,

In the closed microcosm of the garden, time flows, like the unveiling of scenery before an advancing walker contemplating a roll of landscape paintings, or in the reading of a *tianyuan* poem which develops to the counterpoint of its stanzas. Between reality and illusion, references and quotations, suggestion and symbolism, the garden takes root through space and time in the heart of its designer and of the stroller, through fleeting views and fugitive sensations, in incessant transmutations that give the Chinese garden the infinity of facets of a perpetually evolving universe. ⓘ

H——At the heart of the bamboos, a path leads to the retreat; To the side, amidst the pines, the cabin hides.
Ji Cheng, *Yuanye. Treatise on the Garden*, "Assessing a site", p. 102.
Garden for walking every day (Rishi yuan), Taizhou, (Jiangsu province). © Chiu Che Bing

Bibliography

Chen, Congzhou, *Suzhou yuanlin* (" 苏州园林 ", *Suzhou Gardens*), Shanghai, Tongji daxue jianzhuxi, 1956; *Shuoyuan* (" 说圜 ", *On the Chinese Garden*), Shanghai, Tongji University Press, 1984.

François Cheng, *Souffle-Esprit. Textes théoriques chinois de l'art pictural*, Paris, Seuil, 1989.

Chung, Wah Nan, *Tha Art of Chinese Gardens* (" 中国园林艺术 "), Hong Kong, University Press, 1982.

Frodsham, J. D., *The Murmuring Stream, the Life and the works of Hsieh Ling-yün*, Kuala Lumpur, University of Malaya Press, 1967. *Jardin du lettré. Synthèse des arts en Chine*, Boulogne-Billancourt, Musée Albert-Kahn, 2004, p. 209-217.

Ji Cheng, *Yuanye. Le Traité du jardin*, translated into French by Che Bing Chiu, Besançon, Éditions de l'Imprimeur, 1997.

Liu, Dunzhen, *Suzhou gudian yuanlin* (" 苏州古典园林 ", Traditional Gardens of *Suzhou*), Beijing, Zhongguo jianzhu gongye chubanshe, 1979.

Sirén, Osvald, *Garden of China*, New York, The Ronald Press Company, 1949.

Tao Yuanming, *Œuvre complète*, translated into French, introduced and annotated by Paul Jacob, Paris, Gallimard, 1990.

Tong, Jun, *Jiangnan yuanlin zhi* (" 江南园林志 ", *Chronicle of the Gardens south of the River*), Beijing, Zhongguo gongye chubanshe, 1963.

Wang, Wei, *Les Saisons bleues, l'œuvre de Wang Wei*, French text by Patrick Carré, Paris, Phébus, 1989.

I——Choose a Xiao monastery as a neighbour and the chanting of the sutras stays with you.
Surrounded by purple bundles and blue mists, the songs of the cranes reach all the way to the pillow.
Ji Cheng, *Yuanye. Treatise on the Garden*, "On the garden", p. 92-94.
Borrowing from the pagoda of the Northern Monastery (Beisi) from the pond in the Humble Administrator s Garden (Zhuozheng yuan), *Suzhou* (*Jiangsu province*). © Chiu Che Bing

Public spaces and contemporary gardens Arnauld Laffage

Any examination of the theme of the contemporary garden in China, the provision of parks and green spaces, immediately recalls the attachment to landscape in Chinese civilisation and the fact that it was one of the first civilisations to take an interest in landscape (Augustin Berque [1]). Any observation of behaviour shows the extent to which Chinese people remain attracted to natural features and view the spaces around them from the perspective of landscape.

The ban on the teaching of the art of landscaping in universities during the cultural revolution, failed to destroy this culture. However, because the subject was not reintroduced until the late 1980s, works by landscape architects are still too recent for the specificity of the contemporary Chinese garden to be identifiable. We have nevertheless observed that garden designers are primarily influenced by two currents: firstly the culture of traditional Chinese gardens and secondly China's cultural opening up to the world. The ancient process of the "borrowed landscape" (the reconstitution of a distant landscape in the traditional garden) has been transposed to an international dimension and naturally accommodates references to other cultures, in particular through the influence of western gardens.

This leads us to ask two questions: How should we interpret contemporary landscape designs in China? What are the current proposals that represent a response to the expectations of a population with an atavistic attachment to its landscape culture?

The new public gardens

Let us take the example of the Tanghe River Park [2] 汤河 in Qinhuangdao 秦皇岛 (a province of Hebei) designed by Yu Kongjian [3] 俞孔坚. This landscaped urban park, measuring around 1 km in length, includes a variety of features allowing people to reach the previously inaccessible riverbanks and wetland areas. The installation of a so-called "red ribbon" 红飘带 structure provides a playful access route. It is a kind of walkway that snakes its way through the marshy vegetation along the river. It can be seen as a contemporary version of the zigzag bridge or as a dragon moving through the vegetation. This 500 metre long ribbon, both route marker and lighting feature, is also a bench that encourages people to revive traditional garden practices. As landscape furniture and a contemporary landscape gesture, it is an invitation to share with other people as well as with nature. Its smooth, shiny, "finished", highly artificial appearance and composite materials highlight the raw, wild character of the surrounding environment.

1——In *Des raisons du paysage. De la Chine antique aux environnements de synthèse*, éd. Hazan, 1995, "... emergence of landscape, which happened first in China, and more than a thousand years later in Europe...", p. 38.
2——This site on the outskirts of the city (in the process of development, urbanisation and modernisation) was a hard to reach no man's land, characterised by heavy vegetation and safety and cleanliness problems (fly tipping).
3——Yu Kongjian, Director of the School of Landscape, Beijing University, Beijing.

It can be said that it resonates with a particularly Chinese interest in nature, where gardens often constitute a way of staging the relationship between the body and natural features: wind, sounds (listening to the rain, to the songs of caged birds), flying kites, meeting friends, singing, making music, playing cards, chess, etc. All these favoured practices of traditional Chinese gardens are referenced here and give the garden its relevance.

This example reflects a focus on the now and a dialogue with the milieu that takes account of the environmental and ecological dimension. At present, an interest in ecosystems is becoming a crucial element in the landscape designer's quest for an appropriate territorial identity.

Let us consider another location, this time a total spatial transformation ("tabula rasa"): in the sector north of the Olympic site in Beijing, the "*Olympic Forest Park*"[4] 奥林匹克森林公园 forms a series of artificial hills and wetlands created piecemeal.[5] This park includes traditional Chinese garden features (such as scenic rock arrangements) but also wetlands (5.9 hectares) which provide a more contemporary setting for the reed beds, which visitors are invited to walk through on narrow paths dominated by the surrounding reeds. This pathway "between sky and earth" creates an abstract experience that highlights the material, the flexibility and mobility of the plants, an almost tactile immersion where the vegetation seems to lose its substance in the light of these wide open spaces.

A and B——"The red ribbon". Tanghe River Park (2006), Qinhuangdao, Hebei province.
Landscape architect Kongjian Yu. © Kongjian Yu

4——Designed by the Urban Planning and Design Institute of Tsinghua University, under the direction of Mr. Hu Jie.
5——Total area: 680 hectares. Water area: 67.7 hectares. Planting of 570,000 trees and creation of a global ecosystem (fauna and flora) by all the aquatic plants which are not only ornamental.

This way of emphasising natural agricultural features in the staging can be found in other experiments: at the University of Architecture of Shenyang 沈阳, in Liaoning Province, rice fields have been planted like ornamental beds in the midst of the campus.[6] This type of feature changes perceptions, turning agricultural crops into ornamental plantings, which have their own meaning even in an urban environment. By the same account, large-scale landscaping features around infrastructures could perhaps be used to enhance and more directly reflect, without the use of artifice, the surroundings through which they pass (e.g. motorway embankments) and thereby contribute to territorial identity, without the use of excessively "designed" features, which tend to homogenise the landscapes along these infrastructures. It is also worth noting that in China, the term "green spaces" covers several meanings, which differ depending on the relation to the environment.[7]

C and D—"Shenyang Architectural University Campus" (2003), Taizhou, Shenyang, Liaoning Province.
Landscape Architect Kongjian Yu, © Kongjian Yu

6——Designed by the Yu Kongjian Workshop 俞孔坚
7——绿地 *lu di*, green land = green spaces
　　城市绿地 *cheng shi lu di*, green land of the town
　　居住绿地 *ju zhu lu di*, green land housing
　　工业绿地 *gong ye lu di*, industrial green land
　　道路绿地 *dao lu di*, roadside green land
　　公园绿地 *gong yuan lu di*, parkland green land
　　生产绿地 *sheng chan lu di*, green land for production
　　防护绿地 *fang hu lu di*, green land for protection
　　公共设施绿地 *gong gong she shi lu di*, green land of public amenities
　　特殊绿地 *te shu lu di*, special green land
　　其他绿地 *qi ta lu di*, other green land
　　绿带 *lu dai*, green belt
　　绿化 *lu hua*, greenery
　　绿化带 *lu hua dai*, belt of greenery
　　绿化系统 *lu hua xi tong*, system of greenery
　　绿地系统 *lu di xi tong*, green land system
　　绿色空间 *lu se kong jian*, green space
　　绿化广场 *lu hua guang chang*, square in greenery

"Semi-private" gardens

It is also in the "semi-private" gardens within big housing estate blocks that we can see the most common expression of the contemporary garden. Designed for communal use, these local amenities, which are sometimes almost caricatural in their excessive formalism, are primarily seen as places of "spatial practice".

So where we might be content with a square of grass, these spaces have ornamental brooks, bridges, rocks, bamboo thickets, ponds (used as paddling pools in summer), exotic plants, arbours (which provide frames for climbing flowers but also cucumbers or pumpkins), benches, exercise apparatus, etc., all features designed to encourage the practice of space. One of these gardens (in Nankin 南京) even has a cabin with a grand piano for use by inhabitants of the estate. In these recent developments, the contemporary and traditional overlap and it is human behaviour that binds together culture and nature. The elements, the design features, can differ in materials or shapes, but they meet the same demands, the same needs. The Chinese have always been attracted by gardens. You only have to observe the parks, where families stroll, people meet or young newlyweds pose in front of flowering trees, a meandering stream or a humpback bridge, to understand their predilection for the natural features to be found in gardens in the city.

E and F—Semi-private garden within a residential block, Nankin 2001. © Arnauld Laffage
G—Sugarcane Garden, Yu Kongjian. International Flower Show Xiamen 2007. © Tang Jianren

The bridal veil in the wind, the same wind that carries the kite upwards, are the expression of this relationship. It is in this perception of the relation between people and natural features that the contemporary Chinese garden can be understood.

How do the garden designers of today, in their experiments, in their ideas, help to express those living aspects of the garden and its perception, in a contemporary way, by embedding the tradition of the ancient Chinese garden in a modern context?

For the first time, the international flower show in Xiamen 厦门[8] invited designs for gardens by landscape architects. In their proposals, the designers attempt to achieve a fusion between Chinese culture and modernity through the use of local materials and adjustment to the local context. Let us look at two examples:

8——September 23, 2007-March 21, 2008.

Ⓗ——Bamboo Garden, Wang Xiangrong. International Flower Show Xiamen, © Wang Xiangrong

The Sugarcane garden[9] 蔗园 stages essential local features in the quest for a minimalist aesthetic. The choice of plants and the raw, unlandscaped layout, promote dialogue with the rural surroundings. The garden's central excavation is designed to isolate the walker visually and thereby foster the multi-sensory dimension of the relation to space: the sound of the countryside and the distant music of farm work can spontaneously awaken a memory of pastoral life.

The Bamboo Garden[10] 竹园 is more an encouragement to strolling, to exploration, to a kinetic relationship with the landscape. It is another way of reflecting the context. It uses the traditional principle of the frame opening on to the outside world. The garden stages the interplay of materials and light. It emphasises graininess, the contrast of features, the way the white wall is dematerialised into light by the graphic play of the bamboo plants.

It is in this union between the richness of the traditional Chinese garden, the openness to other cultural references and the accommodation of the ecological and environmental dimension, that contemporary landscape architecture in China is currently forging its own specifically Chinese identity.

9——*Yu Kongjia n* 俞孔坚 Workshop. Garden area: approximately 1000 m².
10——Atelier *Wang Xiangrong* 王向荣. Garden area: 1300 m² approx.

字

Character

For the Chinese, learning to write is a character-forming process in both the literal and figurative sense. The characters, which are the same throughout the country, allow the Chinese to communicate even when they speak different languages, such as Cantonese and Mandarin.

Cities and streets are populated by these signs, which give a dimension to urban space that is sometimes more symbolic, and also more playful, than western writing and the signs that populate our cities. Before the invention of printing, stele engraving was used to reproduce both text and calligraphy, together with representations of the world, heaven, religion and the sciences.

Embossing was the first process used for the transmission and perpetuation of both the content and form of texts, which are to be found almost identically embodied in the development of the architecture and, beyond that, of the layout of imperial cities. The invention of printing, several centuries before Gutenberg, spread this way of perceiving knowledge throughout country.

The spatial dimension of this mental geography has been partly lost, and is now dominated by the image. The resulting loss in terms of urban design has nevertheless had an unexpected upside: the transcription of Chinese characters into pinyin (the western alphabet), which might have led to cultural impoverishment, has instead democratised the use of signs, which—now through the medium of information technology—can be read without being written.

As a result, understanding of the Chinese world has been enhanced by the alliance of both ways of thinking, without more being lost on either side than they had already left behind in the course of recent history.

China: street scene in Canton. © mission 21: BMA A-30.17.021

Structures

2.1

Liu Yanjun

Calligraphy architecture city space

Calligraphy and architecture are two arts that are both parts of Chinese tradition and operate in the dimension of space. Moreover, they also belong to the category of the visual and static arts.

Under the influence of traditional philosophy and aesthetic thought, the writing of Chinese characters developed as an artistic form to the point that calligraphy became "the very foundation of Chinese aesthetics", in the words of the great writer Lin Yutang (1895-1976). Originally no more than the quest for an attractive line, it rose to the rank of a major art, the ultimate sublimation of existence through artistic expression.

For their part, in the Chinese tradition, architecture and city organisation offer a synthetic perception of space, in which the building, structure and overall composition develop as an expression of the wellsprings of Chinese thought and aesthetic criteria.

Thus, calligraphy and architecture have in common the fact that they belong to the same cultural system, whilst emanating from different expressive categories. Equally from the point of view of construction principles, aesthetic characteristics and spatial composition, these artistic forms reveal their community of inspiration in structure and in formal expression.

Constitutive principles

In the disciplines considered here, the principles of composition are the same; they entail the combination of a limited number of basic elements, assembled in accordance with a certain system of organisation and particular aesthetic rules, for the purpose of achieving a harmonious, proportioned and balanced whole. Chinese characters or "sinograms" are made up of simple fundamental strokes. The art of calligraphy consists in combining these different strokes (dots, hooks, etc.) in accordance with specific rules of composition, in order to form characters that combine to form words, which themselves create sentences that in turn are structured into texts. In this process, entailing the organisation of structures composed of strokes into coherent combinations, an important factor is the relations between the strokes and their assembly in space, in order to achieve wholes that are structured by flexible links and natural sequences.

The principles of calligraphy, as just stated, could also apply to architecture, as a description of the way a structure is formed. Wooden architecture in the Chinese tradition is composed of a linear succession of elements, comparable to the basic strokes in calligraphy: posts, beams, tie beams, brackets, lintels, purlins, rafters and battens. Raising posts on which beams and tie beams are placed is equivalent to the calligrapher's gesture in drawing in space "a horizontal stroke then a vertical stroke, an oblique stroke on the left then an oblique stroke on the right". The aim in both cases is to form a solid and balanced overall structure.

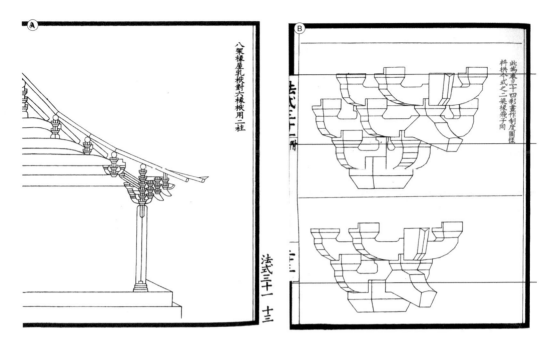

In addition, the architect like the calligrapher has no hesitation in showing the links and combinations between the different posts, beams and other structural elements: the overall beauty is expressed through simplicity, clarity and authenticity. The two components that together form the bracket and the bracket post (斗拱 *dougong*) constitute a whole that represents this quest for balance.

Indeed, the superimposition and juxtaposition of these successive overhangs, creating the junction between the verticality of the posts and the horizontality of the beams, forms complex and subtle corbels. Seen from below, the awning roof seems to rest on this succession of brackets and bracket posts, like a stack of clouds Ⓑ Ⓒ Ⓓ. The basic module of Chinese architecture, it is used to distribute weight between vertical and horizontal elements; it is also a marvellous illustration of the Taoist saying: "The Tao produced one, one produced two, two produced three, three produced all beings."[1]

These traditional principles of composition, which are equally found in music, dance and painting, also apply—on a wider scale—to the organisational composition of the ancient Chinese city.

A—*Yingzao Fashi*, Extract

1—Tao-te-king (or Daodejing). The term *Tao* (or *Dao* "way") is a word used commonly in ancient literature, meaning "road", "path, and by extension "method", "way of doing"." (Anne Cheng, History of Chinese Philosophy, Seuil 1997).

In traditional architecture, whose basic materials are earth and wood, we find that the fundamental unit is the same, whatever the category of building, from simple houses to palaces, temples and administrative or business premises. The variety lies in the shape of the roofs, the colours or the size of the building. For this reason, if we look at the layout of cities, the arrangement of most of the buildings shows a characteristic similarity in the basic composition into "lines and dots", where the only difference is in the thickness of the line. To meet the specific needs arising from the function of the building, Chinese architecture developed along organic lines, in which spaces are extended or enlarged by combining and multiplying preconstituted elements. Window bays (间 jian) are the building units: they are juxtaposed to form buildings, which are themselves arranged to create L-shaped or U-shaped edifices, or quadrangles around a courtyard. Ⓔ Ⓕ Ⓖ These structures can be made up of several successive courtyards or "entrances" (进 jin), and can extend to share a lateral alleyway punctuated with different entrances to form a uniform block of buildings.

These blocks are grouped into districts, bounded by grids of wide streets and organised around a centre where the palace or administrative and legal headquarters is located. The bell towers and drum towers are then placed on a central axis.

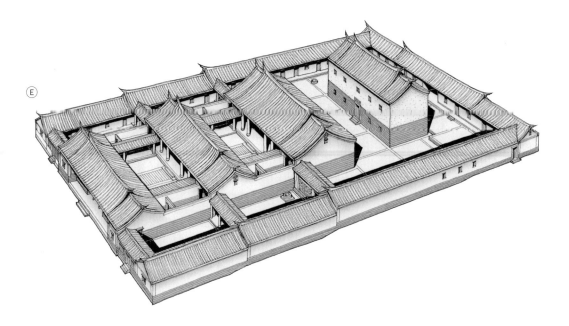

E——Axonometric view of a house in the village of Dingtan, Fujian.
F——View of Lijiang, Yunnan. © OACC
G——Old houses near Nanshizi alley Suzhou.
© Municipal committee for the compilation of local Suzhou records.

Aesthetic characteristics

Calligraphy, like architecture, is a way of combining lines in pursuit of a global aesthetic.

The beauty of a calligraphy lies in the way that the elements of the drawing unfurl, in accordance with the underlying form and general harmony of the composition. It is not a beauty based on symmetry or regularity, but a flowing, free and multiple beauty, conveyed by the expressions: "flow like clouds in motion", "firmness and rapidity of the stroke", "correctly arranged curves and angles". As for the brush that performs the stroke, it must be handled with a quest for balance between "heaviness and lightness, slowness and speed", a "variation in densities and spacings", "subtly alternating curves and straight lines", all precepts that have permitted the expression of infinite diversity and the emergence of many different styles and schools.

In architecture likewise, it is enough to contemplate the great roofs unfurling like the wings of a bird, to appreciate the lively and weightless beauty of the lines that they can produce. Every temple, every palace hall, is the fruit of an alliance between the curved lines of the roofs and the straight lines of the columns. As in calligraphy, they illustrate the fundamental importance attributed to the harmony between the masses and the contrasting forces, between densities and rhythms, between the alternation of straight lines and curves, between rigidity and flexibility. This can be seen in the actual composition of many characters relating to architecture: 宫 *gong* (palace)、室 *shi* (hall)、家 *jia* (house)、亭 *ting* (pavilion).

H——The Forbidden City, seen from Wumen Gate Beijing. © OACC

The goal is not to emphasise the stone, as western architecture seeks to do, but the quest for an aesthetics of line, in terms of lightness, grace and vigour, but above all in terms of dynamics and rhythm.

However, whilst each of the buildings that constitute a city possesses its own beauty, there is no disorder in their juxtaposition, which in fact unfurls with a powerful and energetic elegance and clarity. Indeed, the predominant characteristic of architectural aesthetics in the Chinese tradition, is precisely the quest for global harmony.

Whether in the line of a character in calligraphy, or in architecture the production of pavilions, belvederes or entire groups of compositions in the city, from single houses to entire districts, the beauty of each of these units is not the final goal. Much more important is the total composition, which seeks a balanced distribution in the density and dimensions of buildings, in the rhythm and continuity of communications; it is only in this way, through a perfectly homogeneous and unified totality, that the internal energy specific to a work of art can be expressed. All the more so when it comes to the composition of cities, the aim is to develop an organic ecology based on the different channels of internal circulation, in connection with those greater entities that are the harmonies "of the winds and waters" (风水 fengshui) and cosmic interaction.

The soul of a city only develops through spatial and temporal patterns, as manifested in those categories of "fengshui" and of "cosmos". Likewise, in calligraphy, the gesture and the line must achieve a perfect match between movement and internal circulation to allow access to the spheres where "heaven and man are one". This guiding concept is the founding principle of the composition of cities in ancient China. As Joseph Needham has said in reference to Chinese architecture, "in no field have the Chinese so powerfully expressed their grandiose presupposition: "the human is inseparable from nature", that "human" in question not being man considered apart from society. Palaces, temples and other significant edifices of this type are the structures to which this principle primarily applies, of course, but rural or urban housing, whether grouped or single, expresses the same sense of being part of "a universal perspective", because it incorporates the symbolism of the cardinal points, of the seasons, of the winds and of the stars." In applying this postulate of a quest for unity, rulers, when planning their capitals, used as the foundation of the necessity and legitimacy of their power the principles expressed in the saying "in the image of heaven and by earthly laws": this kind of spatial composition of land is expressed in terms of astral configurations or through abstractions and metaphors which illustrate the original and structural relationship between architecture and cosmogony. The Forbidden City, in Beijing, is the best illustration of the phrase "heaven and man are one".

Yin and yang: the art of organising space

In ancient China, the origin of the universe was explained in a number of ways. The explanation given in Lao Tseu's Taoist philosophy had considerable influence: Taoism states that the world was formed from the two entities, *yin* and *yang*. This concept of *yin* and *yang* applies to all the phenomena and paradoxes of our life, and is based on the principle of the union of opposites. As a philosophical system, it expresses this complementarity at work in the harmony and balance of the universe, with notions such as passive and active, female and male, moon and sun, mountain and water, black and white, etc. It should be emphasised that this conception relates primarily to the relationship between two objects, not the object itself.

This philosophy profoundly influenced the aesthetics of space in traditional Chinese culture. Indeed, whether in calligraphy or construction, the importance attributed to the beauty of full physical form is subordinate to the sequence and interaction between "masses" and "voids". In calligraphy, this is expressed in the general arrangement and distribution of empty spaces (page layout), rather than in the characters alone [1]. This aesthetic applies to all space, in such a way as to: "create interdependence between that which is within the norm and that which is not", "create volumes by playing on variations in densities", "take account of the white (the paper) as much as of the black (the ink)", "make the vital energies and interior harmony interpenetrate". In calligraphy, black represents the mass and white the void. Masses and voids engender each other mutually to create a whole with a perfect and complete existence. In the case of a composition in cursive writing, the result is a particularly elaborate and exuberant form.

Similarly, the inventiveness specific to traditional woodframe Chinese architecture does not lie in the diversity and multiplicity of autonomous models, but in the artistry of the overall spatial composition: the beauty of the juxtapositions,

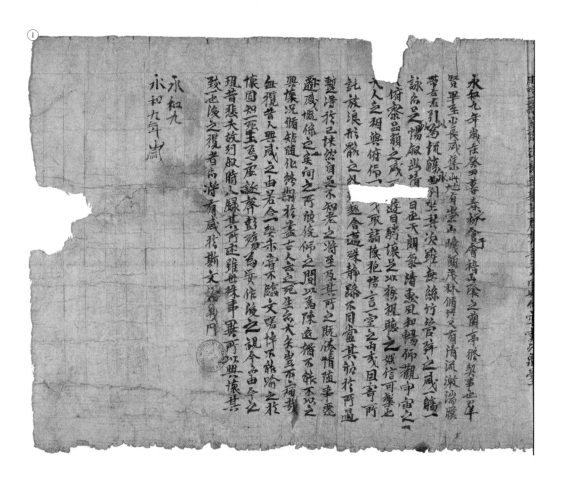

永和九年歳在癸丑暮春之初會于會稽山陰之蘭亭脩禊事也羣賢畢至少長咸集此地有崇山峻嶺茂林脩竹又有清流激湍映帶左右引以為流觴曲水列坐其次雖無絲竹管弦之盛一觴一詠亦足以暢敘幽情是日也天朗氣清惠風和暢仰觀宇宙之大俯察品類之盛所以遊目騁懷足以極視聽之娛信可樂也夫人之相與俯仰一世或取諸懷抱悟言一室之內或因寄所託放浪形骸之外雖趣舍萬殊靜躁不同當其欣於所遇暫得於己快然自足不知老之將至及其所之既倦情隨事遷感慨係之矣向之所欣俛仰之間以為陳迹猶不能不以之興懷況脩短隨化終期於盡古人云死生亦大矣豈不痛哉每覽昔人興感之由若合一契未嘗不臨文嗟悼不能喻之於懷固知一死生為虛誕齊彭殤為妄作後之視今亦由今之視昔悲夫故列敘時人錄其所述雖世殊事異所以興懷其致一也後之覽者亦將有感於斯文

永和九
永和九年歳
致正後之覽者高游有感於斯文永

transitions, confrontations and permutations, of the sequences, insertions, convergences, closures, openings, encounters, mobilities; the aesthetic here is primarily visual, but it can also be auditory and tactile, in the contrast of sharp and blurred, hidden or overt, etc. The starting point is the line, the field of intervention space, the final objective deployment and extension over the whole of the area concerned. Galleries, walls, pavilions, belvederes, terraces, kiosks, etc., are akin to lines that we draw on the ground, with the ink of a brush. And in the space that they punctuate operate all the natural elements—wind, plants, snow, moon, sun, heaven and earth—that the Chinese love and venerate. Masses and voids mutually engender each other, interact through the deployment of vertical and horizontal lines, around an axis, in uninterrupted continuity, to give birth to courtyard houses, palaces, villages and cities.

1—*Lantingxu* or press first to the orchid pavilion. © Bibliothèque Nationale de France

With such a capacity for extension, this type of spatial organisation is highly adaptable to the function and rank of buildings and their environment. Built spaces and free spaces represent the essential components—"masses" and "voids", "black" and "white"—and the art of composition lies in the subtle use of the oppositions between concentrated and diffuse, dense and fluid, hard and soft, mobile and immobile, normal and eccentric, lively and constrained, giving rise to a succession of rhythmically and organically organised spatial and temporal sequences. The spirit that emerges from this process has a great diversity of tones, such as gravity and elegance, or charm and vivacity. It is equally applicable to the halls of a palace and the rooms of a private house, as it is to a mountain hamlet. Thus the spatial composition employed in the Imperial Palace or in the Liu garden in Suzhou can be compared to different styles of calligraphy: the former like a vast composition in the sigillary style, solemn and finished, which proclaims the supremacy of the emperor's power and the hierarchical order embodied in the rituals; the latter like calligraphy in the cursive style, a free and joyful expression of personal emotion. Both manifest the wish to be in harmony with nature.

As the philosopher and poet Zong Baihua (1897-1986) has put it: "Our conception of space is embodied not in the rectilinear alleys of ancient Egypt, nor the volumes of Greek sculpture nor the unbounded spaces of modern Europe, but in pathways ("ways" 道 dao), undulating and winding, uninterrupted and subtle, which open on to their goal from afar! Our universe is the time that governs space, in this way, with the measure and melody of music, we can work for "time and space to be joined in a single whole".

Tasting traditional Chinese architecture is like appreciating a calligraphy scroll: one must be able to stay within it, constantly changing point of view, to grasp the work in its entirety and perceive what it contains in terms of time and space. Thus, it is not the man who moves within the architecture, it is the architecture that unfurls around him, and the means of tasting it lie not in a contemplation of the space that is not static, but dynamic. By moving around, the man who examines the columns, beams, lintels, tie beams, rafters and brackets is able to appreciate the network created by the intersection of all these "lines", to understand the respective roles of masses and voids, of spaces of fluidity or density, each step leading to a new perspective and reference, the places left empty providing space for an unlimited expansion of the mind: it is in this context that we see the full meaning of the aphorism "masses and voids engender each other mutually, the place where nothing is written thus becomes a sublime location".

地

Earth

Earth, heaven and man

China, *Zhongguo*, a name with two constituent characters, one meaning middle, centre, and the other country or kingdom, commonly rendered in English as "Middle Kingdom", is first of all an immense area of land—ten million square kilometres— formed of ancient kingdoms fused by wars and treaties.

Sometimes perceived as a threat, the old empire and each of its constituent kingdoms, sought to protect themselves from external invasion. This was the reason for the building of the great walls unified by the first short-lived Qin dynasty (221-206 BCE). When invaders did succeed in taking China, they themselves were absorbed into the civilisation under their control, adopting the customs of the occupied country at least as much as they imposed their own. This was true of the Jurchens from the North, ancestors of the Manchus known as the Jin dynasty (1115-1234), of the Mongols who chose to name their dynasty Yuan some sixty years after taking power (1279-1368) or of the Qing dynasty of the Manchus (1644-1911).

With the Manchus, Chinese civilisation spread beyond its existing borders to Tibet and all the western territories grouped within the modern province of Xinjiang, to Manchuria and for a while to Outer Mongolia.

It might be said that the unity of China—a country that was home to five hundred million people in 1900, more than six hundred million in 1960 and had reached one billion when the single child policy was introduced—has always been multiple.

Wei Dezhong 魏德忠, The "Great Wall of water", 1970, Henan. © Wei Dezhong

A sho.t histo.y of Chinese cartography

Yves Kirchner

Western researchers have tended to find Chinese cartography disconcerting. Because they resemble pictographic works, Chinese maps often convey not visible reality but another, more intellectual reality, one which reflects a hierarchical vision of the world. In addition, these drawings, which primarily draw attention to the presence in the place of the thing depicted, are not always essential, since information that is considered important is set out in marginal texts. And finally, the Chinese, whatever their origin—Han, Jurchen, Mongol, Manchu, or any of the many ethnolinguistic minorities that populate China—and perhaps because of this diversity, sought to embed the present in a continuity, believing that the only sense in any creation lay in the quest to return to a former golden age. For this reason, until quite recently, the first Chinese maps were seen as primitive productions and treated with condescension.

On the one hand, it is easy to understand why an emperor should wish to draw up a map of his territory—simply put, it is a way of appropriating it, subjugating it and governing it from a distance. On the other hand, it is harder for a western reader to understand why the successors of that emperor should continue to use the same map, despite the fact that it is manifestly "inaccurate". But what is meant by inaccurate? Do we not already have here the first signs of incomprehension between two radically different cultures? How could a map drawn from a work rooted in tradition, and therefore venerated—in this case the *Tribute of Yu*—be considered "inaccurate"? In order to understand how the Chinese have negotiated the twists and turns of the history of cartography, therefore, we need to set aside any notion of chronology or idea of progress, concepts that have ruled the western world since the 19th century, guiding and confusing its perception. China—without any sense of incongruity or paradox—has accepted the coexistence of different models of maps, which have been recognized and adopted at different periods. These originals may be lost, but they have nevertheless survived in the form of numerous copies and annotated compilations. This means that all these maps may have existed at the same time and been considered "accurate".

The Yugong

The first geographical descriptions of China come from the *Shu Jing* or "Classic of History", one of the three canonical Chinese books dating from the third century BCE, from the chapter entitled *The Tribute of Yu*. This document relates myths about the 2nd century BCE, when king Shun, after a number of fruitless attempts, asks his minister Yu, soon to be renamed Yu the Great, to "tame the water and the land". [1] This task, which was to "maintain the water at the level of the land", led him to travel throughout the "civilised world". The book which recounts these events contains very detailed descriptions of the "nine provinces" of China, each ordered in the following way: boundaries of the province; public works carried out in it; quality of the land; nature of the tribute; roads by which it is brought to the capital. A second section deals with the boundaries of the territory, stabilised by five sacred mountains [2] (one at each cardinal point and the fifth in the centre), and with the kingdom's great waterways. The work finishes with a description of Yu's hydrographic achievements. In addition, *the Tribute of Yu* provides a description of the world as imagined by the Chinese. This representation, called the *Yugong*, is centred on the Emperor from whose person imperial power radiates in successive symbolic strata each with a thickness of 500 Chinese *li* (around 250 km) until it encompasses the whole world. The first boundary corresponds to the imperial sphere; the second encompasses the domains of the feudal princes; the third is the zone of pacification, or the zone of the marches partly civilised by China; the fourth is the zone of the barbarian allies; and finally, the outer zone is inhabited by uncivilised savages. This semblance of imperial authority in fact encompassed multiple local specificities of writing, language and belief, which would gradually become uniform. Although the *Yugong* says nothing about the shape of the different zones, they are depicted as rectangles, following the convention that the earth is square or rectangular (the Chinese word makes no distinction) and the sky that envelops it round. Traditionally, therefore, China adopted the shape of a square divided into nine equal parts (the nine provinces), a symbolic shape that can be discerned in the design layout of cities.(A)

These feats of hydraulic engineering, which in 486 BCE led to Emperor Wu's construction of a canal linking the Yangtze in the south to the modern province of Shandong, [3] were instrumental in giving China under the Zhou Dynasty (1046-221 BCE) measuring devices such as the surveyor's chain, and tools such as

---

1——*Mémoires historiques*, translated into French by Édouard Chavannes, t. 1, p. 21.
2——The creation of the world is related in the *Yishi*, a massive compilation executed by Ma Su (1621-1673), which, on the basis of various ancient mythological narratives, gives a description of the world which includes only China: "When [Pangu] was at the point of death, he transformed his body: his breath became the winds and the clouds, his voice the roar of thunder, his left eye the sun, his right eye the moon, his four limbs and the five (parts of his) body the four extremes and the five sacred mountains, his blood and his humours the Blue River and the Yellow River, his nerves and his arteries the veins of the earth, his muscles the soil of the fields, his hair and his moustaches the stars and constellations, the hair on his body the vegetation, his teeth and his bones metals and stones, his essences and his marrow pearls and jades, his sweat and secretions rain and marshland."
3——Jacques Gernet, *Le Monde chinois*, Armand Colin, 1972, p. 605.

the plumbline and spirit level.[4] At this time, the technique used was to cover the territory on foot and to convert these strides into a scale drawing, transforming the reality of a landscape into abstract signs. The Zhou Dynasty ushered in a true culture of writing. However, from the 3rd century of the common era, the Chinese would use a combination of a scale ratio for distances and a rectangular grid —a geometrical system based on the *Yugong*— to estimate the distances between points.

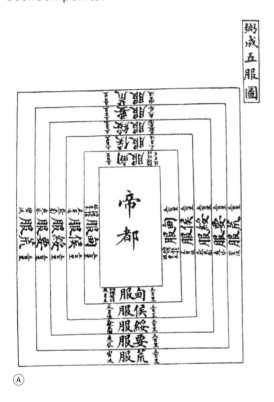

(A)

Meeting the "barbarians"

The Han Dynasty (206 BCE–220 CE), which was cosmopolitan and curious in its attitudes, encouraged the production of maps in different perspectives. One early map, in painted silk, found on the Mawangdui archaeological site in a tomb dating from 168 BCE, draws a fairly accurate topographical picture of the region south of the town of Changsha, which runs along the modern river Xiaoshui. By contrast with western practice, the map is oriented south to north. The Han empire under Huidi, which had its capital at Chang'an (modern Xi'an), was already governed according to a strict administrative and military system which controlled and managed the peasantry. The territory was divided into commanderies (*jun*) and prefectures (*xian*) linked directly to the central authority.

A——Yugong.

4——"In his left hand, he held the level and measuring tape; in his right hand, the dividers and set square." Shiji, chap. 2, p. 50-51.

In 167 BCE, punishment by mutilation was replaced by forced labour, which gave the Empire the manpower needed to carry out major engineering projects (defensive walls, canals, etc.). The map, which is known as the *Garrison map* (*Changsha guo nanbu dixing tu*) and assumed to have been used by an educated person—it was placed in a lacquered box alongside books—as yet unidentified, is drawn on a scale of one Chinese inch (3.33 cm) to ten *li* (approximately 5000 m).

It mentions the streams and rivers and their sources; the contours of the mountains and valleys are shown in different colours, which highlight the altitude changes with surprising modernity; the location of eight towns and seventy-four villages is shown. To the west, a note specifies the suppose resting place of Emperor Shun. The catalogue notice [5] states that as well as being used for administrative purposes, the map was employed in war, which implies that its topographical detail was considered of great value. This fact is sufficiently unusual to merit comment, since most of the Han Dynasty maps were made for a single purpose, for example agriculture, forest or water management, or else the layout of a mausoleum, as is attested by the oldest map so far found in the province of Hebei, the map of the mausoleum of the King of Zhongshan, called Cuo, who reigned at the time of the Warring Kingdoms (475-221 BCE).

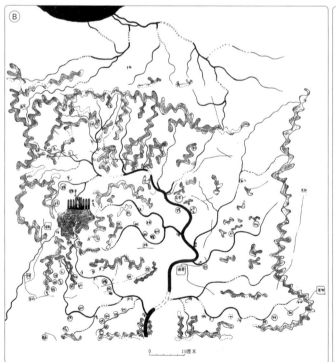

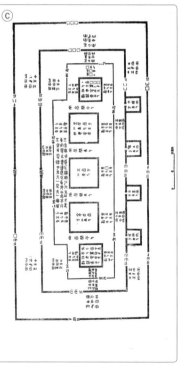

B——Garrison map, exhumed from the tomb n°3 of Mawangdui (Changsha, Hunan).
C——Plan of king of Zhongshan mausoleum (Hebei).

5——*China in Ancient and Modern Maps*, eds. Ancient Map Research Team of the Institute of Surveying and Mapping Sciences Staff.

In 126 BCE, Zhang Qian, the emissary of the Han emperor Wudi, returning from a twelve-year journey to form an alliance with the Yuezhi from north of the Oxus (the Amou-Daria Valley in Afghanistan), against the Xiongnu, visited the Valley of Ferghana (the upper Syr-Darya basin) and Sogdiane (in the modern Republic of Uzbekistan). He brought back from his journey reports of a West that was populous and rich, and showed the routes that he had taken to arrive there across Central Asia. He identified the source of the Yellow River, which he located in the Tarim. He opened the Silk Road which runs south of the Yangtze River by southwestern China and India. These embassies to the "barbarians" show, if that were needed, that China was not as isolationist as has been said. Even if the initial purpose was to assess a potential danger, the Chinese considered the "barbarians" to be "subjects".

The beginnings of a science

One Chinese map which was widely referred to in books dating from the era of the Three Kingdoms (220-589) until the time of the Song (960-1279)—but which has not survived in the original—is the so-called *Fangzhang tu* map by Pei Xiu (224-271), the founder of quantitative cartography. Appointed minister of public works in 267, Pei Xiu presented a map some 3 metres long to the emperor, who kept it in his secret archives. In the presentation of his work, Pei Xiu tried to lay the foundations of cartography:

"In *the Tribute of Yu* I examined the mountains and the seas, the courses of the rivers, the plateaux and the plains, the hills and the marshes, then the boundaries and position of the nine provinces of Antiquity and of the sixteen modern provinces, including the commanderies and kingdoms, the prefectures and towns, then the former names of the places where the kingdoms of the past established treaties or held meetings, then the routes by water and by land, the tracks and roads, and I made a geographical map in eighteen sheets."

In producing his maps, Pei Xiu employed five principles: the use of the traditional grid; measuring the sides of right-angled triangles to define distances; identifying high points and low points; measuring right angles and acute angles; and finally, measuring curves and straight lines. "Thus, continues Pei Xiu, when you combine these principles and look at the map, then the reality of the distances is determined by the rectilinear divisions [the grid]; the reality of the relative positions is determined by the *li* of road between them; the reality of the measurements in numbers is determined by calculating the top and the bottom, the angles and obliques, the curves and straight lines. [...] When the principle of the grid is properly applied, then there is nothing hidden in the form of the curve and of the straight line, of the far and of the near."

The system proposed by Pei Xiu lasted through the Sui (581-618) and Tang (618-907) dynasties. One of his followers, Jia Dan, specifies that texts are useful additions to the maps: "Not everything can be represented on a map [when one has to represent mountains, rivers, springs, etc.], so its reliability also depends on the notes appended to it." The tradition of accompanying commentary to the classical texts, introduced in the 3rd century by the philosopher Wang Bi, also spread to cartography, based on the principle that "if the image reveals the meaning, it is the word that clarifies the image".

In its diplomatic missions to the peoples of the Northern and Northwestern steppes, China collected information, generally of an ethnographic nature, to further its understanding of the customs of potentially threatening populations on its borders. A similar concern had prompted the establishment of military colonies beyond the frontiers, and the building of walls based on a knowledge of the topography and routes used by invaders. The different dynasties tried obstinately to establish forward positions in Tibet to forestall invasion. In 91 CE, under the Han dynasty, the armies of general Pan Chao took up positions there to control the Tarim basin (Karashar, Khotan, Kachgar, etc.), before losing these towns to Hun offensives. However, the energy the Chinese invested in retaining this region shows how crucial they considered its strategic importance. In the 7th century, the Tang dynasty recaptured the region from the Uyghur. The Chinese established four garrisons there, to oversee a territory that stretched to Lake Balkhash and as far as Samarkand. However, in the following century, the Arab conquerors overcame the Chinese at Talas in 751, opening the way for the conversion to Islam of the Uyghur, who were previously Nestorians. For a long time, Chinese power was driven eastwards, replaced by the autonomous Turkish principalities Xinjiang's relations with China were then confined to trade, to caravans passing through on the Silk Road, and also to religious contacts. Islam gradually penetrated from the oases of the Tarim into the whole of northwestern China, as far as Gansu and Shanxi.

Mapmaking and tradition

From the time of the Song dynasty (960-1279), the spread of the examination system and the remarkable explosion of printed publications that followed, permitted the coexistence of different types of maps. Certain authors follow the ancient paths, compiling and annotating texts taken from classical works. Others exploited improvements in calculation methods to draw more accurate maps. These encyclopaedias reveal the riches contained in several thousand earlier texts. But they also sow confusion about their dates, and about the motives behind these purportedly timeless and universal writings. Each contributor—whether commentator, scribe or draughtsman—adds material that he thinks might be of value, and removes what he considers improper.

Under the Song dynasty, it became an unavoidable obligation for each prefect to create a map of their territory. In addition, these maps had to be verified and updated every three years, and a printed copy sent to the authorities through hierarchical channels. The large quantities of available information undoubtedly fostered their production, with the government seeking to collate the different accounts sent by its emissaries in the Empire. For example, numerous local monographs (*fangzhi*)—accompanying the maps of the prefectures or provinces described—were used by court-appointed officials to familiarise themselves with the history, economy, flora and fauna and principal families of the region they were appointed to govern.

In the 1960s, a stele engraved in 1121 (*Jiu yu shouling tu*) depicting China in the Song era, under the reign of Emperor Huizong (1082-1135), was found in the Sichuan region. It divided the country into 9 administrative regions on a grid drawn on canvas. In the mid-11th century, significant inequalities in taxation had caused a peasant uprising. The administration was considered corrupt and the army was prone to pillage. Five years after this stele was engraved, the capital (Kaifeng) fell into the hands of the Jürchen Tartars. The map is orientated north, which is unusual for the era, when the Chinese compass favoured the south; it includes Baoding, Guangxing and the Shandong peninsula in the north, shows the line of the coast, and very recognizably the Bay of Hangzhou in the east, Hainan Island in the south, and the Chengdu region in the West. The mountains, the Yellow and Yangtze Rivers and their tributaries, Lakes Tai, Poyang and Dongting, together with more than 1400 locations, are shown with considerable accuracy.

D—Stele *Jiu yu shouling tu*. Map with 9 administrative regions.

Another stele, engraved in 1136, the *Map of China and the Barbarian Countries (Huayi tu)* provides older and less precise information than the previous stele. An inscription on the top right nevertheless stipulates that "the venerable Jia Dan of the Tang Dynasty [618-907] is the author of a census of more than a hundred localities, conducted using the chronicles of ancient times" compiled and reported by the author of this map. This suggests that behind this anonymous work there lies the outline of the much commentated map by Jia Dan entitled *Hainei huayi tu,* which included, amongst other marginal observations, the sea route from Canton to Baghdad. To the north-east of the Korean peninsula, one can make out two sections of the Great Wall and to the south the island of Hainan. More than 500 towns are mentioned, together with some 30 rivers, their tributaries and the main lakes. The texts around the map relate to the history and customs of "several hundred remote tribes".

On the back of this stele is another map called the *Map of the development of the waterways by the Emperor Yu (Yu ji tu)* which, although engraved around 1080, is astonishingly "modern". It uses the famous grid recommended by Pei Xiu, contains almost no commentary and is remarkably accurate. The representation of China's coastline is so remarkable, given its production in the 11th century, that Joseph Needham wrote of it: "Anyone who compares this map with contemporary productions [...] can only be astonished by the level achieved by Chinese geography at that time in China."

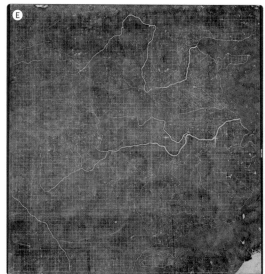
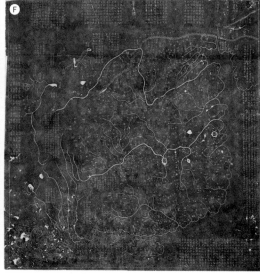

E—— *Map of the development of the waterways by the Emperor Yu (Yu ji tu),*
F——*Map of China and the Barbarian Countries (Huayi tu),*

Around the same time, a *Guide to the Geography of the Dynasties of the Past* (*Lidai dili zhizhang tu*), probably compiled by Shui Anli, was engraved on wood and then printed. This work, which covers the period of the legendary Dynasty King Ku, contains 44 maps, a foreword and a treatise for students preparing the imperial examinations. The Great Wall, represented in two sections, crosses the top of the map from one side to the other. China's 27 administrative regions are duly represented, together with the remote tribes, with accompanying commentary. The outlines of the general map, representing China as a whole, reproduce—in even more abbreviated form—those of the *Map of China and the Barbarian countries* (*Huayi tu*), both in the shape of its coastlines and in the technique. These are the oldest printed historical maps found in China.

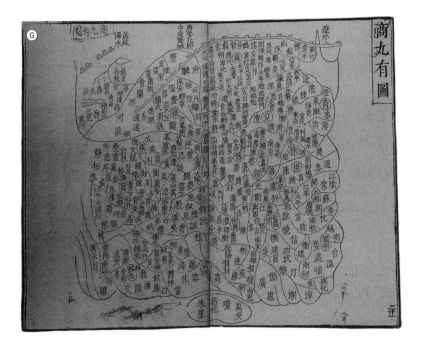

The *Map of the mountains and rivers* (*Yu Gong suozai Suishan Junchuan zhitu*), taken from the six volumes of *Annotations on past dynasties*, the *Shu Ji Zhuan* compiled by Cai Shen, combines work from the Song, Ming and Qing dynasties. It is considered to be a summary for the use of students preparing to take the imperial exams, a rival to the previous work. Although dating from 1209, the maps are based on the *Tribute of Yu*, in which, according to the *Yugong* tradition, the nine regions Ji, Yan, Qing, Xu, Yu, Yang, Jing, Yong and Liang are represented and compared with current administrative divisions. It shows the sacred mountain Kunlun in the west—the source of the Yellow River—and the coastlines in the east, with an axonometric representation of the rivers and mountains.

G——*Map of the nine regions*, from the *Guide to the Geography of the Dynasties of the Past*. Droits réservés.

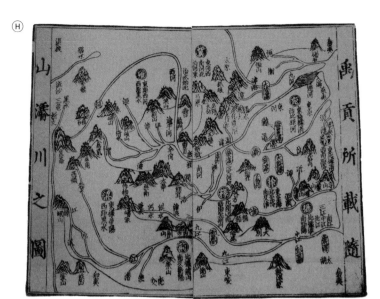

This type of commentary on the *Tribute of Yu* continued over subsequent centuries, as is evidenced by the *Yu Gong Shanchuan Zonghui zhitu* published by Fu Yin during the reign of Emperor Yongle (1403-1424). The regions depicted are those of northern China, site of the modern Beijing, together with Shanxi, the central parts of Zhejiang, Jiangxi and Hunan in the south, the provinces of Xinjiang, Qinghai, Sichuan, Guizhou and Yunnan in the west, and the coasts in the east. The mountains, the rivers (the nine branches of the lower Yellow River are particularly remarkable), the lakes and sand dunes, together with the nine regions, are depicted in a stylised manner. Many features are simply represented by their name, depending on the availability of space.

By contrast with Europe, where hand-drawn maps disappeared with the invention of copperplate engraving at the end of the 15th century, Chinese hand-drawn maps continued to proliferate. They have more to do with art than science, and sometimes even with *fengshui*, the landscapes being "adapted" by the artists to receive the best *qi* possible—as if the simple fact of arranging the pictorial representation of the place could benefit the place itself.

The impact of the Mongol invasion
After the conquest of northern China by Genghis Khan in 1227, then of the south by his grandson Kublai Khan in 1279, the territory of China became part of a larger whole corresponding to Eurasia. In the course of the 13th century, other Mongol troops occupied Persia, took Baghdad, invaded Syria and reached eastern Europe. This expansion could have led to the establishment of a strong

H—*Map of the mountains and rivers*, compiled by Cai Shen en 1209.

federation, in which geographical knowledge would have expanded, but the Empire quickly disintegrated. The Mongols adopted the different cultural traditions of the societies they encountered, and the Mongol empire acted as an intermediary between China, the Islamic world and Europe. This factor played an important role in exchanges of technology and cultural practices, but not, it would seem, in the sphere of cartography. In the absence of an equivalent of the Christian church, with its dual ecclesiastical and educational role, or of the Confucianism of China's administration, with its bureaucratic and educational function, the sum of existing geographical knowledge did not lead to the development of a specific cartographical culture. It would seem that no necessity was felt to incorporate it into spiritual systems other than *fengshui*. It remained restricted to military tasks alone.

With a few significant exceptions, most Chinese cartographers did not record scale in their work. During the Yuan dynasty (1279-1368), when Islamic cartographic influence penetrated China, the Chinese produced two maps of the world: the first, called *Map of the Earth*, by Zhu Siben (*Yutu*, published in 1320), used the grid system developed by Pei Xiu; the second, called *Map of the resounding teaching [of the khan] which prevails throughout the world*, by Li Zemin (*Shengjiao guangbei tu*, published in 1330), did not. According to several sources, Zhu and Li were colleagues who worked closely together, and their maps, although built on different models of representation, both had a profound impact on the history of Asian cartography. Neither of these works has been found, so the only versions we have come from copies.

One of the versions inspired by the *Map of the resounding teaching [of the khan]* is a Korean work, the *Historical map of countries and towns* (*Honil kangni yoktae kukto chi*, 1402), often abbreviated to *Kangnido*. According to the introduction, it was drawn by combining Li Zemin's map with the map by Quan Jin entitled *Map of the integrated regions [of China]* (*Hunyi jiangli tu*, produced in 1370). This work also became a source of inspiration for a popular type of Korean map which would be widespread until the 19th century, known by the generic name *Map of the world under the sky* (*Ch'onhado*). Eighty-one countries are represented on an earth roughly centred on China's sacred Kunlun Mountains. Most of them are mythical countries taken from an ancient Chinese work, the *Shan hai jing*—places like the land of the "Cyclops", of the "three headed" people, of the "long armed" race, etc.

The map called *Kangnido* gives a very detailed description of the empire of China, together with Korea and Japan, although the relative positions of the three countries are inaccurate. China and Korea are too large, whereas Southeast Asia (with its promontory and multiple islands) is roughly drawn, as is India which is lost in the overall mass of the continent. To the west, the Arabic Peninsula, Africa and Europe are represented, although very small in comparison with China. There are more than 100 names for the European territories alone. The familiarity with the outline of Africa suggests early exploration of the region, before Vasco de Gama's voyage, which only reached the Indies in 1498. Most of the Chinese transcriptions of place names in South-East Asia, Africa and Europe come from persianised Arabic originals, implying that the Kangnido map drew largely on knowledge originating in the Middle East.

However, between 1405 and 1433, mainly under the Ming emperor Yongle, an admiral named Zheng He headed seven naval expeditions to Java, Sumatra, Indonesia, Sri Lanka, Persia, Arabia and twice East Africa as far as Mozambique.[6] This fleet, which contained up to 70 vessels, some of them as long as 138 m, was then much in advance of the West.

These were not really trading expeditions, but part of the Chinese tradition of establishing relations with numerous nations, some of which for a while paid tribute to the empire. These voyages were recorded by Ma Huan.[7] Addressed to the emperor, the journal records precise ethnographical observations about the peoples encountered, but also includes scientific entries on geography, climate, etc. These seagoing expeditions, which mark the apogee of Chinese maritime expansion—already significant under the Southern Song dynasty (1127-1279)—nevertheless ended on the death of Zheng He in 1433, as they were considered extremely costly.

One of the versions clearly inspired by Zhu Siben's *Map of the Earth* is a map by Luo Hongxian entitled *Guang Yutu* (1579), which is an enlargement of the Chinese part. In creating it, Luo Hongxian used different maps, including not only the *Map of the Earth* but also the *Map of the resounding teaching [of the khan]* together with a certain number of other Yuan dynasty works. He also consulted several illustrated Ming sources, including various studies of the "barbarians of the southwestern seas". Like the *Map of the Earth*, the *Guang Yutu* uses a grid in which each square is supposed to represent 100 li, i.e. approximately 50 km. But unlike

I—*Historical map of countries and towns (Kangnido)*, produced in 1402 by Korean Kim Sa-hueong. All rights reserved.

6—In a book entitled *1421, The Year China Discovered the World* (2002), Gavin Menzies, a retired officer of the British Royal Navy, claims to have discovered a map dating from 1763, a copy of a probably lost 1418 map, supposedly proving that the great Chinese admiral also discovered America 77 years before Christopher Columbus.

7—*The Overall Survey of the Ocean's Shores (1433)*, by Ma Huan, White Lotus Press, Bangkok, 1997.

Zhu Siben's map, for the first time in Chinese cartography it includes a cartouche of 24 symbols to represent mountains, rivers, borders, roads, etc.

Joseph Needham claims that the Chinese overtook the Europeans in cartography in the 16th century. In reality, it is hard to find anything in the history of Chinese cartography that resembles a linear process of gradual improvement. The Chinese continued to produce two distinct types of map, one based on relatively accurate scientific observations, the other based on existing maps, relying on "cultural data" drawn from earlier treatises. Whilst it is unlikely that there was real competition between these two conceptions, it has nevertheless been observed that there were considerably more maps of the second type than of the first, not just until the 16th century but also up to the 19th.

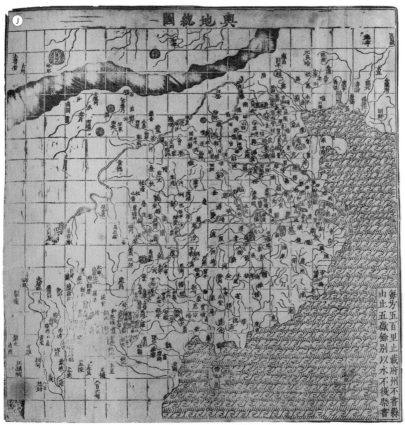

J—Luo Hongxian (first Ming Atlas produced in China in 1541).

The Jesuit contribution

The Jesuits played an important role by introducing new cartographic techniques into China, as well as contributing significantly to advances in knowledge of astronomy, the calendar and mathematics in the Middle Kingdom. Nevertheless, to impress the Chinese, the Jesuits chose to link western scientific superiority with the Christian religion. For that reason, they were reluctant to keep the Chinese informed of modern scientific progress in the West, for fear that scientific doubt might also spread doubt regarding their religious doctrine. The knowledge brought by the first Jesuits very quickly became obsolete. The pioneer of this enterprise was Father Matteo Ricci (1552-1610), who arrived in Macao in 1582 and immediately began to learn Chinese. Gifted with a prodigious memory, Ricci quickly made numerous Chinese friends amongst the local functionaries in the southern town of Zhaoqing where he lived. Their curiosity about his native land and the different countries he had visited during his travels had been increased by a world map from Europe presented to them by Ricci, where China occupied a relatively modest portion of the world.

The Jesuit was asked to produce a map with the names of the countries and towns transcribed into Chinese. Believing that Chinese maps were more accurate than those made in Europe, Ricci compiled both western and Chinese sources (in particular Luo Hongxian's *Guang Yutu*). This first map was known by the name *Complete Map of the Mountains and Seas of the Earth* (*Yudi shan hai quantu*, 1584). Neither the original nor its immediate successor (published in 1600)

K——*Chungguk sipsamsong to*: Korean map. On the left, the Ming Empire (1368-1644); on the right, the world in 1800, approx. © Library of Congress (Washington)

has been found, but a version of the first map is available in the *Tushu bian* by Zhang Huang, a work published in 1613. According to this, Ricci's map was put together from a projection of the world developed in 1570 by the Belgian cartographer Abraham Ortelius (1527-1598). Its centre is situated somewhere in the middle of the Atlantic Ocean, with China shown on the right and roughly to the correct proportions.

The third edition of Ricci's map was produced in 1602 in Peking on six sheets each measuring 70 cm x 80 cm, intended for attachment to a screen. In this version, entitled *Complete map of the innumerable countries of the world* (*Kunyu wanguo quantu*), Ricci had markedly improved on his earlier work, with the Chinese empire represented as no more than a part of the Asian continent. According to Father Ricci and several of his western contemporaries, most of their Chinese followers who saw this map were shocked. One of them, Li Zhizao, distributed several thousands of copies, one of which reached Emperor Wanli in 1608. The emperor was so impressed that he ordered twelve additional copies.

Ricci enjoyed his fame as a mapmaker and took special delight in the thought that he was the first person to present a concrete illustration of the roundness of the earth in China. In reality, Chinese texts report that a Persian astronomer, an emissary of Kublai Khan, had already showed them a globe (or perhaps a picture) in 1267, but no one in Ricci's entourage had reported this precedent. For all of them, the Jesuit's maps and globes gave a new and surprising picture of the world. The fact that this image was based on a Copernican representation of the universe was not a significant problem. One of Ricci's most striking demonstrations was to show how the meridians could be used to determine precise geographical positions. He explained the process in his introduction:

"[Ideally] there should be a line for each degree of longitude and latitude, but in [... this particular map] we have drawn a line every ten degrees to avoid making it too confusing. By this method, we can place each country in its correct position."

The Jesuit priest had understood the need to make cultural concessions to the Chinese, whilst presenting them with radically new geographical and scientific information. For example, the preface to the *Complete map of the innumerable countries of the world* emphasises that he had come from the West "full of admiration for the great Chinese empire, whose fame extends beyond ten thousand *li*". In deference to the domestic notion of China's cultural and geographical centrality, Ricci changed the projection of Ortelius' map to place China nearer the centre. He also used the myth of the Creation by the Taoist philosopher Huainan, describing the universe as hatching from an egg, to explain his Ptolemaic conception of the universe. And, "in keeping with the Chinese genius [for commentary]", he provided abundant notes.

The description of the Middle Kingdom simply says: "China is the country most famous for its culture and its products. It covers an area of latitude extending from 15 degrees to 42 degrees north, and numerous countries pay tribute to it. This map contains only [the chief mountains, rivers, provinces and roads]. For the details, a variety of nomenclatures may be consulted."

Part of Ricci's material is taken from Chinese sources—in particular the famous 13th century work *Complete Critical Examination of the Classics and Archives* (*Wenxian Tongkao*) by Ma Duanlin. Certain accounts, in particular "the land of one-eyed people", are borrowed from the mythological tradition of the *Book of Mountains and Seas* (*Shan hai jing*, 3rd century BCE).

However, despite the use of Chinese material and his other concessions to Chinese culture, Father Ricci faced criticism from a certain number of cartographers. Wei Jun accused Ricci of "delivering false teachings to deceive people". According to him, Ricci's supposed map of the world contains not only "fabulous and mysterious" information which could not be verified, but by placing China to the west of the centre and tilting it to the north, he had displaced the Middle Kingdom from its legitimate position at the "centre of the world". How, wonders Wei, "can China be treated as a little country of no importance?" She Que, another contemporary hostile to Ricci, asserts that "the idea of a kingdom beyond the ocean (i.e. Europe) is a complete fiction, intended to disguise the fact that the Westerners have settled near China (near the provinces of Fujian and Guangdong, he declares) and constitute an immediate military threat."

Chinese cartography forced to evolve

From the end of the 17th century to the beginning of the 19th century, the great majority of Chinese mapmakers largely ignored Jesuit representations of the world. The atlases published in 1673, 1743 and 1819, each a 6 or 14 page document, reflect the main cartographical current of the time, a tradition founded solidly on models originating in the Song dynasty, such as the *Map of China and the Barbarian Countries* (*Huayi tu*), and explicitly reproducing Liang Zhou's 16th century drawings. None of these maps seeks to question the traditional representations, and all of them include amongst the various non-Chinese countries arbitrarily distributed around the edge of China (usually represented as unimportant islands) a certain number of mythical lands taken mainly from the *Classic of the Mountains and Seas* (*Shan hai jing*), a compilation dating from the 3rd century BCE.

With the western imperial expansion into China, few significant changes took place. And despite the threat, the need to acquire western knowledge of the world was not always evident. In 1838, on the eve of the first Opium War, few Chinese had reliable information about the West. The official Qing accounts of the "tributary peoples known by the name of the map *Huang Qing zhigong tu*" left the Chinese uncomprehending. Other Qing sources of information, originating with the White Lotus secret society *Mingshi*, were equally fallacious. As for the "accounts of foreign lands" brought by the Jesuits, they were also obsolete. To a large degree, the representation of the world that inhabited both the popular mind and that of the elites had not really changed since the Song dynasty.

Although most Chinese mapmakers had abandoned the western models, a rare few had continued to apply foreign knowledge. In particular, in 1819, the Taoist priest Li Mingzhe produced an *Illustration of the contours of the sky* (*Huatian tushuo*) in which he presented two relatively "modern" maps of the western and eastern hemispheres, which include the lines of latitude and longitude.

In 1842, Wei Yuan, commissioned by the Governor of Hunan, Lin Zexu, produced a four volume *Illustrated geography of the world* (*Sizhou zhi*), in which he provides a systematic description of various countries (location, climate, history, culture, customs, technology, etc.). Exceptionally, his work was based on translations of western works. Published at the height of the negotiations for the Treaty of Nankin, which ended the first Opium War, during which the Governor Lin Zexu had distinguished himself by burning the opium of the English, its aim was to explore "the foreign aggression" and study ways of resisting it. Although this newly acquired knowledge came too late to change the course of history, it reflects the emerging awareness of the need for reform. At the request of the English, Lin Zexu was banished to Chinese Turkestan.

Nevertheless, this work, which had circulated privately amongst colleagues, inspired the publication of two other books: the *Illustrated repertory of seagoing countries* (*Haiguo tuzhi*, published in 1843) by Wei Yuan and the *Description of sea routes* (*Yinghuan zhilüe*, 1849) by Xu Jiyu. Whilst this second book concentrates on the accuracy of geographical charts, the first by Wei Yuan provides a geopolitical analysis of the speed of western maritime expansion. Their joint aim, as expressed by Wei Yuan, was to "describe the West as it appears to Westerners".

Wei Yuan's treatise had a practical purpose: it was intended to show "how to use barbarians to combat barbarians, how to pacify different barbarians [to our advantage], and how to use the techniques of the barbarians to control the barbarians". Xu Jiyu's book, although also motivated by a desire to improve Chine's strategic position in relation to the West, was more a learned encyclopaedic atlas, much of which had been borrowed from the Westerners.

Given that Chinese cartography followed a radically different path from that of the West, it seems somewhat futile to compare them. Until relatively recent times, the aims were simply different. Nevertheless, one of a number of aspects worth considering is the link that the Chinese established between time and space, in which time is perceived as an implacable sequence of reversals which require man to "adjust to its measure" while "uniting with the moment". The man who "experiences change whilst holding on to the principle of the *dao* knows how to control the rear when he is at the front and the front when he is at the rear". [8] Thus space—as it were immutable—sees the passing of a time that is untamed, capricious as the wind, sometimes violent, but also gentle as a breeze, and it is the task of man to record it on the page as if recording a series of changes in the weather.

L—*Illustrated geography of the world (Haiguo tuzhi),* compiled by Wei Yuan, published in three editions 1842, 1847 and 1852.

8—*Huainan zi,* chap. I "Of the original "dao"", 16a.

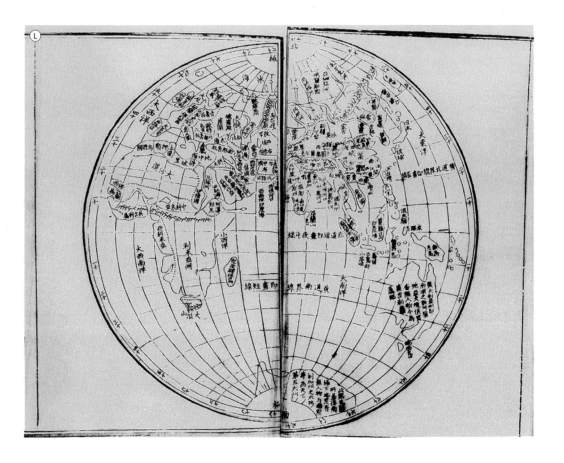

Bibliography

J. B. Harley and David Woodwards
The History of Cartography vol. II, 2, Cartography in the Traditional East and Southeast Asian Societies, Chicago-London, The University of Chicago Press, 1994.
J. Needham, *Science and Civilisation in China,* Cambridge University Press, 1971.
R. J. Smith, *Chinese Maps, Images of "All Under Heaven" (Images of Asian),* Oxford University Press, 1996.

Of the land and its mythologies

Catherine Bourzat

The economic and social transformations of China at the turn of the 21st century have occupied centre stage against a backdrop of massive geographical upheavals. *Zhongguo*, the Middle Kingdom, has become a polarised space of megacities with populations of multimillions. The agrarian empire has traded in its countryside for urban garments, new, overflowing cities, with all-engulfing suburbs, motorway networks and real estate speculation, market gardens, rice fields and age-old orchards. As for the population, after a long history of compulsory and resigned immobility, it has suddenly been propelled wholesale into mobility.

As the price of this XXL size transformation, China's leaders have put the country on the loom. China's clothes have always been ill-fitting, despite the centuries of central control and of massive engineering projects. A multi-segmented great wall, built to create a tangible limit and boundary to the northern steppes; water management enacted on two of the planet's biggest rivers, flowing down from the Roof of the World: the Yangtze (6380 km) and the Yellow River (4845 km); a tight network of canals to connect the country's great water basins; massive population displacements to plug the holes and to colonise and supply the border regions. Nothing worked in a decisive and satisfactory manner: China remains a country of limited space. A sequence of deserts and a barrier of mountains have pushed the population eastwards, as if through a funnel: 9/10th of China's people live on 1/6th of the territory. Nine tenths of a population of 1.3 billion, the largest on the planet, is a lot for a territory which, although vast, has a surface area only seventeen times that of France. Inevitably, the result of this equation is a recurring shortage of arable land... with its consequent share of landless peasants, poverty and anger. Today, this territory condemns more than 150 million men and women to uprootedness and homelessness; cast aside in their country's intense growth, they eke out a precarious existence as day workers.

A——Wang Wenlan 王文澜, Bicycle kingdom, Shanghai, 1991. © Wang Wenlan
B——Zhang Xinmin 张新民, Ten square metres, ten families. Living quarters for migrant workers from Sichuan, Shenzhen, Guangdong, 1997. © Zhang Xinmin

A crisis of growth for a country whose economic feats have put all the planet's capitalist heads in a spin? Yes: three decades of accelerated transformation have inevitably produced side-effects, fractures, faultlines, which the leaders have tried to contain nationally by a series of massive and breathtaking infrastructure projects. In order to move forward, Maoist propaganda gambled on a combination of the power of large numbers and the time factor. Launched in 1979 by Deng Xiaoping, then boosted in 1989 by Jiang Zemin with the switch to market economics, the Chinese rocket has fuelled itself with capital and cutting edge technology in its drive to catch up. As a response to a cultivable area reduced to 1/10th of the territory, the attempted reclamation of coastal tidal flats (Hebei, Shandong, Jiangsu, Zhejiang, Fujian) only shows up the limitations of sheer graft in dealing with the haemorrhage of arable land, caused primarily by urban growth. Between 1996 and 2004, almost one million hectares of farmland were lost each year, falling from 130 to 122 million hectares. Eight million swallowed up by concrete and tarmac in less than 10 years.

Far from resolving its ancient territorial pressures, China's growth has exacerbated them, forcing the regime into a race against time, reflected in the pharaonic infrastructure projects of the 10th five-year plan (2000-2005). For the first time in its history, the country is attempting to deal simultaneously with its entire land area.

C——Zhang Xinmin 张新民, *A small alley*, Chengdu, Sichuan, 1995. © Zhang Xinmin
D——Tang Haowu 唐浩武, Migrant workers escaping from the heat of their sleeping quarters, Wuxi, Jiangsu, 2003. © Tang Haowu

Thus, one of the aims of the Three Gorges Project on the Yangtze is to enable large cargo ships to travel upstream, carrying goods from the coastal zone of Shanghai to Chongqing, a city of 30 million situated 2000 km in the interior. The purpose of this dam is to trigger economic growth in the West of the country. In Shanghai, large-scale synergies are being created on either side of the Yangtze Delta by the construction of an extensive motorway network, including a 36 km long bridge over Hangzhou Bay. The triple dam diverting water from the Yangtze to the Yellow River basin, where levels are low, is part of the same process of network creation, this time on the south-north axis.

In *La Face cachée de la Terre*, Philippe Pinchemel[1] brings geography into the social science sphere, by suggesting that it is society that creates space. A significant proportion of China's myths are about land and land management. In Chinese, the term for landscape has two components, *shan* and *shui*, mountains and water, the very features that control the land and its occupation and overhang the challenges

E——Wang Shilong 王世龙, 3000 workers digging a canal, Henan, 1974. © Wang Shilong

1——Philippe Pinchemel, *La Face cachée de la Terre*, Armand Colin, 1998.

that 21st century China faces. In antiquity, before the country's ideological and cultural unification under central imperial authority, the rulers sacrificed to these omnipotent entities, to the "Illustrious Mountains and Great Rivers". Princes and lords were invested with the same obligations over the lands they governed. In return, *shan* and *shui* guaranteed power and stability for rulers, protection and fertility for the people. The space then was much more confined than it is today. For the purposes of State ritual, there were four "great rivers"—the Yellow River, the Yangtze, the Huai and the Ji—and five "illustrious Mountains". Together with a cosmogonical system based on Five Orients (the four cardinal points plus the centre), the cult of the Five Peaks continued under the empire, on either side of the Christian era. They formed the symbolic and sacred outlines of the Middle Kingdom and nationally were the sites of the sacrifice that the emperors made to Heaven; called *feng*, this ceremony took place annually in special temples. As sons of Heaven, according to a tradition inherited from the Zhou Dynasty (c.1046-771 BCE), the rulers addressed the sky through this ceremony as a symbolic renewal of their mandate. The tradition survived until the end of the imperial institution in 1911.

As long as order reigns over the mountains and waters, there is peace; chaos ensues on their excesses, the earthquakes and floods that plunge the country into ruin. The earth still shakes in China and the rivers' moods continue to threaten. From the scarce fragments of ancient Chinese mythology emerges the figure of a hero, who became the first sovereign of the first royal dynasty, the Xia (2207-1766 BCE), for having successfully triumphed over the great flood by taming and controlling the waters. His name is Yu the Great and the *Huainan zi*, the Book of the Master of Huainan (139 BCE), says of him that he "contained the overflowing waters with living earth to form the upstanding mountains". "Living earth", but also the assistance of magical creatures—Ying the dragon and the tortoise Baini, Mud-Helper—and of divinities, who gave him talismans, in the form of *tu*, paintings depicting the world and its phenomena, enabled Yu to succeed in his task. He returned the rivers to their beds and guided their courses to the East and their great outlet in the China Sea. Confucian commentators attribute further virtues to him and emphasise his disinterested commitment to the task; it is these qualities, they say, that persuaded the legendary emperor Shun to make Yu his successor. After this, the imperial succession became hereditary and mythology became history.

The fragments of text that record Yu's projects also describe him as being the first to practise hydromancy to restore order to the waters. The hero only sets to work once he has collected information on the dimensions of the land and the position of the sources of each river, assisted by the maps-talismans given him by the divinities. Before taking on the roles of hydraulic and civil engineer, he explores every corner of his world. Carrying his survey right to the margins of his territory, he brings back data, measurements and an inventory of creatures, benign and malign, which, once emperor, he has depicted on nine bronze tripods placed on the terrace of his palace. In his role as ruler, he continues to carry out inspection tours of the country, combining the function of sovereign and ministers. His tripods became the insignia of power, handed down from king to king under later dynasties. Once again according to myth, they were lost for ever when a Qin king sought to take them for himself.

In Chinese, *zhi*, the word that means "to govern", refers in the written language to the "imperious words that control the waters", according to the etymology established from its form by Kyril Ryjik. [2] The same word is also used to mean "care for". The territory has imposed its constraints on the exercise of power. Governing China is about showing one's capacity to overcome it. At the time of the first empires, this notion took the form of an institution called *Mingtang*, the Hall of Light or House of the Calendar. It was a building in the capital which was designed to represent the ancient cosmogony. Constructed on a square terrace (the shape of the Earth as then perceived by the Chinese), its superstructure had the circular shape of the vault of the sky. Its roof was held up by columns that formed the subdivisions of the interior space: a square hall in the centre, divided into nine intercolumniations, based on the nine provinces of the Middle Kingdom, and subdivided into twelve rectangular annexes for the twelve stations of heaven, which form the seasons and the months. In the course of the year, the sovereign visited this symbolic architecture of the cosmos in sequence. He moved from room to room, following the calendar. The ritual symbolically embodied the conception of imperial power: in correspondence with the working of the cosmos, the virtue of the Son of Heaven could ensure that harmony (*he*) and peace (*ping*) reigned. This is neither more, not less, than the concepts underpinning the programme of the country's current rulers: leaving behind the class war of the Maoist area, the stated purpose of Hu Jintao and his team is to "build a harmonious society".

Harmony and peace are two crucial necessities, since China's limited space also needs to be shared to accommodate a multinational unified State. For there is a further facet to the cartographic equation of people and land: a little under 7% of Chinese belong to 55 ethnic minorities. They are thinly spread, since they cover two thirds of the territory. These are affected by physical and climatic constraints.

2——Kyril Ryjik, *L'Idiot chinois*, Payot, 1980.

There is also a 56th ethnic grouping, an overwhelming majority encompassing 93% of the remaining population. They are the Han, descendants of the people of the first empires which unified the land from the end of the third century BCE. Their identity is cemented by history and maintained through ancestor worship and through Chinese culture and language. One of the reasons why the State periodically emptied its countrysides of their supernumerary peasantry to move them elsewhere, was to restore the Hanzu balance in regions inhabited by ethnic minorities. The same concern for a harmonious population mix explains one of the technological feats of the 10th five-year plan. On July 1, 2006, the anniversary of the foundation of the Chinese Communist Party, the first train travelled the world's highest railway, which rises to a height of 4000 m. It links Golmud to Lhassa and brings Tibet within a train ride of Beijing. Much more decisively than with the troop deployment of 1959, the Tibetan plateau fell within the orbit of Chinese territory. With a single railroad, confines ceased to be boundaries.

F——Li Lang 黎朗, *Wumatang train station under construction*, Tibet, 2006. © Li Lang

The inauguration of the Roof of the World train was a source of glee for investors in a prosperous sector directly concerned with the meshwork of revolutionary infrastructures woven across China in the last two decades: tourism. "A trip to Tibet is considered by many Chinese as a trip to heaven and is a dream of many", commented Zhao Hongyu of CYTS, one of the country's biggest travel agencies. Tourism represents a major aspect of the new mobility of the Chinese. It is a recent phenomenon. The Chinese first discovered the weekend in 1995, when Saturday ceased to be a day set aside for political education. In 2000, they acquired three weeks of paid holiday, divided between the New Year, May Day and the National Festival. An immediate success! The trains carried 4 million passengers a day during the Labour Day holidays. In 2004, 1.1 billion journeys were taken, generating revenues of 470 billion yuans (47 billion euros). Taking no notice of the landless migrants around them, Chinese tourists now crisscross their country en masse. Formerly, in the Empire, this mobility was confined to a privileged few: the educated, who travelled to chance their arm in the recruitment exams, regional functionaries fulfilling their assignments and inspection duties, wandering monks and merchants. Today, given sufficient wealth, everyone can travel and experience this piece of freedom.

The Chinese language does not distinguish between "tourism" and "travel". The word for both is *lüyou*, a term which refers to the ritual journeys taken by the rulers of antiquity to the country's mountains and waterways (*lü*) and to the vagabond wanderings of the curious-minded (*you*). *Lüyou* is "mobility associated with imagination", to use the definition of tourism suggested by Rachid Amirou,[3] a "secular form of pilgrimage" which, in China, follows the itineraries laid out in tourist leaflets, alongside travel books and guides, whose growing numbers reflect the success of the tourist economy. They all work like inventories, similar to those depicted by Yu the Great on the ancient insignia of power, collections of pictures, like the "trip to heaven" described by Mr Zhao in reference to Tibet. It is the task of tourists to collect these pictures in their travels. It is in this way that the land is reinvented, outlining a new geographical reality moulded out of culture and mythology.

3——Rachid Amirou, *Imaginaire touristique et sociabilité du voyage*, Paris, PUF, 1995.

G——Zhang Xinmin 张新民, *Line for buying train tickets at the Guangzhou station*, Guangdong, 1995. © Zhang Xinmin

A population on the move

Pierre Haski

Urumqi Station, capital of Xinjiang: passengers hurry to board a brand-new train preparing to leave for the far west of China. Around a third of them are ordinary travellers, a third soldiers garrisoned on the western borders, the rest new immigrants who have come from the overpopulated provinces of the east, with a meagre bundle and their families, to seek a new life in the Chinese "Far West".

Dongting Lake, Hunan Province: "You see, it was in Chairman Mao's time"... That is how an old peasant woman explains her presence on this reclaimed land, "stolen" from the lake, which has since exacted revenge by frequent floods, forcing the army to reinforce the ever higher, ever more vulnerable dikes. In the 1950s, the Great Leader had sent thousands of people—parias, convicts, landless peasants—to dry out the marshes of Lake Dongting. [1] They succeeded at the cost of infinite sacrifice, but the lake still has a point to make.

Three Gorges Dam, Sichuan Province: the world's biggest dam, on the Yangtze River, has become a reality. The objective is twofold: to regulate the flow of the great river and to produce as much electricity as 18 nuclear power stations. The price: 1.4 million people living along the Yangtze have already been displaced, and in autumn 2007, the authorities, fearing an "ecological disaster caused by the dam", announced a new development plan with the displacement of a further 3 million people.

Dongguan, Pearl River Delta: taking advantage of a break, two young workers down a bowl of noodles in a cheap cafe opposite their factory. They are part of the 150 to 200 million Chinese on the move in the biggest rural exodus in history, an inexorable process of urbanisation in a country where, just a few years ago, two thirds of the population were farmers. Migrants who provide the cheap labour that feeds the economic machine in its chaotic, headlong, double-figure growth.

Xinjiang, Dongting Lake, the Three Gorges Dam, or the Pearl River Delta... Four snapshots of a population on the move, not always voluntarily. In the immensity of China, these migrations have several causes, ideological, political, economic, or simply the individual initiative of Chinese who have been rooted to the land for thousand of years, and who have rediscovered, as has happened many times in the history of China, a sudden mobility.

The motive may sometimes have been ideological, as when Mao Zedong sent almost 17 million young Chinese from the cities to the countryside, between

---

1—Judith Shapiro, Mao's war against nature. Politics and the environment in Revolutionary China, Cambridge University Press, 2001.

1968 and 1980, at the height of the cultural revolution.[2] For Michel Bonnin, "this experience profoundly marked a whole generation of city dwellers. It disrupted the lives of millions of young people (almost half their generation) and influenced the lives of their parents, their brothers and sisters, the whole of urban society, as well as a good part of rural society, obliged to make space for these unwelcome guests". We know what happened next: this experiment in social alchemy was gradually brought to an end after Mao's death in 1976, and the return to the big cities of most of these young people—even though it is not unusual to meet some who stayed in the country—too broken to start again.

A few decades later, it is the youth of rural China that is travelling in the opposite direction. But this time, it didn't take an order from the top to get tens of millions of men and women on the move: the economic reforms had the same effect. What began as a modest stream in the early 1980s, towards the famous "special economic areas" and particularly the most famous of them, Shenzhen, on the Hong Kong border, has been transformed, with the acceleration of the Chinese economy, into a succession of waves and counter-waves.

The numbers can scarcely express the scale of the phenomenon, and the department that manages the "hukou", the residence certificates that strictly controlled all mobility, is finding it hard to keep pace. How many people are there, today, in this "floating population" that moves between city and countryside, the new spearhead of China PLC, the strong arm of the country that has gained the most from globalisation through its entry into the World Trade Organisation (WTO) in 2001. Around 150 million? Perhaps 200 million...

A——Intellectuals leaving Suzhou for the countryside, Jiangsu, 1969.
© Municipal committee for the compilation of local Suzhou records
B——Zhang Xinmin 张新民, Workers' residence, Shenzhen, Guangdong, 1991. © Zhang Xinmin

2——Michel Bonnin, Génération perdue, *Le mouvement d'envoi des jeunes instruits à la campagne en Chine, 1968-1980*, Éditions de l'École des Hautes études en sciences sociales, 2004.

The scale of the phenomenon is such that it is visible to the naked eye. In southern China, obviously, where some of the megacities of seven to 10 million people have grown by dozens of kilometres, with lines of factories whose top floors, decorated by the linen drying in the windows, provide accommodation for the migrants... In the Yangtze Delta, in Shanghai and its backcountry, the second and now most dynamic of the development areas. And even in Beijing, the grey, austere capital, which has been stimulated, transformed, remoulded by the prospect of the Olympic Games in August 2008.

In Beijing, three million migrants work, eat and sleep on hundreds of building sites that are preparing the Olympic capital, were in the shops and industries, or else live off the parallel economy on the outskirts. Go southward from Tianamen Square, and you pass through an area of steel and glass buildings symbolising 21st-century Beijing, and then congested orbital roads, before the city returns to ground level, a jumble of·shops, workshops, dilapidated streets and a population of subcontractors to the urban economy, made up of migrants freshly arrived from the country, who pass through this social and cultural airlock before crossing the orbital roads one after another.

Some have come alone, leaving wife and child in the village where they return when it is the season to work in the fields; others have taken the plunge, bringing their families with them, turning their villages into dying places for the old. It is hardly an enviable fate: whether they work in the modern or underground economy, they are exploited, despised, at the mercy of the authorities who leave them vegetating in a huge legal grey area, without status, without the citizenship they are entitled to.

But the coin also has another, less sinister side. When you ask these young migrants if it is not too hard to work seven days a week, 13 or 15 hours a day, they don't understand the question. The countryside they have left behind is not paradise: if it were, they would have stayed. [3] The work there is hard, fruitless, and brings in no money because of the fragmentation of plots, the lack of resources, the often hostile natural conditions.© Millions of them, moreover, lost everything when their land was confiscated to make way for urban expansion, motorways or industries. Given almost no compensation, they have no choice but to emigrate. In the city, however, they are able to send a bit of money to the village, they experience a social and sexual mix that they had never known, they are released from the weight of tradition and discover an urban culture that they make their own and transform.

Nonetheless, these migrants are not a coherent, organised social group. Despite their impressive numbers, they are a collection of individual, fragmented experience. Though the signs of a few new organisations are appearing here and there, or real collective phenomena. Thus, the Pearl River Delta region has begun to experience labour shortages because of its reputation for low salaries, with migrants preferring to try their luck first in the Yangtze Delta. So the *"Mingong"* (peasant-workers) are voting with their feet, and starting to express objections to their working conditions, especially in the south of the country.

Alongside these voluntary departures, however, whether by individuals or small groups, China continues to displace its population by the millions. The construction of the Three Gorges Dam, in the centre of the country, was the most spectacular example, and it is not over. [4] The millions of people displaced, either to new towns built higher up to replace the homes now underwater, or elsewhere in the country, apparently submit unflinchingly to their fate... The only protests we hear about relate to swindles around compensation.

C—Zhou Zhenhua 周振华, Working in the fields, Yinsigou, Henan, 1968. ©Zhou Zhenhua

3—Chen Guidi and Wu Chuntao, *Les Paysans chinois aujourd'hui, trois années d'enquête au cœur de la Chine*, Bourin Éditions, 2007.
4—The film *Still Life*, by Jia Zhangke, which came out in 2007, is probably the work that best shows the scale of the upheavals caused by the building of the dam and its social and human impact.

The same is true in the cities, with the gigantic urban renovation projects. When you wake up in the morning with the character "for demolition" painted on your house, you only have one month to reorganise your life. It has happened to millions of people in Beijing, Shanghai and most of China's big cities. China is into much of a hurry to worry about individual suffering: an indifference that has been internalised by the population, encouraged to believe that the communal happiness generated by economic growth and progress is more important than the price paid individually by those caught up or crushed in this strategy.

That will perhaps not always be true, but today, in this China in its headlong rush, cities disappear and are reborn, others grow where before was nothing but a village, millions of people move a few kilometres or to the other end of this immense territory...

Obviously, there is not—there cannot be—any great conductor orchestrating this gigantic stew. The State initiates big programmes, like the decision to transform Beijing or to invest in the far west. But it can no longer decide, as before, the life and choices of dozens, of hundreds of millions of people engaged in a race first for survival, and then for wealth. For many of China's 1.3 billion people, this emancipation from poverty entails an uprooting, sometimes voluntary, sometimes successful.

D——Wang Jinsong 王劲松, Character *chai* (demolish), 1999. © Wang Jinsong

水

Water

Virtue in an emperor in China was defined as his capacity, through the observance and performance of rituals, to maintain the peace and well-being of his subjects.

The harmony of the world depended on him. The primary sign of this harmony was the abundance of the harvest, and therefore benevolent rains and regular river flows. Drought and floods were consequently signs of the wrath of Heaven.

Control of water, a central element of life, the yin element that balanced out the yang of fire, thus became the primary sign of healthy government and sound institutions. In day-to-day life, each person experienced the emperor's problems at their own humble level. In the early 20th century, the lack of sewers and the natural smells of the city were the characteristics that travellers noticed most. Hot water, with or without tea, protected people from fickle bacteria and as today, there was widespread fear of devastating floods, though not yet of pollution.

From the creation of the Grand Canal (1800 km built between the 6th and 15th century) to that of the Three Gorges Dam, from the crossing of the Yangtze by Mao Zedong (1966) to the annexation of Tibet (1959)—the Republic's primary reservoir—water has long been the mark of sovereign power.

However, water also brings disaster and death. It can become a permanent source of danger, as it is for those who live alongside the great rivers, in the past threatened by floods, now by the bursting of the great hydroelectric dams, and even more immediately by the pollution of lakes and rivers, drought, melting glaciers, etc.

Since the 8th century, these engraved stones have been used to show the level of the Yangtze River over a span of 1600 metres. These ancient artefacts have disappeared with the rise of the water following the construction of the Three Gorges Dam. An underwater museum now provides public access to the place.
© Yan Changjiang

Cities and water Ruan Yisan

^{4.1}

A——Sichuan province. The ancient city of Zhaohua was located in a loop of the Yangtze. © Chen Yang and Jiang Nan.

Water is the source of life, and in China the history of the cities, of their emergence and development, is particularly intertwined with the role of water. It is water that governs the birth and development of many cities. In the traditional theories on the choice of sites by geomancy or *fengshui* ("winds and waters"), water is one of the fundamental elements on which the examination of the site is based. Since Antiquity, water, a resource that is essential to life, has also—in the form of rivers and canals—provided crucial routes for transport and communication, a means of trade and interchange between populations. Today, technological advances have changed the role of water in the urban economy, but despite these changes it remains an essential component of the urban environment.

Water management and the siting of cities

In ancient China, *fengshui* governed the foundation of all cities and the construction of all buildings. Its theories developed over time, through observation of the environment and the accumulation of experience and knowledge about climate, ecology, land topology and geology. By these means the ancient Chinese, in order to decide the ideal site for building, constructed a theory of the environment which developed into a sort of simple and natural philosophy based on the harmonious coexistence between man and nature.

The precepts of *fengshui* sum up the basic principles for deciding the side of a city in eight words: "probe the dragons, observe the rocks, direct the waters, decide the propitious location." Mountain ranges suggest the shape of a dragon, and their study is recommended in the words: "probe the dragons". The "rocks" refer to hills situated apart from the mountain ranges, which is why they need to be "observed". And finally, water in Chinese culture has always been considered as a symbol of wealth, and it is often said that: "to control the waters is to control wealth." A town site cannot be selected without considering water resources, water systems and water quality; the methods for managing them, referred to in the words "directing the waters", also include rainwater drainage, flood prevention and the use of water in daily life. In Chinese gardens, "directing the waters" also means using them to create scenery. As for the final words, "decide the propitious location", this is the perfect place for siting the town, in an area surrounded by mountains and protected from the waters.

There are many ancient capitals of China that were built in a perfect location in *fengshui* terms, because it "carries *yin* on its back and *yang* in its arms."[1] For example, the Sui and Tang dynasty capital Chang'an (today's Xi'an) was cited in the so-called "within the passes" region, in the Shaanxi, an alluvial plain fed by rivers. Bordered to the north by a tributary of the Yellow River, the Wei, and backed by the Qingling massif and seven other rivers—the Jing, the Ba, the Chan, the Feng, the Hao, the Yu and the Lao—the city was moulded by the configuration of the site, "eight rivers surrounding its walls": it is these abundant water resources, the dense network of waterways and the well-irrigated farmland that made Chang'an a prosperous and flourishing city. Similarly Hangzhou, described as "paradise on earth", is situated at the confluence of the Qiantang and the Grand Canal, not far to the east of the Tianmu chain, near the Western Lake, a site known for its landscapes of clear waters and hills.

Water and the emergence of the cities

Rivers gave birth to civilisation, because they created the conditions for the emergence of cities and governed their growth and development. For the people of antiquity, the "rampart" *cheng*[2] initially referred to the wall that protected them from floods. It defended their settlements by retrenchments made up of rows of dikes that protected their houses, fields and storehouses from damage by water. These earth and stone barriers were an embryonic form of of city walls. Apart from their flood prevention function, they provided protection from animals and enemy attack, and then the location for the first steps in the trading of goods, the "market" *shi*. The flat and accessible land on the edges of rivers was an ideal place for markets, provided access to water for irrigating crops and supplying provisions, for fishing and for communication.Ⓑ

The city of Shanghai was originally a fishing village on the banks of the Yangtze where it joins the sea; as the wealth of the area increased with the development of fishing, other villages were built on the banks of the Wusong tributary (now called the Suzhou River), and in the late 13th century a large market spawned a merchant townof significant size. Subsequently, at the beginning of the 15th century, as the Wusong became silted up and the waters of the Huangpu rose to form a much wider riverbed, a port became established under the Ming dynasty, with even more significant social and economic consequences for Shanghai.

1—— A Taoist saying, with multiple meanings. Here it suggests that the site has a mountain range behind it to the north, protecting it from the wind, and opens to the south, to plains and water.
2——The Chinese word for city—*chengshi*—is formed of the two characters *cheng* and *shi*, which mean "rampart" and "market".

At Jingdezhen, the presence of Lake Poyang, which feeds into the Yangtze, was decisive. Jingdezhen became the capital of the porcelain industry and also its main trading centre. The porcelain industry requires a great deal of water and access to the sea allowed goods to be transported abroad.

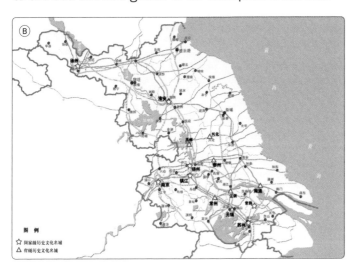

Historically, many cities flourished as a result of the building of the Grand Canal from Beijing to Hangzhou. At a time when production levels were low and land transportation difficult and costly, waterways and the regions they flowed through became advantageous places for the transport of people and goods, and for cultural exchanges. Because of the topography of the country, highlands in the west and lowlands in the east, in China the Yangtze, Huang, Huai, and Pearl Rivers flow almost exclusively from the west to join the sea in the east. These great waterways greatly facilitated east to west relations, whereas by contrast north to south communications encountered a range of obstacles. The digging of the Grand Canal between Beijing and Hangzhou established a link and gave momentum to cultural exchanges between the North and South of the country, allowing cities to grow and prosper: the great cities of Beijing, Tianjin, Yangzhou, Zhenjiang, Wuxi, Suzhou, Hangzhou all started out as settlements along the Grand Canal. Successive governments arranged for the capital to be supplied with basic goods and cereals by river. This activity, which was regulated by central government, also fed the rise of new cities such as Liaocheng, Jining, Yangliuqing, Beicang, Hexiwu, Duliu, which provided warehousing facilities, trading centres, etc.

B—Historic and cultural towns along the Grand Canal in Jiangsu Province. The stars indicate towns with national protected status such as, from north to south, Xuzhou, Huaian, Yangzhou, Nankin or Suzhou; the triangle indicates towns with regional protected status, such as Gaoyou and Taizhou in the centre of the map, or Nantong in the Yangtze Delta.
© Ruan Yisan

The Jiangnan region, the "water country", where the cities of Suzhou, Jiaxing and Huzhou are located, is home to a dense network of rivers—the Yangtze, the Fuchun—and to Lakes Tai and Yangcheng, forming an area of canals where all the villages grew up around water. Zhouzhuang, at the intersection of five lakes, and also Luzhi, Nanxun, Wuzhen and Xitang, are all towns that developed long ago, providing a transition between the canals that feed the region and Lake Tai, the Grand Canal, the Yangtze River and the sea. That is why, for generations, most transportation was provided by boatmen. Trade developed through ease of communications and produce from the surrounding land was carried through all these conurbations, contributing to the emergence of flourishing cities, with large and prosperous populations. In the "water country", water determines the street networks and construction boundaries, runs alongside and provides access to every home; its ubiquity is responsible for the characteristics typical of cities throughout this region.

China's cities and their interdependence with water

Most of the ancient cities are built in areas with a water supply, and make full use of the natural possibilities provided by waterways or springs, in particular for irrigation purposes. In the Jiangnan region, the natural conditions created by the waterway network were highly favourable to agriculture, silkworm breeding, fishing and livestock, and constituted a system of river transportation based on a tight and organic mesh of waterways offering communications between numerous marketplaces. These towns specialised in a wide range of complementary activities, which transformed the structure of the trading networks: thus Zhouzhuang and Tongli specialised in rice and oil production, whereas towns like Nanxun or Wuzhen concentrated on activities associated with cereal crops. The configuration of the canals also gave the towns their shape: linear when they ran along a single waterway; star-shaped when they stood at the intersection of two or more canals, like Nanxun, Luzhi, Wuzhen; or else quadrangular when they were located on four canals intersecting at right angles, like Zhouzhuang; or finally circular, when situated at the confluence of two waterways or on a more complex branching, as with Tongli and Xitang.

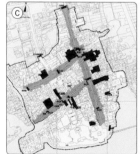

The connection between the inhabitants and the water is permanent. At Suzhou, situated on a lake basin with numerous waterways, the urban structure has moulded to this network, with a juxtaposition of roads and rivers, forming the shape of a double chessboard. The buildings are connected to the water, which determines their architecture; they give onto the street at the front, and onto a canal at the rear, and in some cases secondary waterways even flow through the larger buildings. The habitat is in harmony with nature. In the past, the canals were the main routes for communication and transportation. People also used them to wash their clothes and vegetables, and as a place to meet and talk. Water routes and land routes make it possible for different methods of travel to coexist without competing, and the places where they meet, around bridges and landing stages, perform the function of public squares. These communication nodes where people meet and distribute goods are the places of most intense activity.

However, whilst waterside towns benefit from this proximity in terms of supplies, transportation and irrigation, they also run a high risk of flooding. That is why governments under all dynasties were obliged to invest heavily in resolving this problem. The Tang capital Chang'an had a very comprehensive drainage system, with gutters on both sides of the streets and a network of brick sewers, enclosed or open-topped, running beneath the alleyways. In Suzhou, the canals themselves constituted a major system of flood protection. Some were filled in 1958 and, after 1972, when the city was damaged following torrential rains, new measures were introduced to remedy this error of judgement and its potentially serious consequences.

C——Different types of small town in Jiangsu: Zhouzhuang, Tongli and Luzhi © Ruan Yisan
D——City of Wuzhen © Ruan Yisan
E——City of Zhouzhuang © Ruan Yisan

In addition to its functions as a resource and a means of transportation and irrigation, water in the cities is used to enhance the environment and improve the ecological conditions. Lijiang, which stands on the plateau of Yunnan province, is a city of canals, with numerous bridges, where the presence of water has moulded the urban space. The architecture of the houses is matched to the conditions, with every house opening on to a canal. The canals even flow through the houses, creating a cool and peaceful urban environment. The inhabitants work to protect the water, which they venerate. The close connection with water has given the city its atmosphere, the sense of harmony between man and nature. Here there are: "wilted vines, old trees, drowsy crows; dwelling places, little bridges, flowing water.[3]

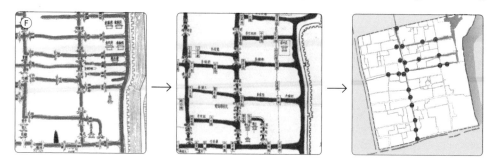

The new challenges

With time, the functions of urban water systems have changed. Shanghai initially grew because of the Huangpu, which became a focus of intense maritime transport activity. Later, its eastern bank—Pudong—expanded to such a degree that the river became a route within the city itself. The importance of the river for the maritime transport sector diminished, whereas its social and cultural functions became dominant, bringing the inhabitants new needs and new aspirations. The 2010 Universal Exhibition will spread across both banks of the Huangpu, which will accentuate their role by highlighting the areas where human beings and water interact and imbue them with increased vitality. These places possess formidable social, economic and cultural potential. Concerted development of riverside areas, in a way that is sensitive to ecology and aesthetics, can make a city more competitive in terms of quality of life and cultural factors, and thereby further growth.

F——Old district of Suzhou, historic development of the canals © Ruan Yisan

3——Poem by Ma Zhiyuan (13th century)

With the development of rail and air transport, the Grand Canal between Beijing and Hangzhou has lost its dominant position in communications between North and South, but we continue to use it to carry coal from the North and flows of goods from the Yangtze Delta. It helps to regulate water surpluses in the South, and many people still live on its banks. Because of poor irrigation in the North, it is unfortunately no longer navigable in certain parts and waste has accumulated, a worrying development that is being treated with the seriousness it deserves. The land adjacent to the canal is an integral part of our ecology and of the environment. As a part of our historical legacy, the canal will inevitably influence the future ecological, cultural and environmental development of many cities.

In urban development and modernisation, it is essential that water supplies and water systems should be properly managed, that genuine architectural efforts should be made to maintain a harmonious symbiosis between this natural element and the urban environment. In Suzhou, for example, although water transport has virtually disappeared, the canals have survived, the urban landscape that bears the traces of past lives has been preserved, bearing witness to the way people lived in close harmony with the water and to this city's specific architectural style. Development and renovation projects have sought to protect these qualities, by preserving the layout and dimensions of the canals, and the character of the buildings on their banks.

The culture that developed around water represents a sedimentation of the knowledge and history of peoples. It embodies and concentrates a whole essential component of our civilisation. Today, the culture of water is part of our mental landscape, inseparable from our belief in the need to modify our behaviour so the human beings and water can coexist in harmony. This coexistence, in this era of new models and rapid change, will only be possible if we treat water and its environment with all the respect they deserve. Only in this way will the rivers that flow through the cities of China be able to pursue their indefatigable and civilising progress.

City water supplies from the end of the 19th century to the 21st century

Delphine Spicq

Water, an element that is central to life, and to human and economic activity, is one of the major challenges of the coming century. In a world where water resources are increasingly sparse, the tensions and conflicts associated with access to and use of water are on the rise; many countries are now involved in major disputes over the sharing of cross-border resources. Pessimistic forecasts about future availability suggest the likelihood of increased tensions associated with access to water.

In principle, China is a country with access to abundant quantities of water.[1] In reality, this observation hides wide disparities between regions. Indeed, hydrological conditions in China are very different in the North of the country, which lacks water, and the South, which has it in abundance. There are additional difficulties: the disposition of the waterways and land contours. In the Northern and Central regions, the water descends from steep mountains onto plains where the gradient is shallow. At flood periods, millions of cubic metres of water rush into river beds that are often elevated several metres above the plain, lifted over the centuries by the large quantities of silt transported and deposited by the current. Sudden violent floods descend from the mountains, draining the arable land on their route, in a few hours flooding the surrounding plains and overflowing onto the cultivated land below, where the water stagnates. Alongside this curse, there is another equally ancient one that primarily affects the North of the country: drought, which equally limits the country's capacity to feed its population.

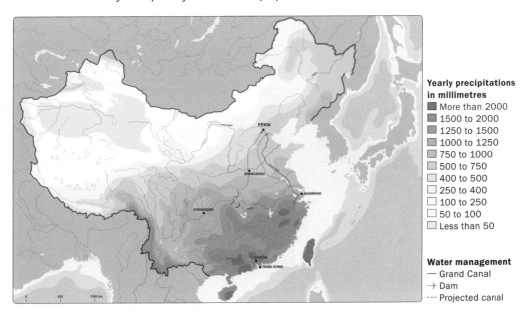

Yearly precipitations in millimetres
- More than 2000
- 1500 to 2000
- 1250 to 1500
- 1000 to 1250
- 750 to 1000
- 500 to 750
- 400 to 500
- 250 to 400
- 100 to 250
- 50 to 100
- Less than 50

Water management
- — Grand Canal
- → Dam
- --- Projected canal

1—With 2800 km³ per year, China is ranked fourth in the world in terms of water resources, behind Brazil, Russia and Canada but ahead of the USA, cf. Peter Gleick, *Water in Crisis*, p. 129-133.

Its most extreme form, desertification, is expanding in the northwestern and central part of the country. Finally, the picture would be incomplete without mentioning pollution, which is today supplanting the other water-related problems. As a result of economic development, both cities and countryside are now experiencing water supply difficulties. Here, we will focus on the description of changes in urban water supplies from the end of the 19th century until today, with an emphasis on the transformation of the processes and problems associated with recent economic development, primarily in the cities of the North.

Urban water supplies

Before the introduction of modern water conveyance systems, the populations of Chinese cities used traditional methods, involving the physical carrying of small volumes of water compared with the quantities that can be stored today. Water was drawn from wells or nearby watercourses, then carried by hand in buckets or barrels, either on people's backs—using the famous shoulder pieces—or in wheelbarrows or donkey carts. The water carriers then sold it to the population at different points in the city. The cost was high, since the water sellers demanded a significant price for their labour. Moreover, they never missed an opportunity to cheat customers on quantity or to cite multiple reasons—difficulty, but also cold, rain, frost, festivals, etc.—to increase the price.

A——Probably Yongdingmen dajie ("Avenue of the Gate of Eternal Stability") in Beijing, January 1909.
Albert Dutertre. © Albert Kahn Museum
B——Chaoyangmen waidajie ("avenue outside the gate facing the rising sun") in Beijing, a water carrier in 1912.
Stéphane Passet. © Albert Kahn Museum

The precious liquid was stored in big jars where it was clarified with alum (aluminium sulphate). Suspended particles in the water clumped around the alum molecules and fell to the bottom of the container, where they were removed using a bamboo stick. The water was then ready for consumption. It was clear but not necessarily pure or safe, free of bacteria. For this reason, it was sometimes treated a second time with beans or charcoal. Beans were believed to eliminate the bacteria. Charcoal, which is still used today, is both a good filter and an effective way of combating microbes.

Drinkable water could also be bought from outlets or street sellers offering boiled water or glasses of tea.

Some of the water came from wells. In Chinese cities, these were private or community owned: people from the courtyard houses, the temple or the district had access to them. Often mediocre in quality, since the water table was polluted from wastewater and the latrines, the well was often used as a backup supply and rarely for drinking.

The arrival of westerners in China, following the Opium Wars (1838-1842 and 1856-1860), and their gradual settlement in the main urban centres changed this traditional supply system. In the concessions, the westerners gradually introduced the urban services which existed in most Western and Japanese cities at the time: electricity, waste collection, transportation (trams), telephones and running water. Reasons of public health (epidemic prevention) and safety (fire prevention) were behind the creation of the first water companies in the foreign concessions. ⓒⓄ

The first modern water conveyance company was created in Shanghai, for the international concession, in 1883. The Shanghai Waterworks only supplied that district, with the exclusion of its French counterpart and the Chinese city. First viewed with suspicion, at least by the Chinese, the example was followed by foreigners living in China and then by the Chinese, and several water conveyance companies emerged within a few years. In Tianjin, the first company came into being in the British concession in 1897, the Tientsin Waterworks—the second to be built in China—then a second in 1902, in the Chinese area, which supplied most of the city. The Tientsin Native City Waterworks was financed by foreign and Chinese capital, but run exclusively by British managers. In 1905, the Chinese city of Shanghai, and in the following year the cities of Guangzhou, Wuchang and Chengdu, introduced this service. The creation of modern water conveyance systems continued across the country over the next ten years. Beijing received

C——Dingzijie, ("T-shaped street"), a man draws water from a well in Beijing, January 1909.
Albert Dutertre. © Albert Kahn Museum
D——"In Kunming's past", before 2000, courtyard water tap. © Geng Yunsheng
E——Well with tiger pattern, funerary object, Han Dynasty (206 BCE - 220 CE), terracotta. The Chinese character jing 井 depicts and means a well. L: 13 cm, H: 9.9 cm. Cernuschi Museum, inv: MC 06036. © Cernuschi Museum – Roger Viollet

running water in 1908, supplied by a company run by Chinese managers. In 1916, there were seventeen water companies, four of them in the city of Shanghai alone (the water company for the international concession, for the French concession, for the Chinese city and finally for the Zhapei district). By the beginning of the 1920s, China's twenty biggest cities had modern water supply networks.

However, the modernity was relative, since in most of these cities, the average quantities consumed (less than 100 litres per person per day) were low compared with their American or European equivalents (around 700 litres in American cities). In addition, this average conceals significant disparities: in Tianjin, for example, on the eve of the Second World War, daily consumption per inhabitant was scarcely 50 litres, a very low figure explained by the fact that the conveyance systems differed from their western counterparts, in that they combined modern elements with others inherited from traditional supply methods. That is why, although the elites were directly connected to the network and received water at home via plumbing systems—a method of connection already present in most developed countries—the rest of the population fetched their water from a water point in the street or a tap installed in the courtyards of traditional houses. These water points were managed by the water companies which did the selling. Their staff, mostly former water carriers become traders, thus kept control of the water supply to most of the population. In Tianjin, their control increased further after 1935, with the tacit agreement of the Sino-British company, which was more interested in increasing profits than guaranteeing equal access to the distribution system.

The water outlets created in the new districts held a monopoly over several streets, or even over an entire neighbourhood, and the traders employed prohibitive pricing and intimidation without any action by the water company. It was only after the Communists took power in Tianjin, in 1947, that these practices would disappear. It should nevertheless be added that water from the supply network was of much better quality and much cheaper than under the old system, even if the quantities available at the outlets were low.

Broadly speaking, after a promising start and sustained development in the 1920s, political instability severely restricted the construction of new networks. The Second World War, far from reversing the trend, exacerbated it and led to widespread destruction.

A new era opened with the arrival of the People's Republic in 1949. Reconstruction and extension of the water systems, a condition of health policy, were Party priorities in all towns and cities. The few specialists, mostly foreign educated, were put to work on this titanic task. The results achieved in less than 10 years were immense and the success undeniable, despite the weakness of the available technical resources, the necessity to train staff rapidly on the job and the difficulty of importing much of the equipment needed. Per capita consumption, though higher, was low compared with western standards, but the progress nevertheless represented both a qualitative and a quantitative advance.

Whether under Mao or in the 1980s, the two major difficulties confronting the cities were firstly the diminution in available resources, at a time of continually rising demand, and secondly pollution, which grew as the country developed economically. Moreover, the reduction in resources concentrates pollution which, in turn, makes part of those resources unusable.

The challenges of water

The cases of Tianjin and Beijing, the two megacities of the Northern China plain, speak volumes. The city of Tianjin, situated 120 kilometres southeast of Beijing, is the confluence point of nine waterways which flow into the river Hai. Tianjin is surrounded by salty, wet land, edged with marshlands linked by innumerable streams. The city and its environs were regularly subject to floods, which the dikes, though constantly reinforced, were unable to contain. The situation changed after

1950, with the digging of numerous canals which steered the water towards the sea, and the construction of small reservoirs which dried out the the outskirts of the city. However, the new danger was no longer an excess, but a shortage of water: the river level fell because of the increasing volumes pumped from the tributaries of the Hai, notably for irrigation. At the same time, the quintupling of the population between 1960 and 2000 made it necessary to seek new resources, which is why two big reservoirs and four drinking water treatment plants were built between 1950 and 1980. Nonetheless, these measures quickly proved inadequate, and from 1975 onwards, the city had to supplement its supply by importing water from the Miyun reservoir, north-east of Beijing, also the capital's principal supply source. The problem recurred at the beginning of the 1980s but, with demand also rising fast in Beijing, the government reserved the water from the Miyun reservoir for the capital and Tianjin turned to another resource: water from the Yellow River was diverted to Tianjin.

Over the course of that decade, two plants were created, one of them Xinkaihe, which takes water from a major tributary, the Luan. The revival of economic reforms in 1992 generated new growth and water shortages reemerged.
Water had to be found further and further afield in the mountains, where it was stored in great reservoirs. In 1997, one of the city water companies was sold to a French company. This "manoeuvre" allowed part of the production system to be modernised at less cost. But problems remained: the conveyance system is obsolete and needs repair and modernisation, and the quantities produced are inadequate to meet growing demand.

Wells provided an alternative resource during the 1970s. The city had almost 1200, a third public and the rest private. They were used mainly as backup in case of supply failures. However, withdrawals in excess of the replacement rate resulted in subsidence, and most wells were closed after 1986. They are now used very little.

In Beijing, the situation is quite similar. The two great Guanting and Miyun reservoirs, built respectively in 1954 and 1960 to resolve the water shortage, have now become inadequate. The urban population increased from two million in 1950, to fourteen million at the beginning of the 21st century. Further water shortages occurred in the mid-1970s, becoming more acute after the reforms of 1978. As in Tianjin, when landslips became increasingly common, pumping from the water table was quickly restricted.

The water allocated to farming around the two big cities is gradually being sacrificed to maintain supply to the urban centres, since the authorities prefer to import cereals rather than face water riots.

As regards pollution, a major problem that has threatened urban water supplies since the 1990s, the anarchic development of large numbers of small factories in the cities and towns has led to increased pollution in all the waterways. Most of these factories, which use chemical products, heavy metals, etc. in their production processes, dump their waste water without treatment, in contravention of regulations. Many harmful products are dumped directly into the natural environment, which deteriorates a little more each day. International companies are also responsible for such pollution.

It has a range of consequences: some pollution is accidental and easily identifiable, like the aminobenzene spilt into the river Songhua upstream of Harbin in November 2005, or else the abnormal development of blue-green algae or cyanobacteria, which has created risks to the health of Lake Tai, near Wuxi, interrupting the water supply to the city for several days in June 2007. The proliferation of these algae, due to the ever-increasing presence of phosphorus in wastewater (fertiliser, manure), is mainly caused by waste discharged from a factory on the edge of the lake. There are many examples of this kind. Often spectacular, and now reported in the press, these one-off episodes are not the most damaging. Another type of pollution, less visible and more diffuse, is no less dangerous: the pollution caused by fertiliser, pesticides, or manure from animals or urban waste systems, which is often discharged without treatment. Certain villages in the Hai River Valley have to use water so polluted that it affects the people's health. The long-term effects are such that in certain places the quotas of young men fit enough for military service are never met. In other villages, cancer and death rates have increased markedly in the last two decades.

Between environment protection and economic development, the Chinese government seems, up to now, and perhaps understandably, to have chosen the second. However, this constant pursuit of uncontrolled and polluting industrial development could in the long run threaten the potential for future growth and the general health of the population.

Bibliography

Ma Jun, *China's Water Crisis*, Norwalk, Eastbridge, 2004.
Delphine Spicq, *La Politique de l'eau et l'hydraulique urbaine dans la plaine du Nord de la Chine: le cas de Tianjin, 1900-1949*, Doctoral thesis, University Paris VII
Denis Diderot, Paris, 2003.
Peter H. Gleick, *Water in Crisis: a Guide to the World's Fresh Water Resources*, Oxford University Press, Oxford, 1993.

Water policy: the cracks begin to show

Brice Pedroletti

It was one of those long-distance buses that link Shanghai with the interior, full of migrants. Some of them were going home. Others were visiting relatives. Rain was falling on Badong county when it happened. The avalanche of rocks and mud first carried away workers who were repainting a railway tunnel through the hillside. It took four days to realise that the bus, which had never reached its destination, had been swallowed up on the road below. Thirty five dead, including the three unfortunate painters. Landslides are common in this region. A tributary of the Yangtze River flows through it and it is not far from the Three Gorges Dam, whose waters have already swallowed up part of the county capital Badong, which has been rebuilt higher up.

A——*Pair of workers by the Peiling River, in 2004* © Yan Changjiang 颜长江

An over-exploited river

But the news on that November Friday, in all its horror—there were families, four children, and DNA tests were required to identify the bodies—came at a very bad time: a few days earlier, the official Xinhua (New China) press agency had reported the reassurances uttered by Wang Xiaofeng, the member of the Council of State responsible for the Three Gorges, claiming that "the impact of the Three Gorges Dam on the ecosystem has been no greater than predicted in our feasibility studies". A U-turn: at the end of September, the same official had sung a very different tune at a forum of experts in Wuhan. He had referred to the "hidden dangers" of the project and warned that the intense pressures exercised by this enormous mass of water (39 billion cubic metres once the reservoir is full) on the sides of the submerged valleys might well "cause pollution, landslides and other geological disasters". Those Chinese experts who had vainly criticised the project stepped up to the plate. The headline on Xinhua's English-language pages was: "China warns of environmental catastrophe from Three Gorges Dam". In the weeks that followed, dozens of foreign journalists dispatched to the area described the symptoms of a worrying pathology: houses riddled with cracks, collapsing embankments, new towns abandoned, populations in fear of further landslides. The water level has now risen above 150 m and will reach its final level of 175 m in 2009.

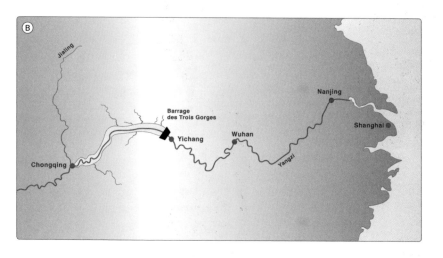

B—*View of the Three Gorges Dam in 2005.* © *OACC*

Since the bus incident, the mandarins have kept their heads down. With its titanic dimensions (2309 m long and 185 m high), *Sanxia Daba*, the world's largest and most modern dam, embodies China's genius for hydrographic engineering—and its madness. Taming the waters brings an atavistic echo of imperial times: 4000 years ago, China's first emperor, Yu the Great, entered into legend for taming the rivers and inventing irrigation. Later on, another large structure, the Grand Canal, would play a major role in feudal China. In the early 1950s, Mao Zedong launched the first big dam projects of the communist era, on the Yellow River and in the Huai River Basin. The Great Leader was able to order *"mountains to bow and rivers to change course"*. Often with unintended consequences: an even more serious decline of certain rivers—the Yellow River is only a shadow of its former self—and a few spectacular failures, such as the domino collapse of the Banqiao and Shuimanqiao dams on the Huai River (a tributary of the left bank of the Yangtze), which killed 240,000 people in 1975.

The Three Gorges project was initially a pipedream (proposed at the creation of the Chinese Republic headed by Sun Yat-sen in 1912) before a vote by the National People's Congress in 1992, under Li Peng, gave it the green light—with one third of members abstaining, a rare event in China. Today, the responsibility for this feat of Promethean socialism has been inherited by two engineers, one trained in hydroelectricity, the other in geology: as new converts to the cause of sustainable development, Hu Jintao and Wen Jiabao are nevertheless unable to sober up the Chinese economy. Instead, they are trying to crisis manage the succession of fits that have shaken this overburdened organism: not a month goes by without tens of thousands of residents, somewhere in China, finding themselves waterless because of mini ecological disasters. No risk that the Three Gorges Dam might crack—it is virtually indestructible—but the fault lines are all around, in the country's alarming environmental health record and its hydrographic network.

It is a matter of common knowledge that there is a shortage of water in China: "some 400 to 600 Chinese towns are short of water and the quantity of water consumed per person is a quarter of the world average" notes Ma Jun, Director of the Institute of Public and Environmental Affairs, which publishes a water pollution map of China [carte de la pollution]. Not only is less than 60% of waste water treated, but half the water treatment plants on the four most polluted rivers (Yangtze, Yellow River, and the Hai and Huai Rivers) do not work properly, according to the environmental protection agency Sepa. 70% of streams and rivers are

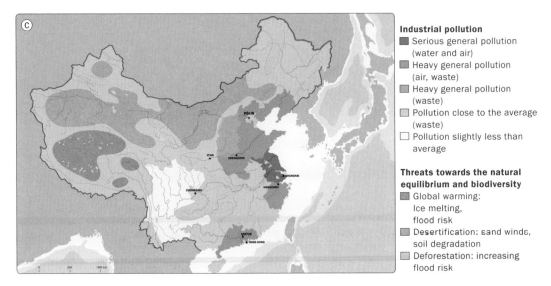

Industrial pollution
■ Serious general pollution
  (water and air)
■ Heavy general pollution
  (air, waste)
■ Heavy general pollution
  (waste)
▨ Pollution close to the average
  (waste)
□ Pollution slightly less than
  average

**Threats towards the natural
equilibrium and biodiversity**
▨ Global warming:
  Ice melting,
  flood risk
▨ Desertification: sand winds,
  soil degradation
▨ Deforestation: increasing
  flood risk

seriously polluted. In this context of systemic crisis, the current overexploitation of the Yangtze, China's longest and most generous river, is worrying. In 2007, the Baiji, the freshwater dolphin, was officially declared extinct by China's Academy of Sciences. According to the Chinese press, some 30.5 billion tonnes of industrial, agricultural and human waste were discharged into the "long river" last year.

Celebrated as one of the biggest sources of clean energy in the world, the Three Rivers Dam has deleterious effects on this overburdened environment, one of which is the formation of a gigantic basin of polluted water. Whilst it will help to control the river's devastating floods, there is a risk that it will become clogged with sand whilst inhibiting downstream sedimentation, causing a deepening of the river bed.

Variations in the ecosystem, combined with industrial waste, have led to algae blooms (cyanobacteria) in two large downstream lakes, Chao Lake in the Anhui region and Tai in the Jiangsu region. As China's hydrographic backbone, the Yangtze is earmarked for further large-scale development: upstream of Sanxia Daba, there are plans for around a hundred hydroelectric plants on the River or its tributaries, including the Xiluodu plant on the River Jinsha in Sichuan province, which is set to become China's second biggest dam in 2015. Initial work has already begun, despite controversial impact studies.

C——Pollution map

Mother Nature bites back

They are also relying on the Yangtze to irrigate Beijing and the dry regions of North China. Work has now begun on two of the three routes designed to divert water from south to north, the gigantic so-called "Nan Shui Bei Diao" project devised by Mao and approved in 2002.

The central route will carry water from the Danjiangkou reservoir in the Hubei region (the River Han, a tributary of the Yangtze) to the capital. But here again, nothing is simple: the building of two giant tunnels under the Yellow River looks likely to take longer than planned. In addition, the widening of the Danjiangkou Dam and the canal will flood hundreds of historic sites. The excavation is well behind schedule. Only part of the route will be ready for the 2008 Olympics in Beijing: the section carrying water from Shijuazhang, in the Hebei region, to nearby Beijing. However, Hebei is also short of water. The eastern route, where work has also begun, is intended to carry water from Shandong to Beijing, along the old Grand Canal. This route was supposed to be ready by 2007, but will not now be finished before 2010.

Moreover, the water will be too polluted and will need treatment. As for the western route, on the plateaus of Qinghai Province, the technical challenges are unprecedented, and no work will start before 2010.

D——*Construction of the Shimen reservoir, in Henan, 1975. Dyke 90 m high, capacity 30 million cubic metres.*
© Zhou Zhenhua 周振华

In the immense Yangtze Delta, water is more than abundant: for centuries it has been a world of canals, lakes and rivers. The historian Christine Cornet, who started out last year on the trail of a missionary called Father Jo, who had photographed the region in the 1930s, expresses her surprise at the continuing intensity of transport activity on the waterways, with their boatmen and miniature boatyards. However, the industrial fever of the last 15 years has transformed the region: in the backcountry of Shanghai, between Wuxi, Jiangsu province's industrial metropolis, and its backyard Yixing, there is nothing but an endless succession of chemical plants, workshops, hamlets and rice fields, a chaotic motorway grid, superimposed on the network of canals, crisscrossed by trucks full of barrels, mopeds and heavily laden delivery tricycles. In every village, a proportion of the houses are rented to workers from other provinces —often Anhui—whilst their owners are themselves in Wuxi or Shanghai. We are near Lake Tai, a huge expanse of water measuring 2428 square kilometres, which rarely exceeds two metres in depth. At our last visit in November, there were almost no more signs of the algae which poisoned the lake last May, a sort of bacterial monster generated by an excess of nutrients, partly from the factories around, but also from fertilisers and the sewers. In Wuxi, 2 million people then found themselves without water.

E—View of the Three Gorges Dam in 2005. © OACC

In a China now highly sensitive to pollution issues, this disaster had a major impact: the lake was subjected to one of those shock treatments which the country specialises in, with thousands of volunteers sent to drain off the algae, chemical products to dissolve them and an influx of water, once again, from the Yangtze. In October, the government of Jiangsu province announced a budget of 10 million to clean the lake and close thousands of factories. However, this is not the first time that there have been promises to restore Lake Tai to its former health. Hundreds of factories which should already have moved are still running. These derisory efforts won Yixing the title of model city in 2006: the height of hypocrisy for Wu Lihong, the environmental activist who for 10 years has toured the disfigured country of his childhood, tirelessly collecting evidence of crimes against the environment in small plastic bottles. After years of harassment by the local authorities, he was arrested last April, just before the Lake Tai ecosystem imploded, and given a four-year jail sentence in a rigged trial (for fraud). His appeal has just been rejected. Gare, the monster of Lake Tai, could well awaken next summer: whatever the great orchestrators-in-chief of the *workshop of the corporate world* may say, the truly titanic enterprise today lies in pollution control.

F——Pollution around Lake Tai, Suzhou, 2005. © *Li Lang* 黎朗

風水

Fengshui

All around the world, *fengshui* has become an inexhaustible source of superstitions, along with the associated moneymaking opportunities. Nonetheless, it is impossible to understand the structure of Chinese space without *fengshui* and the rituals, whether religious or secular, connected with it. *Fengshui* itself has been used to organise the houses of the dead and of the living since at least the 6th century BCE. This means that both urban and rural China has been organised in accordance with principles that can still be read in every site and in every landscape.

Fengshui is supposed to protect from misfortune and promote luck. Over time, *fengshui* masters combined their compass—the *luopan*—with all the practices associated with the *Book of Changes* (*Yi Jing* or *Yi King*)—an interpretation of the world based on *yin* and *yang* and the eight trigrams—and then, over the centuries, with various interpretations of *qi* (vital energy), and with the dragons that populate the heavens, the earth, the mountains, water or fire...

Taoism was also naturally involved in the rules of construction. It would transform the legendary master builder Lu Ban into a divinity recognizable by his fly whisk, the guardian of customs and techniques, inventor of a thousand and one tricks for keeping furniture straight, flying kites, building the most delicate pavilions, designing bird cages.

A——Chuandixia Village, Beijing. © Françoise Descamps

Rituals and traditions of Chinese space

Yves Kirchner

Definitions

Fengshui (literally "wind and water"), explains an eminent specialist on Chinese thought, Marcel Granet (1884-1940), "seeks to determine the value of sites by considering the flowing waters (*shui*) and the air currents (*feng*)", and to harmonise them in such a way as to promote the health, well-being and prosperity of their occupants. Sometimes called "the technique of reason", the Chinese referred to *fengshui* in designing their cities, building their houses and burying their dead. An essential aspect of the Chinese perception of the world, according to Needham (1900-1995), author of a monumental encyclopaedia *Science and Civilisation in China*, is that they do not see things "mechanistically" but "organically"; a way of seeing in which "each phenomenon is linked with all others in a hierarchical order". Thus, the Chinese believe that there is a network of correspondences between man and the universe in which he lives, the place where he chooses to live and his ancestors. According to the definition proposed by the *Encyclopedia Sinica*, *fengshui* is "the art of adapting the dwelling places of the living and the dead so that they co-operate and harmonise with the local currents of the cosmic breath (what the Chinese call *qi*)". The *Zhongwen Dazidian*, Great Dictionary of the Chinese Language, links this practice with the School of *yin yang*, specifying that it "consists in observing the orientation of the mountains and the flow of the rivers to decide the location of tombs and dwellings". Moreover, the primary meaning of the terms *yin* and *yang* seems to correspond, if we believe Marcel Granet, with the *ubac* (northern side of a mountain) and the *adret* (side of a mountain exposed to the sun). Finally the *Zangjing* (*The Book of Tombs*), the burial classic by Guo Pu, provides this explanation: "Entombing means dominating the vital breath. Now the breath rides on the wind to disperse, and stops where water sets a boundary: the Ancients assembled them (the winds) so that there should be no dispersal and traced them (the watercourses) to make a stopping place."

The Chinese often refer to the mysterious forces of the earth which circulate beneath our feet, within our being, and govern health, prosperity and luck. The goal of *fengshui* is to "channel" them, in order to harmonise our interior being with the external world, like the harmony of a building with the environment around it. *Fengshui* refers to natural features. The shapes of hills and valleys, the flow of streams and rivers, are the most important factors; but it also takes account of the height and appearance of buildings, of the direction of roads and bridges. In addition, as the strengths and nature of the invisible currents can be modified by the position of the celestial bodies, the aspect of the latter is also taken into account. In the course of its development, *fengshui* has encompassed human constructions, such as houses, dams, roads, elements that play a preponderant role in today's publications, sometimes giving rise to distortions.

History

Such practices feature in books dating back to the 4th century BCE. Two centuries later, the *Historical Memoirs* by Sima Qian mention the existence of a category of soothsayer, the *kanyujia* (Soothsayers by the canopy of Heaven and the chariot of Earth). The geomantic system was consolidated under the Three Kingdoms, in the third century CE, with the text *Guanshi dili zhi meng* (*The geomagnetic guide of Master Guan*) attributed to Guan Luo. In it, two currents on the surface of the Earth—*yin* and *yang*—are linked with two symbols that apply to the eastern and western quarters of Heaven, the Green Dragon of spring (East) and the White Tiger of autumn (West). It was thought that each of these symbols matched configurations on the Earth, the Green Dragon on the left and the White Tiger on the right of any inhabited place, to protect it as if it lay in the crook of an arm.

Yin and Yang

First under the Sui dynasty (581-618), then under the Tang (618-907), harmony was sought in the balance of the forces of *yin* and *yang* present in each everyday item. The balance of a building is as much about its proportions as the materials used and its location (its indescribable logic, its intrinsic strength). According to Needham, the ideal site had a proportion of "three fifths yang and two fifths yin". The impalpable, intangible force, resulting from this, *qi*, is described in the Chinese work *Zhuzhai yu fengshui* as follows: "It cannot be touched, it cannot be seen, it is a form of perception. To use a more concrete description, it could be said that it is 'the first impression', the impression immediately experienced on entering a new place." Zong Bing (375-443) nevertheless specifies in a treatise on landscape painting, the *Hua shan shui xu*, that the reality that surrounds us "is not limited to its external appearance".

The analysis does not end here: one has also to take account of the trigrams [a combination of three *yin* (broken) or *yang* (continuous) lines], of the hexagrams (in all, there are eight possible combinations of trigrams which combined form 64 hexagrams), of the cyclical characters (branches and trunks) and of the Five Elements.

There are several kinds of *qi*, the most important of which are vitalising *qi* (*shengqi*) and deathly *qi* (*siqi*). On a given site, the aim of *fengshui* will be to promote the expansion of *shengqi*, and to restrict *siqi*. To achieve this, the geomancer will arrange the site in such a way that there is not excessive wind, to prevent dispersal, and that the water flows without threatening the dwellings.

He will recommend the planting of trees and bamboos as windbreaks and the creation of reserves of water; the art of the *fengshui* master, whose profession resembles that of a doctor of nature, is to exploit the qualities of a plot whilst optimising its resources. He heals the wounds of the dragons and helps the vital *qi* to flow through the houses. By detecting the pulse of the earth, he can determine the ideal place for human beings to live.

The two schools: "shapes" and "compass"

Any human arrangement must be harmonised with the complex configurations of nature. Under the Song dynasty (960-1279), two currents emerged: the compass school and the shape school. The first perfected the use of the "geomancer's compass", a flat disk with a magnetic needle in the centre, whose concentric circles are engraved with the "eight trigrams", the five elements and the signs of the Chinese duodecimal calendar, the "celestial trunks" and the "terrestrial branches", together with other astronomical and cosmological symbols. "There is now no doubt, Joseph Needham tells us, that the compass was developed for geomancy, and that it derives from the soothsayer's compass (*shi*). This compass had two flat sections: the upper section, disk shaped, corresponded to Heaven, and the lower section, square, to the Earth. The stars of the Great Bear were marked on the upper section, whilst on both the disk and the square were characters representing the compass points. Such instruments probably already existed as early as the 3rd century BCE, and apparently already played a role in direction finding, even in cloudy weather."

The members of the second school were more interested in the characteristics of the landscape which the geomancer surveyed to find the hidden currents, called "dragons' veins", which must not be "injured" by buildings.

In earth geography, the dragon dwells under the sinuous curves of the mountain chains. Straight lines and flat plots are places where he is weak, whereas changes of direction, elevations, mountains, symbolise his "pulsations". Tong Kog, author of the *Book of the science of Dili* (1979), explains that *qi* energy, like blood, also flows in the veins, and that the individual's personality and health both depend on its quality. And, just as a good doctor checks a patient's health by taking his pulse, a good *fengshui* expert will distinguish between lucky and unlucky, good and bad sites, by examining the arteries, the pulses of the mountain. "Dragons, the *Book of Mingtang* tells us, have a thousand forms and ten thousand appearances, large or small, standing or crouching, angry or docile, hidden or exuberant. They are in infinite metamorphosis, diving down, surging up, flying and leaping."

The source of *qi* on earth is at Mount Kunlun, the Great Progenitor, which rises to 7,724 m between Tibet and the province of Qinghai. For energy to flow, one must protect oneself from the wind that may disperse it and use the water that carries it and concentrates its beneficial influence. Mountains and water, earthly manifestations of the energies of the Universe, are two primordial factors to take into account when seeking and analysing a place to build.

According to Chapter 1 of the *Yellow Emperor's Treatise on Buildings*, the curves of a chain of mountains and of a river are to be considered as the belly and back of the dragon. The waters of rivers and lakes are his blood, the surface of the earth his skin, vegetation his hair, and buildings his clothes. The dragon's main arteries, which come from the heart, will therefore appear in the form of ridges or chains of hills, or else winding watercourses. The ideal site is called "the dragon's antrum" (*xue* in Chinese). To find a *xue*, one must first face southwards. Then, one decides whether the site is ideal by reference to various factors: the topographical characteristics of the environment, the astrology of different members of the family, and events that may have affected the site.

The ideal shape is that of a horseshoe or armchair: the protecting black tortoise to the north (a mountain high enough to block the winds and negative *qi*), the white tiger to the west (a fairly steep mountain), the blue dragon to the east (a mountain slightly higher than the one in the west, to demonstrate the superiority of this animal which carries the flow of *qi*) and a view of the purple phoenix (a mountain slightly further away to the south).

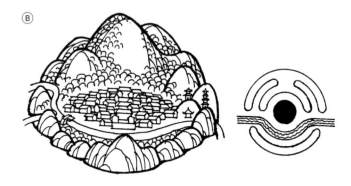

B—Ideal site to settle a village according to *fengshui* principles
Source: Wang Qiheng, ed., *Research of Fengshui Theory*, Tianjin University Press, 1992.

Fengshui today

Accused of causing multiple conflicts and court cases, *fengshui* was condemned in the reform movement of May 4, 1919, and dismissed as superstition under Mao. It nevertheless retains its influence throughout Asia, where it plays an ambiguous role in the cities of the south; nobody really believes in it but no one is quite prepared to reject it. In Hong Kong in particular, companies attach great importance to the view from their headquarters, and in particular to the presence of an area of water. Mirrors are carefully placed to reflect a pleasant view and summon the positive *qi*. Some might claim that this is just a way of pleasing customers. But is it the only reason? Making good deals has become the essential focus of *fengshui*. The ideal position, for a business, is the corner of a street, with a diagonal entrance to attract *qi*, customers and money from two directions. Generally, oblique lines are avoided—they attract misfortune and intrigue—but in some cases they are very useful. In the past, gambling houses used oblique doors

C——Hong Kong & Shanghai Bank Tower, architect Norman Foster, 1979-1986, Hong Kong.
© Ian Lambot / Foster and Partners

for somewhat shameful reasons: they were the best way to retain the gamblers' *qi* and money. Years later, some embittered or perspicacious spirits complained that a respectable Chinese bank in Hong Kong used the same type of entrance. Is it enough to laugh about an influence so manifestly pernicious? And what should we think about the smug amusement with which the western press reported that, in 2003, right in the middle of an MRSA epidemic, property developers in the suburbs of Beijing tried to stop the building of a hospital (or was it a clinic?) for the sole reason that the site chosen by the authorities could damage the "veins of the dragon" carrying *qi* to the capital?

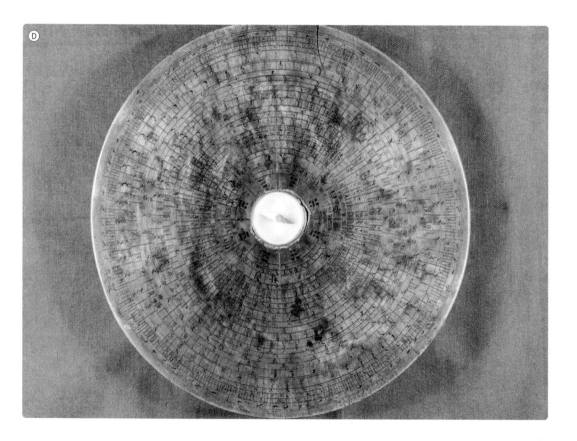

D——Geomancer's compass. Frédéric Edelmann Collection. © Dominique Delaunay
E——HSBC tower and a *fengshui* master at the entrance of the building during work. © Foster and Partners

Interview with Zhong Ruzhong, a geomancer from Hunan

Patrice Fava and Shi Cuijie

There are different rules for determining the right *fengshui* for a house and for a tomb. What are the main differences?

Houses are part of the *yang* world, tombs belong to the *yin* world. For houses, you need to think about the environment, the natural exposure in the four directions. You have to study winds and draughts. For tombs, the most important thing is the veins of the dragons (*longmai* 龍脈). You have to see where the mountain range begins (*shan de yuantou* 山的源頭), which corresponds with the location of the dragon (*lai long* 來龍). You also have to consider the mountain range behind, its shape and where it begins. After conducting this geographical and geological analysis, you have to find the pressure point (*dianxue* 點穴) where the tomb will be located. That is the most important stage. Everything depends on this choice. You have to consider the direction in which the waters flow. For houses, the access routes are of great importance, for tombs what matters is water. In summary, it could be said that the predominant factors for determining *fengshui* are: the *mai* 脈 (the underground veins), the mountain range 山 and water 水.

In observing the geomantic context, you must first identify possible dangers, unpropitious signs. For example, a river that flows in a straight line near a house represents a danger. On the other hand, if it arrives in a zigzag or if the house is surrounded by water, that is a positive factor.

A few years ago, when we were walking in the mountains, you said that you could look at the location of a tomb and say what would happen to the dead person's descendants, and that your predictions were almost always right. How do you do this?

There are many factors. The most important thing is the shape of the mountain range and the flow of the waters. These principles are equally valid for tombs and houses. When you look at the gate to the village of Zhongjiacun and analyse the direction of the waters and the way the river flows, you understand how this village managed to produce so many scholars and senior officials. That gate is 660 years old. It dates back to the Ming and is still there today.

We also went together to the village of Zhangguying, just nearby, which also dates back to the 15th century and has been very well preserved because of its *fengshui*. Zhang Guying was himself in fact a geomancer. What do you think of the *fengshui* of that village?

In Zhangguying, the "dragon veins" (*longmai*) come from very far away. The mountains form an excellent protection all around. The mountain range behind is the dragon range. The water that comes in from both sides joins up and flows out of the village (*shuikou* 水口) at the Point of Longevity (*changshengwei* 長生位) on the eight trigram system. The fact that Zhang Guying, the founder of this village, had such exceptional descendants is explained by the *fengshui*.

How do you use the eight trigrams in the construction of a house?

The orientation of a house, based on the directions associated with the eight trigrams, is of great importance. It must be oriented along the "point of longevity" (*changsheng wei*). The same technique is used to determine the orientation and location of the front door.

When you are designing a tomb, do you consider the dead person's horoscope?

Of course. You have to know his eight birth characters (*bazi* 八字), in other words the signs of his destiny. You have to combine the dead person's personality and *fengshui*. There is no ideal *fengshui* that applies to everyone. The *fengshui* has to match the *bazi*.

How do you relate the element that is predominant in an individual's destiny and the environment. For example, if a person's element is Wood, what will be the most favourable type of tomb?

If the mountain range corresponds to the element Metal (*jin*) and the deceased to Wood (*mu*), he must not be buried there. On the other hand, if he is Water (*shui*), it is perfect. You apply the system by which the elements engender and destroy each other. It is not because there is a word in a place, that the landscape belongs to the element Wood. It is the direction of the compass that tells you whether the place is Metal (*jin*), Wood (*mu*), Water (*shui*), Fire (*huo*) or Earth (*tu*). Our house, for example, is associated with the element Metal, as indicated by the compass. It is enough to know someone's eight birth characters to know their dominant element, and what star they are governed by.

According to the lunar calendar, my daughter Xuanxuan was born on the 29th day of the 3rd lunar months of the year 2006, at 10:30 a.m.. Can you calculate her *bazi* and her astrological associations?

2006 is a *bingxu* 丙戌 year, the third month is a *renchen* 壬辰 month, the 29th day has the binomial *yiyou* 乙酉 and the time of her birth corresponds to *dinghai* 丁亥. These are her eight characters. The dominant element in her future is Wood (*mu*). Wood is attracted to Earth and Metal destroys Wood (*mu xi tu* 木喜土, *jin ke mu* 金克木). The Wood element is calculated from the binomial of the date of birth (*riyuan* 日元), whereas the three others correspond to three calendar spirits (*shensha* 神煞): Shangguan 傷官, Zhengyin 正印, Shishen 食神, which will play a crucial role in her future.

Do you belong to a particular *fengshui* school? The landform school (*xingjia* 形家), the compass school (*lijia* 曆家)? How was this tradition passed down to you?

I don't belong to any school. When I was 25 years old, I studied with a Liuyang master and then I worked alone with the books that I inherited from my ancestors.

You have a very ancient compass. I know that it isn't possible to sum up what a geomancer's compass represents in a few sentences, but could you briefly tell us something about this object steeped in history?

The compass contains the whole system called: *yin, yang* and the five elements (*yin yang wuxing* 陰陽五行), the eight trigrams (*bagua* 八卦), the ten heavenly stems and the twelve earthly branches (*tiangan dizhi* 天干地支), the constellations (*xingxiu* 星宿), the twenty-four solar periods of the year (*jieqi* 節氣), etc. In order to analyse the good and bad aspects of *fengshui*, you have to use the correspondences between all these spatiotemporal factors, but to decide the orientation of a house, the location of the front door, you refer to the concentric circles one by one. In fact, you have to know all these series and the correspondences between them by heart.

Bibliographical sources

Monique Cohen et Nathalie Monnet, *Impressions de Chine*, catalogue of the National Library exhibition, 1992.

Henri Doré, *Recherches sur les superstitions en Chine*, IIe partie Tome XI, Chang-hai, T'ou-se-we printing press, 1919, p. 1030-1038. Reprinted by You-feng publishing house.

J. Edkins, "Feng-shui", in *Chinese Recorder and Missionary Journal*, March, 1872.

E. J. Eitel, *Feng-shui or the Rudiments of Natural Science in China*, Hong Kong, 1873.

Stephan D. R. Feuchtwang, *An Anthropological Analysis of Chinese Geomancy*, Editions Vithagna, Vientiane, Laos, 1974. p. 18-27.

Marcel Granet, *La Pensée chinoise*, Albin Michel, 1934 (particularly the chapter on numbers, p 151-299).

J.J. M. De Groot, *The Religious system of China*, 6 vols, Brill, Leiden, 1872; reed. Ch'eng-wen Pulishing Company, Taipei, 1972. (see vol. 3: "Fengshui")

Marc Kalinowski, *Cosmologie et divination dans la Chine ancienne: le Compendium des cinq agents* (Wuxing dayi, VIe siècle), E.F.E.O, Paris, 1991.

Max Kaltenmark, "Ling-pao: note sur un terme du taoïsme religieux", Institut des Hautes Études chinoises, 2 (1960), 559-588.

Joseph Needham, *Science and Civilisation in China*, vol. II, III, IV.1, Cambridge University Press, Cambridge, 1962.

Frédéric Obringer, *Fengshui, l'art d'habiter la terre*, Philippe Picquier, Paris, 2000.

Klaas Ruitenbeek, *Carpentry and Building in Late Imperial China—A Study of the Fifteenth Century's Manual Lu Ban Jing*, E.J. Brill, 1993.

Stephen Skinner, *Fengshui, terre vivante: traité de géomancie chinoise*, Les Deux Océans, Paris, 1989.

The tools of the geomancer

Patrice Fava

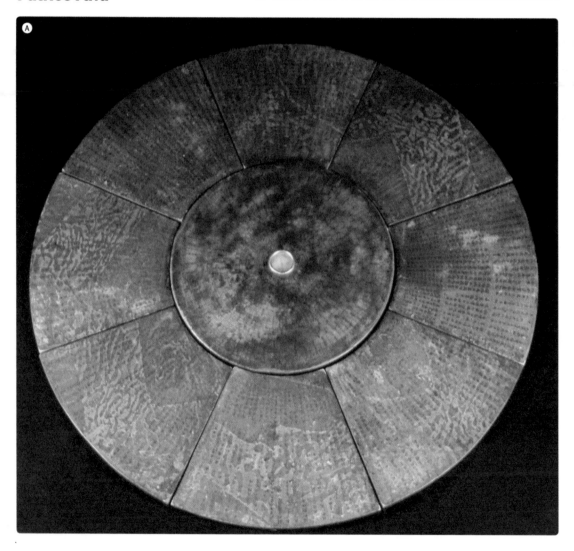

The geomancer's compass and the theory of the Nine Stars [1]

Geomancy is the art of placing a house or tomb in the landscape, and the instrument which, since the Song Dynasty (11th century), has embodied the whole science of the geomancer is the compass, called *luopan* 羅盤. Each of the circles surrounding the Heavenly Lake (*tianchi* 天池) containing the magnetic needle is a concentration of cosmological, divinatory, astrological and calendar information. The biggest compasses can have thirty-eight circles. These different loops have been extensively explained and discussed by the eminent historian of science Joseph Needham and by the English anthropologist Stephan Feuchtwang.

The originality of the compass shown here is that it has eight mobile "wings", arranged in a circle around the body of the instrument. There are inscriptions on both sides. Side A describes the system of the Nine Stars (*jiuxing* 九星), which are located in the constellation of the Great Bear. They have evocative names, originating in soothsayer tradition: Greedy Wolf (*tanlang* 貪狼), Great Gate (*jumen* 巨門), Warlike Column (*wuqu* 武曲), Literary Curve (*wenqu* 文曲), Destroying Army (*pojun* 破軍), Pure Honesty (*lianzhen* 廉真), Wealth Preserved (*lucun* 祿存), Left Assistant (*zuofu* 左輔) and Right Assistant (*youbi* 右弼). All these stars are connected, in geomantic texts, with the eight trigrams, the five elements, the twelve palaces, the heavenly stems and the earthly branches of the sexagesimal cycle. The concept underlying the theory of the Nine Stars is that the cosmic forces that they represent are projected onto the earth and can be identified in the landscape. The task of the geomancer is therefore to identify the presence of these stellar figures in the different natural configurations and to be familiar with their qualities, so that they know what long-term effects, favourable or unfavourable, they may have on their immediate surroundings. The text on the eight wings of the compass covers sixty-four different situations and announces what effects each of one of them will have: discord, births, deaths, wealth, etc. The presentation of the nine stars that appears in the centre of each "wing" is taken from a two-volume Ming era treatise on geomancy, *The correct use of the compass points* (*Luojing dingmen zhen* 羅經頂門針). The Wolf star, for example, is described as *yang*, corresponding to the element Wood, and, if it coincides with the trigram orientations *li* 離, *zhen* 震 and *xun* 巽, is said to spread beneficial influences.

A——Geomancer's compass, with eight mobile wings: diameter 71 cm. Image: Compass © D. Delaunay

1——Article written with the collaboration of Marc Kalinowski.

The texts inscribed on side B are divided into two parts. On the inside loop is a series of twenty-four calendar spirits governed, here again, by the seven stars of the Great Bear flanked by their assistants, but this time with the names that they have in the astronomical tradition: Heavenly Pillar (*tianshu* 天樞), Heavenly Jewel (*tianxuan*天璇), Mizar (*kaiyang* 開陽), Heavenly Weight (*tianquan*天權), Sparkling (*yaoguang* 搖光), Jade Scales (*yuheng* 玉衡), Heavenly Pearl (*tianji*天機) and the Heavenly Assistants (*tianfu*天輔). The stars come with short texts describing the virtues and prognoses associated with them. On the outside loop is the list of the twenty-four compass directions (*xiang* 嚮) reproduced identically on each of the eight wings. For each position, different prognoses specify the propitious or unpropitious circumstances associated with the presence of one or other of the elements.

Discussions on the fundamentals of geomantic theory remain contradictory, but efforts are now being made to understand how the system works, instead of a total denial of its validity, as was often the case in the past.

After a house was finished, a ritual was performed called "Installing the Dragon god" (*anwei longshen* 安位龍神). To do this, an intaglio woodcut was impregnated with black ink and then used to emboss the image on rice paper. This paper was then glued to the lower part of the altar of the earth god (Tudigong土地公), who was identified with the dragon god of the underworld (*dixia longshen* 地下龍神). At the top is the diagram of the *taiji* 太極 (the supreme pinnacle) surrounded by the eight trigrams (*bagua* 八卦), then, on either side of a talismanic sign, the secret names (*hui* 諱) of the sun (*taiyang* 太陽) and of the moon (*taiyin* 太陰). The two characters after *lingbao* 靈寶 mean "sacred jewel", a Taoist term that refers to a wide group of fourth and fifth century liturgical texts, but also to the earthly treasures whose counterpart is to be found in heaven. The charts, symbols and talismans, of which this plate is an example, belonged to this category of transcendent objects (*ling* 靈).

The figure that appears on the second third of the board, above the character *xing* 星 (constellations) represents the earth god. On the next line are four characters: 年 (*nian*, year), 月 (*yue*, month) , 日 (*ri*, day), 時 (*shi*, hour) which are completed when the date of the ritual is decided. Below, the characters中宮 (*zhonggong*, Palace of the centre), on the right (到此 *daoci*: arrive here) and on the left 鎮宅 (*zhenzhai*: place the house) form a sentence that means: "may the earth god come here to establish the favourable geomantic context for this dwelling" and gives the general meaning of the talisman which has a protective and propitiatory function.

Building a new house modifies the natural environment and the hidden forces of the underworld, of which the dragon is the emblematic figure. Under geomantic principles, therefore, a ritual must be carried out to "pacify and thank the dragon."

B—Woodcut (*muban* 木板) dating from the Qianlong period (18th century), 120 x 15 cm. Hunan Province.
© D. Delaunay

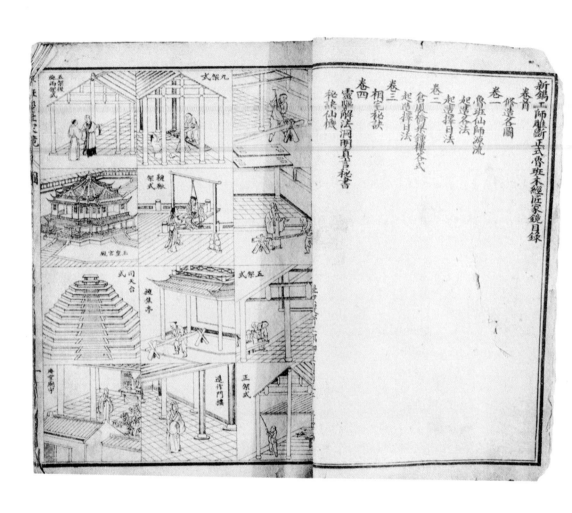

C——*Illustrated Book of Lu Ban* 繪圖魯班經, published by the Jiangdong Bookshop in Shanghai 上海江東書局, woodcut in 4 fascicles of 17 folios 19.7 x 19 cm, including 134 illustrations, undated. It mentions the names of Superintendant Wu Rong of the Bureau of Imperial Carpenters in the Beijing Ministry of Public Works 北京提督工部禦匠司司正午榮匯編, of Zhang Yan, Head of the Bureau of Craftsmen 局匠所把總章嚴仝輯 and of Zhou Yan, from the Bureau Of Craftsmen of Nanjing 南京遞匠司司承周言校正, which indicates that it is a reprint based on the Ming edition compiled between 1425 and 1450.
© D. Delaunay

The Book of Lu Ban

The *Lu Ban jing* 魯班經 (Book of Lu Ban) was not written by the divine carpenter who lived in the 5th century BCE, but by an official of the Ministry of Public Works apparently given the job of recruiting building specialists at the time when Emperor Yongle was transferring his capital to Beijing. The oldest edition of this work, with more than a hundred illustrations, was printed for the first time from woodcuts at the end of the Ming Dynasty. Numerous editions followed. It contains much of the expertise of builders and carpenters in different fields: the construction of houses, temples, palaces, bell towers and drum towers, pagodas, bridges, leisure pavilions, lofts, cowsheds, and also furniture. Alongside the technical information that makes it a valuable architectural manual, with certain elements dating from the Song dynasty, it also contains much of the esoteric tradition of the carpentry trade. Like blacksmiths, doctors or soothsayers, carpenters formed a brotherhood of specialists skilled in the occult arts, numerology and astrology. Half of the *Lu Ban jing* is in fact a secret book (*miben* 秘本), which describes some of the rituals, talismans, propitiatory formulas, geomantic rules and magic processes that accompany different stages in the construction of a house, and which are based primarily in the Taoist tradition. Carpenters preside over people's future, over good relations between the spirit world and human beings. They need to know the natural dangers and the forces of evil that threaten human beings, and to ally themselves with good spirits and positive energies. The science of numbers plays a fundamental role in this quest for harmony. Each stage of the construction process must obey very precise calendar recommendations. The *Lu Ban jing* specifies propitious and unpropitious days for cutting trees, beginning work on a house, installing windows. Door width is a subject of particular concern. The *Lu Ban jing* also reviews, with drawings, seventy-two house designs which, depending on their location and access route, will bring their inhabitants good or bad luck. Overall, the principles employed reflect an analogical form of association: a T-shaped road will block the development of the family, and is very bad for fertility; on the other hand, a road that widens in front of the house will bring the family wealth and renown. The front door must never extend beyond the roof, as this will be very damaging to future generations. Two houses should never have doors opposite each other, otherwise one of the families will have problems. At different stages in the building process, the protective gods are invoked. The General of the Tiles 瓦將軍, or a picture of Huang Feihu 黃飛虎, god of the Taishan, is placed on the roof. In certain cases, to modify the geomantic environment, it is necessary to install a "stone that dares to oppose" (*shigandang* 石敢當), or protective tablet, the dimensions of which are specified. The system is highly complex. It involves symbols, correspondences, physical and psychological observations, or is based, as Carl Jung would say, on archetypes.

D——Lu Ban statue, Hunan province, 20 cm height. Image: Lu Ban © D.Delaunay

Lu Ban, the divine carpenter

Lu Ban 鲁班, patron saint of carpenters, is a historical figure whose legend has grown over the years. His real name was Gongshu Ban 公输班 and he came from the village of Dongping 東平村 in the country of Lu 鲁 (now Shandong). He was born into a family of carpenters. His father's first name was Xian 賢 and his mother came from the Wu 吴 clan. He lived under the Eastern Zhou dynasty, in other words at almost the same time as Laozi and Confucius. For a man of the 4th century before our era, we know a remarkable amount about him. He was born on the 7th day of the 5th lunar month of the year *jiaxu* 甲戌, in the 3rd year of Duke Ding of Lu 鲁定公 (507 BCE), at the time *wu* 午 (between 11 a.m. and 1 p.m.). A flock of cranes that was flying overhead that day landed near the house, which is an extremely lucky sign. A delicious perfume spread around and remained for a whole month. He was not much interested in school. At the age of fifteen, he left to be apprenticed to a master carpenter. In a few months, he had learned all the skills of the trade and returned home. As was already common in his time, he refused to serve the tyrant in power and withdrew to the mountains for thirteen years. At the age of forty, after a very active life, he disappeared again to become a hermit and learn the arts of the Tao.

In Chinese chronicles, Lu Ban is seen above all as an inventor of genius and every primary school child knows the clever carpenter who invented the saw after observing a sharp blade of grass edged with small teeth. He is credited with the invention of many other objects: the spirit level, the set square, the measuring tape, the drill, the grindstone, the padlock and even automata. Wang Chong 王充, the author of *Critical Essays* (*Lunheng* 論衡) reports that he gave his mother a cart that moved on the orders of its driver, by means of a highly sophisticated internal mechanism. We also know from his contemporary, the philosopher Mozi 墨子, that Lu Ban had made a giant bird-shaped kite out of bamboo which could stay up for three days. It is also said that he used this bird as a vehicle to return home to his wife, from whom he was often separated because of remoteness of the sites were he worked. It would seem that Mozi had great admiration for this inventor of genius, and advised him, in the name of the great harmony that he sought to promulgate, to stop building catapults for the country of Chu. Lu Ban accepted his arguments without hesitation.

Amongst the many stories told about this divine carpenter, the story of the statue he made of his father reveals that he not only excelled in all domains, but that he was also gifted with supernatural powers. His father, it is said, was executed by people from the kingdom of Wu. In order to honour his memory, Lu Ban created a statue of him with one hand pointing to the country where the assassins came from. A drought immediately took hold, and after three years a delegation was sent to beg him to accept the apologies of the authorities and the gifts offered to him. Remorsefully, the pious son agreed and cut off the statueís arm. The rain immediately began to fall.

In the famous Ming Dynasty novel, *Journey to the West*, Lu Ban is described as the Minister of Public Works for the Jade Emperor (Yuhuang dadi 玉皇大帝), head of the Taoist pantheon.

The worship of Lu Ban, which was originally confined to his region, extended to the whole of China and in different eras he received honorific titles from the Empire's highest dignitaries. The Ming emperor Yongle canonised him ìGreat master protector of the countryî. In Beijing, several sanctuaries were dedicated to him, especially in the great Taoist Eastern Peak Temple (*Dongyuemiao*). Before starting construction work on a house or a bridge, all carpenters invoke his protection and perform a ritual with offerings to him.

What is less well known is that Lu Ban is also the patriarch of a sect of master magicians called *Lu Ban zhengjiao* 鲁班正教, "the orthodox religion of Lu Ban". That is not altogether surprising, for architecture has been linked since antiquity with the magic arts, with cosmology, with geomancy and with the system of correspondences (*yinyang wuxing* 陰陽五行). Like our cathedral builders, Chinese carpenters were also builders of temples and sculptors of gods and lived in permanent contact with the world of the divine. Architecture, as *the Book of Lu Ban (Lu Ban jing* 鲁班經) *clearly shows*, operates within a largely religious context. Representatives of the Lu Ban brotherhood, who are still active in the provinces of Hunan and Jiangxi, continue to perform rituals such as the consecration of statues (*kaiguang* 開光) and invocations of the gods (*qingshen* 請神) and to practise bodily transformation rites (*huashen* 化身). The statue of Lu Ban, their master, is enthroned on their altars, sometimes depicted astride a crane, like the immortals, sometimes with a fly whisk, or else holding the famous *Lu Ban jing in his hand*.

Some two thousand four hundred years after his death, Lu Ban is considered equally as the patron saint of carpenters, one of the most famous inventors of ancient China, a great saint in the Taoist pantheon and a master magician.

Lu Ban's ruler

The quest for ideal proportions in architecture has been a major preoccupation in all civilisations. Lu Ban's ruler 魯般尺, known since the 8th century, is the most explicit material expression of this quest for harmony between heaven and earth, and is primarily based on numerology and astrology. Works produced by the hand of man must be modelled on the spontaneity of creation.

Lu Ban's ruler, which is used to measure the gaps between doors and windows in general, varies in its dimensions depending on eras, schools and local traditions. Using the system of measurement in feet (*chi* 尺), inches (*cun* 寸) and tenths of an inch (*fen* 分), the Book of Lu Ban (*Lu Ban jing*) specifies that the authentic builder's ruler should be 1 foot 44 long (*yichi sicun sifen* 一尺四寸四分), i.e. approximately 45 cm. It is divided into eight equal sections called "gates" (*men* 門). Four of them are propitious and four unpropitious. Each of them is associated with particular functions: wealth (*cai* 財), sickness (*bing* 病), separation (*li* 離), justice (*yi* 義), the civil service (*guan* 官), catastrophes (*jie* 劫), bad luck (*hai* 害), good luck (*ji* 吉) and with the Five Elements: wood (*mu* 木), earth (*tu* 土), water (*shui* 水), metal (*jin* 金), fire (*huo* 火). On the scale marks of Lu Ban's ruler, the width of a door with a single leaf 2 feet 1 inch wide would correspond to the "justice" (*yi* 義) section, while if it was 2 feet 8 inches wide, it would correspond to the good luck (*ji* 吉) section. A two-leafed door 4 feet 38 inches wide would correspond to wealth (*cai*). The ideal measurement, for a large door with two leaves, concludes the *Lu Ban jing*, is 5 feet 66. Each of the eight sections is accompanied by a poem that describes the benefits and dangers associated with one "gate" or another. On certain rulers, these poems are reproduced, but carpenters were expected to know them by heart.

The height and spacing of columns, the depth of rooms, also follow precise rules. The whole house is subject to careful calculations that must also take into account the stars, which are feared for their malignant powers. The other side of the ruler gives the names of the constellations, which can bring wealth, good luck or calamities.

For a long time, Lu Ban's ruler, generally made of wood and with inscriptions written with a brush, was a secret instrument. The master allowed his pupils to copy it when they completed their apprenticeship. It was both an instrument of measurement and a ritual object which, like books, was a repository of transcendental truths.

E——Lu Ban rulers 40 x 5 cm. Image: Lu Ban rulers © D.Delaunay

建筑

Architecture

While the traditional organisation of space is linked, apart from fengshui, with the Confucian rules governing social relations, ancient construction for its part is based on expertise in the assembly of structural timbers which, to different degrees, follow their own hierarchy of rules and principles shared by generations of craftsmen.

At the centre is a rectangular space around which, in accordance with a strict hierarchy, are disposed the areas of the family (or ruler) and the areas of domesticity (or vassals) until the walls of this ensemble meet the street. Urban space is organised in a similarly hierarchical manner, although there are significant differences between cities that represent imperial power and conurbations constructed around commerce or harbour activities.

Until the beginning of the 20th century, even the shape of towns scarcely changed, if we exclude the introduction of western type buildings, which did very little to alter the long-standing forms. Despite the ravages of war and the massive social upheavals wrought by the Maoist revolution, urban structure remained amazingly stable until the end of the 1980s.

It is true that overpopulation and industrialisation caused sometimes dramatic deterioration to traditional structures. And it is also true that new forms of habitat appeared, but it was only with Deng Xiaoping ("To be rich is glorious") and the award of the 2008 Olympic Games (decision by the IOC in 2001), that all of China's cities would move into a ferment of unprecedented transformation, in the course of which long-standing Chinese cultural norms would finally give way to western construction techniques.

Traditional Architecture Museum, Temple of Agriculture, Beijing © OACC

Construction
Rules, models and manuals
and manuals Christophe Gaudier

While the Chinese language has many verbs like: *jian* 建, *ying* 营, *zao* 造 *zhu* 筑, which with various nuances all refer to the action of building, it has no term that can be validly translated as architecture. The dissyllable 建筑 used in modern Chinese is in fact borrowed from the Japanese, who first used the expression in translations of American works, and even a modern dictionary like the *Ci Yuan* 词源, whose first edition dates from 1915, does not include the expression.

The same is true of bibliographies. To take just one example, the *Yingzao fashi* 营造法式 or *"Manual of Building Standards"* appears in the bibliographical section of an encyclopaedia like the *Wenxian tongkao* 文献通考 (c. 1300) in the chapter "Philosophers", subsection *Za yishu* 杂艺术 "Miscellaneous Techniques and crafts" between a work on mathematics and one about a board game. It is cited twice in the bibliographical section of the *Song shi* 宋史 *History of the Song Dynasty*, first in the section "history: ceremonies", and a second time in the section "Philosophers: five elements". In more recent catalogues, it tends to appear in the sections on works of the art of governing, such as the *Guoshi jingji zhi* 國史經籍志 (1594), where it is listed in the "History" section, subsection "Government", alongside the *Lu Ban yingzao zhengshi* 魯班營造正式 or "Lu Ban's authentic rules of construction", a carpentry manual and *Ziren yizhi,* 梓人遺制 *"The art of carpentry"*. In the *Siku quanshu zongmu* 四库全书總目 it appears in the "History" section, subsection "Government", subdivision "Examination of trades", along with a manual on brick making and construction rules under the Yuan dynasty. It will be noted, however, that although technical works on construction are cited together in all these works, they are always associated with other texts covering a wide range of subjects, and therefore do not form a category, or even a subcategory, of their own.

This means that until recently, Chinese civilisation had never felt the need to make the production of the built environment the domain of a specific activity or discipline: architecture. [1] Yet the Chinese did not build without rules or principles. To be persuaded of this, it is enough to consider the permanence of the essential forms of Chinese architecture, which some believe to have been in place by the beginning of our era and probably even long before. This permanence is all the more remarkable in that it is maintained despite the short lifespans of the principal materials used: wood and clay.

1——This work, probably written in the early 13th century, only comes to us through extensive extracts copied in the *Yongle da dian.*

Standardised architecture

A Chinese building consists of:

- A tamped earth terrace protected by a facing of flat stones, then covered with slabs.
- A load-bearing structure of columns and lintels.
- A frame supporting a roof consisting of several layers of tiles.

The three parts of a Chinese building

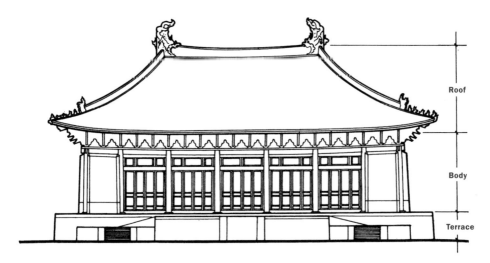

Roof

Body

Terrace

On the top of the surrounding columns and on the lintels there may be assemblies of varying complexity, forming the brackets that support the roof eaves. The structure has no foundations and the columns are not set into the terrace floor, but simply placed on drum-shaped stone pedestals. It is the weight of the roof that maintains the building's stability. The dado joints are not nailed and retain a certain flexibility, which enables the structure to resist stresses such as those caused by storms or even earthquakes.

Chinese construction is a standardised and uniform process. From antiquity, there is a tendency to look for consistent ratios in the dimensions, for example between width and depth, between depth and height. This tendency applies to all aspects of construction, from the most general dimensions to the smallest frame assembly components. Chinese construction is in fact component based. The frame is made up of a large number of identical elements, some of which can be small.

These components are prepared in the workshop and then assembled and mounted in situ. This approach permits a degree of prefabrication and eventually standardisation. This standardisation is achieved by taking a module from part of the frame, then using its cross-section to calculate all the dimensions of the building, and then standardising the dimensions of that module into a restricted number of "classes", to be adapted to the size and category of the building.

Chinese frame type

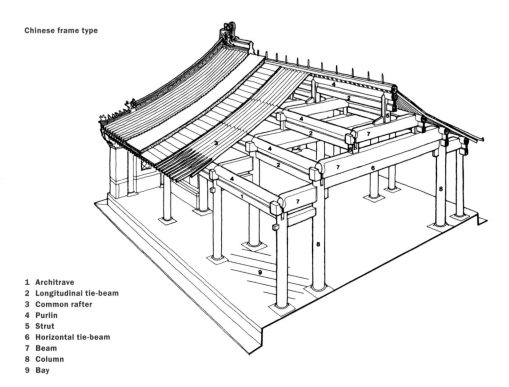

1 Architrave
2 Longitudinal tie-beam
3 Common rafter
4 Purlin
5 Strut
6 Horizontal tie-beam
7 Beam
8 Column
9 Bay

A rule-based architecture

From early times, there emerges a set of rules, ritual in origin, which—depending on titles and ranks—govern the shapes, dimensions and even the colours of what each individual can build. Official architecture, at least, is a regulated and controlled architecture. In the capital, but also in local administrative headquarters, a large proportion of construction was by official order. This applied first of all to palaces and imperial residences, but also to all buildings which, in one way or another, contributed to the administrative panoply of the empire: officials' houses, administrative headquarters, barracks, schools, temples for emperor worship, but also sometimes Buddhist or Taoist temples, some of which were built on the orders of members of the imperial family. In the capital, at several periods and in particular under the Song, a particular department, the *Bureau of Construction*, had the task, among other things, of overseeing both the erection and the maintenance of all these buildings. *The History of the Song* defines its functions as follows: "The inspector was in charge of matters relating to the construction of buildings, ramparts, bridges and ships, and the construction of carts... He had to ensure that there was a permanent stock of the necessary materials and tools, which could be supplied in case of need. He prepared the apprentices by teaching them the necessary methods. He set the periods of work and rest for the different seasons and times of day at the empire's official building sites and workshops. He assigned officials to examine the accounts and expenditure entailed in construction, to verify them and set the terms and amounts..." Public officials

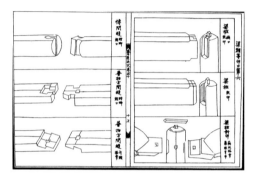 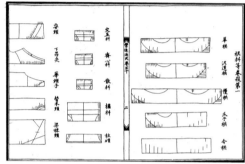

were therefore in charge of public construction and directed and monitored the work. These officials were not themselves technicians, but rather specialists in public administration, and in performing their role they relied not only on official documents but probably also on the exchange of private documents, which were used if not to manage the work, at least to monitor performance. They also employed these documents to manage construction sites, to plan and organise labour and materials, and to maintain the accounts. Li's *Standards* belongs to this category of document.

At the beginning of the *Xining* era (1068-1077), in the course of a civil service reorganisation, the "construction department inspectorate" *(jiangzuojian)* was ordered to produce a *yingzao fashi*, i.e. a set of "building standards", to replace old documents that had become obsolete. These new standards proved too general and unusable, and in 1097 a junior inspector in the department of works, Li Jie, was ordered to revise them. This new version was completed in 1100, printed and circulated around the municipal departments. In 1103, at the request of Li Jie, a new edition was prepared for wider circulation. It is likely that the printing plates and most of the copies were destroyed when Kaifeng was seized by the Jin in 1126. In 1143, during the rehabilitation of the imperial library in Hangzhou, a new edition was printed by officials in Suzhou, from an old copy of 1103 edition that they had found. It is through copies of copies of this latter edition that the *Standards* have reached us.

Little is known about Li Jie. He was apparently born in Henan near today's Zhengzhou and began his career officiating at ceremonies in the dynasty's ancestral temple. In 1103, he had reached the grade of junior inspector in the department of works, and was responsible, amongst other things, for maintaining the out-of-town residence of the emperor's younger brother and for the building of barracks. He must have been in the post for some time, since it was in 1097 that he was given the task of revising the *Standards*. A late and probably exaggerated tradition credits him with building most of the capital's important buildings, but it is certain that his duties gave him practical experience of construction. He is also credited with having written several works, none of which have survived. He is thought to have died in 1110.

The *Standards* are not a private work but an official assignment, and the text is primarily intended for government departments. If they were written for the purpose of replacing old and obsolete documents, we should nevertheless resist the temptation to conclude that this rewrite was prompted by progress in building techniques that had left the old manuals behind. In fact, most of the structural elements are already present in still extant buildings that predate the Song, and apart from a tendency to build taller and lighter buildings, there is no obvious major transformation in building methods. The need for a rewrite perhaps has more to do with the need for standardisation, for improvements in the use of an increasingly rare and expensive material—timber—and for better use of manpower. The *Standards* are intended for public construction and were written during a period of reform of the imperial finances. A wish to control building costs may perhaps have had something to do with the demand for new standards.

Li Jie specifies that in producing these new standards, he relied on: "rules based on ancient traditions relating to building structures, which have proved their efficacy over a long time and have been explained to me in detail by knowledgeable and skilled craftsmen with experience of construction, laws on what is respectively useful or deleterious in different structures and on the formulas of proportion."

The plan used by Li Jie in writing the *Standards* makes no attempt to follow the different stages in the construction of a building, from foundations to roof. The text is organised into four main parts: structures, which describes each of the elements involved in the construction of a building in terms of the types of material used; tasks, which sets the quantities of work required for the completion of each structure; materials, which determine the quantity of raw materials to provide; and finally examples to illustrate the concepts. In the composition of the *Standards,* there is a major effort to organise the material collected. The structure adopted, the arrangement of the parts and chapters, arises directly from the function of the text. Each of the main parts corresponds to an aspect of the work of the officials overseeing a building project: execution and compliance monitoring, manpower management, materials supply. One wonders to what extent the organisational aspect of the text is attributable to Li Jie alone. It is not impossible that he applied an existing plan. The great originality of the *Standards*, and what distinguishes it from a treatise, is that it never approaches construction as a generic topic, but in terms of a breakdown of successive structures, like a set of spare parts each with its own specific description. The *Standards* contains neither an essay on construction methods, nor theories about the art of building, nor references to any constructional system. The approach taken is quite different, a detailed description of each component that may be involved in the construction of a building and an account of the rules for its use.

The content of the *Standards* remains essentially quantitative and normative. Li Jie in no way seeks to define construction methods. The *Standards* is not addressed to craftsmen but to public officials, to give them what they need for oversight purposes.

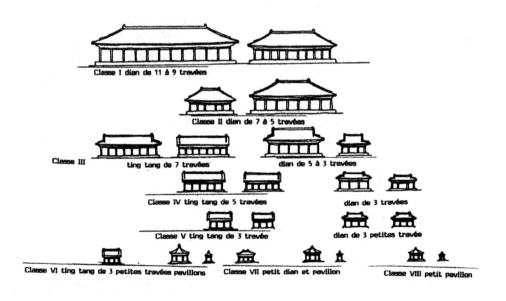

It defines dimensions, proportions, quantities, both of materials and labour, but relatively few processes. A Chinese building is primarily a frame. It entails the assembly of pieces of frame, the repeated use of identical components. The general dimensions of the building, its height, its depth, its width, arise out of the dimensions and quantities of each of its components. The dimensions of a window are defined by the height of the column and the length of the lintel. The length of the building will be defined by the number of windows in the facade, its depth by the number of successive rafters in the roof. So it is quite unnecessary to describe a building in its totality. It is enough for the standards to set the dimensions and shapes of each component, on the basis of a limited number of defined structural models. There is little about actual construction processes. It is not the technical act that interests the public official, but the result. Tools, instruments, processes are therefore described only when the outcome of the building depends on their use. This is the case of the survey instruments or graphic processes used in plotting the curve of the roof.

The module, according to the "Yingzao Fashi:" there are 8 classes of modules that are used depending on the category of the building. The height is divided into 15 units and the width into 10.

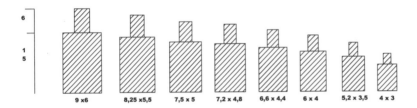

One might wonder what real influence the *Standards* had on actual buildings, and how much they were applied. In fact, no building currently exists which could be said to have been built in line with the recommendations, and there is nothing to say that such buildings ever existed. If, on the other hand, we try to apply these standards to the analysis of buildings, it is quite easy to identify most of the broad outlines of the *Standards* in practically all surviving buildings erected between the 8th century and the end of the 13th century.

For example, the ratio of 3:2 between the height and width of beams sections is a constant found in almost all constructions throughout this period. There are elements in the *Standards* which date back long before it was written, but others that would seem to have developed contemporaneously with it, which only came into general use later on. One example is the crown post on bracket systems, which made it possible to increase roof elevations without extending their span. This feature is described in the *Standards*, although there exist very few buildings where it was used, all of them located in Jiangnan. The *Standards* of Li Jie are valuable for the historian of techniques and of architecture. It is evidence of the role of public officials and public construction in a process of standardisation that is partly the outcome of the very nature of the building. It also provides a detailed and accurate glimpse of the building processes used in the 12th century. But it is pointless to expect the *Standards* to provide answers about the origins and meaning of certain features of Chinese architecture. For example, the *Standards* contains a description of a graphic method for plotting the curve of the roof. It tells us nothing either about the origins of this method or about the reasons for this curve, but it provides evidence that by the 12th century, sophisticated graphic methods for resolving technical problems were known and used.

The degree of sophistication of this method, the geometrical concepts involved (scale reduction, iterative plotting), also show that this process is the outcome of a long development process. A comparison of the *Standards* of Li Jie with surveys carried out on a set of buildings—mostly temples—erected between the eighth century and the late 13th century, reveals differences or correspondences that can be used to identify changes, transformations or the spread of techniques. The *Standards* is therefore a waymark, a reference point that can be used if not to date, at least to identify constants, variations and trials in the solutions found for problems that Chinese builders faced. It is also valuable because it is evidence of the links between the craft practices developed on building sites as a means of rationalising and systematising techniques, standardising components and developing effective methods for determining dimensions, amongst other things by the use of modules taken from the structure of the building, and the involvement of the public official who recorded and regulated these practices for purposes of oversight and management.

Curve of the roof

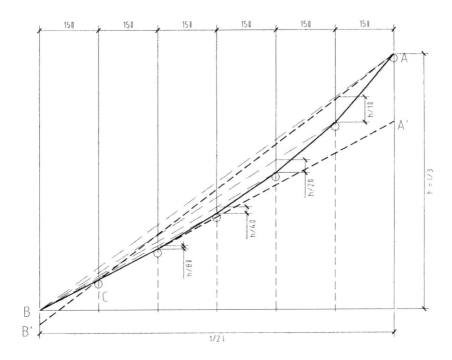

You draw a cross-section of half the building on a scale of 1/10, then you draw the line that joins ridge tile A to the edge of the eaves B. You divide the base depending on the number of rafters. From the ridge tile, you lower the intersection point between AB and the horizontal projection of the first rafter by h/10, which gives you the position of the first intermediate purlin. You draw the line joining the resulting point to point B and you repeat the procedure with a reduction of h/20. Te same operation is repeated until the penultimate rafter.
It will be noted that in order to keep the same length BC in horizontal projection for the eaves without breaking or bending the slope, you have either:
- to reduce point B to B' and damage the buildingís natural lighting
- or to reduce the height and slope of the roof by lowering the eaves from A to A'

Yangshi Lei

Chiu Che Bing

"He is a master builder of talent, one I will not forget"

Aisin Gioro Xuanye, the Emperor Kangxi,
Imperial Chronicle of the Garden of the Glorious Spring

Tradition relates that when the main beam of the *Taihe dian* 太和殿 [1] was raised, the emperor attended in person to perform the ritual of offering the sticks of incense in honour of the gods. The beam would not fit correctly to the frame, and the propitious moment would soon be passed. A master carpenter jumped on to the frame and, with a blow of his axe, shaped the tenon and adjusted the beam in time for the ceremony to be completed correctly. Highly satisfied, on the spot the emperor conferred on the master carpenter the title of *changban*, foreman, in the Office of Construction at the Ministry of Public Works.

The event is reflected in the dictum:

> "In Heaven, Lu Ban; [2]
> On earth, *changban*;
> On his destiny shines the Purple star;
> In the Golden Hall he was made mandarin." [3]

This master-carpenter was called Lei Fada 雷发达 (1619-1693). He was the first in a line of builders and construction supervisors who would distinguish themselves in the design and construction of imperial projects under the Qing dynasty (1644-1911).

Construction under the Qing dynasty and the origin of the Bureau of References

Under the Qing, the start of any project over a certain size [4] signalled the beginning of an administrative process. A memo was sent to the Minister of Public Works for the emperor to appoint two mandarins, one in charge of the project 承修大臣 to set up a Works Office 工程处 to supervise the design and implementation of the project, the other responsible for verification 勘估大臣 to set up the Office of Verification 勘估处 to establish an estimate for the work, consult contractors and carry out inspections. The Office of Public Works was an executive body, the *dangfang* 档房 an archive office which operated in parallel, in the capital, *zaijing dangfang* 在京档房, and on the project site, *gongci dangfang* 工次档房. Two departments were created, the *yangshi fang* 样式房 and the *suanfang* 算房. The first was responsible for project design, the production of plans and drawings and the crafting of models, a task performed by the *yangzi jiang* 样式匠. The second was the task of the *suanshou* 算手 "calculation officials", who established estimates, checked quantities and maintained accounts. The head of each department had the title of *zhangan* 掌案 "head project manager".

1——The Hall of Supreme Harmony is the throne room of the Forbidden City.
2——His real name was Gongshu Ban 公输般, a native of the state of Lu 鲁 in the late Spring-Autumn period (722-481 BCE), hence the name Lu Ban. Gongshu Zi 公输子 (Master Gongshu) as he is often called, was a builder, inventor and strategist, and protector of the society of builders.
3——"上有鲁班, 下有长班, 紫薇照命, 金殿封官。"
4——More than 50 taëls of silver for the work, and 200 taëls for the materials

The term *yangshi fang* is not found in official Qing dynasty documents. From archive materials, it seems that there were two types of *yangshi fang*. The first was a permanent body, such as the *Yuanmingyuan nanmu zuo yangshi fang* 圆明园楠木作样式房, the *nanmu* Workshop Design Bureau in the Gardens of Perfect Clarity. The second was temporary and existed only for the lifetime of a project.

The number of craftsmen working in the *yangshi fang* was not set. According to a memo sent in year XII (1873) of the reign of Emperor Tongzhi (同治, 1856-1875, r. 1862-1875), the department then had sixteen people, including the two *zhangan* Lei Siqi and his son Lei Tingchang.[5]

Members of the Lei family practically monopolised the role of *zhangan* for almost 200 years under the Qing dynasty. They are known in China as Yangshi Lei 样式雷, Lei of the Design [bureau].

Joseph Needham, in his monumental work *Science and Civilisation in China*, in the volume on construction and hydrographic projects, refers to the Yihe yuan and mentions Lei Li 雷礼 (1505-1581), Minister of Public Works in the reign of the Emperor Jiajing (嘉靖, 1507-1566, r. 1521-1566), as the ancestor of this dynasty of master builders. However, although Lei Li and Lei Fada both came from Jiangxi province, they were from two distinct branches.

According to the genealogical record of the Lei 雷氏族谱[6] clan, Lei Fada descended from the branch attached to Lei Qilong 雷起龙 who settled in the district of Jianchang 建昌县[7] in the reign of the Yuan Emperor Renzong (仁宗, r. 1312-1320). Lei Qilong's three children all had brilliant careers either as mandarins, like Lei Hong, 雷洪, Minister of the Civil Service, or in academic circles. Ⓐ

Throughout the whole Ming period (1368-1644), the Lei family lived in Jianchang district. The adopted son of Lei Wenyuan 雷文远, Lei Hong's great-grandson, was involved in the construction of 金陵 (the modern Nanjing 南京), the first dynastic capital of the Ming, under the reign of the founding Emperor Hongwu (洪武, 1328-1398, r. 1368-1398). At the end of the Ming dynasty, the children in Lei Wenyuan's direct lineage, Lei Yucheng 雷玉成 and his sons Lei Zhensheng 雷振声 and Lei Zhenyu 雷振宇 left for Jinling to become traders. They were sufficiently successful, by the inaugural year in the reign of the Emperor Kangxi (康熙, 1654-1722, r. 1662-1723), to bring their wives and children, including Lei Fada and Lei Faxuan 雷发宣, to join them in Jinling.

5——The other names mentioned are Lei Sisen, Lei Siyao, Lei Tingfang and Lei Tingdong. Members of the Lei family account for one third of the bureau's personnel.

6——This document is now kept in the Chinese Heritage Research Institute 中国文物研究所. *Zhongguo yingzao xuesh huikan*, vol. iv-No. 2, p. 156.

7——The district was part of the Nankang prefecture (Jiangxi 江西南康府 province). It is the modern Yongxiu 永修县 district.

A——*Genealogical record of the Lei clan.*
Revised genealogical table of the Lei clan, the branch that migrated to Jinling, then to Beijing.
Source: Chinese Heritage Research Institute. © Wang Qiheng

Tradition relates that in the winter of 1683, in order to meet the needs of his family, Lei Fada and his second cousin Lei Faxuan accepted a call from the Beijing court to work on the imperial construction projects. It is unlikely that this was Lei Fada's first visit to the capital. At this time, he was already 64 years old. It is reasonable to assume that soon after his arrival in Jinling, he travelled to the capital to take part in reconstruction and rehabilitation work on the Forbidden City. Two reconstruction projects were conducted at the Taihe dian, in 1669 and 1695. If it was really Lei Fada who fixed the beam during the ceremony, it could only have been during the 1669 project. He was then 50 years old.

If that is correct, Lei Fada returned to Jingling to put his affairs in order, then returned to the capital with his cousin and children in 1683, and settled at Haidian 海淀. He continued to work on construction sites and only retired at the age of 70, dying four years later. He is buried in Nanjing.

In the genealogical record of the Lei clan, the entry on Lei Fada only mentions the dates of his birth and death, his burial place, his matrimonial status and his children. There is no information on his working life.Ⓑ Ⓒ

B—De Da Qing men, Gate of Great Purity, to Kunning gong, Palace of Earthly Tranquillity. Purple Forbidden City. Elevation drawing. Drawing archive. Source: National Library of China. © Wang Qiheng
C—Project for the reconstruction of Jianfu gong, Palace of Established Happiness. Purple Forbidden City. Axonometric view. Detail. Source: Ancient Palace Museum. © Wang Qiheng
D—Funerary stele of Lei Jinyu. Embossing.
Text underlined in red: "My great-grandfather [...], with respect, took part in the construction work for the pavilions in the gardens at Haidian. He directed the operations of the *nanmu* workshop, and as a result of the fitting of the master beam of the main hall, he was, by imperial grace, received in audience and answered the questions asked by the Emperor. By imperial grace, he was awarded the title of head of the Bureau of General Administration of Imperial Construction, attached to the Neiwu, with the rank of mandarin level 7 and the corresponding rewards."
Source: National Library of China © Wang Qiheng

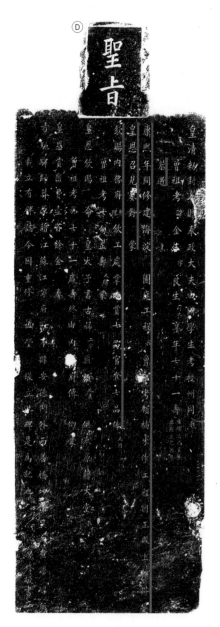

But the facts recorded by the stele commemorating the life and career of Lei Jinyu, Lei Fada's eldest son, cast a different light.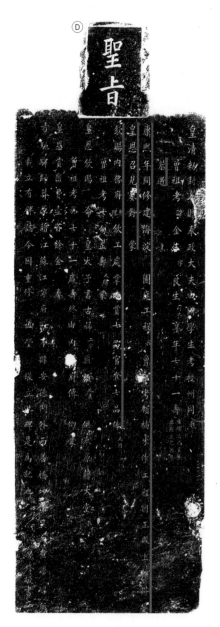

Lei Jinyu (雷金玉, 1659-1729) was educated at Guozi jian 国子监, the imperial college. After the examination to become a mandarin, he obtained the title of *zhoutong* 州同, assistant to the departmental magistrate, with duties in the capital. Probably for convenience and also with an eye to the future, Lei Jinyu joined the *baoyi* 包衣[8], the banner of palace servants.

8——Manchu term meaning "house". A member of the *baoyi* was considered to be a "slave", "servant". There are no existing historical documents proving Lei Jinyu's incorporation into the *baoyi*.

In 1684 and 1689, the Emperor Kangxi conducted a tour of inspection in the south of the Empire and fell in love with the landscapes of Jiangnan 江南. He conceived the idea of building a garden in the capital whose scenery would remind him of the charms of that enchanting region. Zhang Ran 张然[9] and Ye Tao 叶洮,[10] two artists from the Wu 吴 country, were given the task of redesigning Qinghua yuan 清华园, the Gardens of Floral Candour, a former Ming Dynasty Garden.[11] The building of the garden, which was to serve as a place where the Emperor could "escape from the hubbub to deal with affairs of state", began in 1685 and was completed in 1690. The garden was renamed Changchun yuan 畅春园, Garden of Glorious Spring. Ⓔ Lei Jinyu was involved, and according to the terms of the commemorative stele, he "directed the work of the *nanmu* workshop,[12] and as a result of his action in positioning the master beam of the main hall, he was, by imperial grace, received in audience and answered the questions asked by the Emperor". Is it likely that history would have repeated itself within 20 years? It is certainly not impossible, but improbable. It seems quite natural that the oral tradition could have attributed the son's exploit to the father in order to put an extra spin on the foundation of a great lineage. In any case, Lei Jinyu was awarded the title of the head of the Bureau of General Administration of Imperial Construction, attached to the Neiwu fu 内务府总理钦工处掌案,[13] with the rank of a level 7 mandarin and the corresponding rewards.

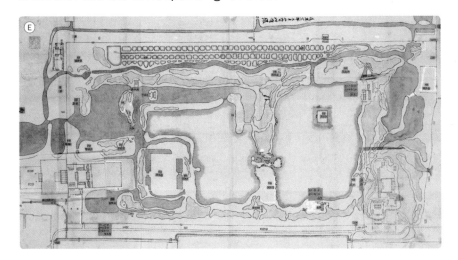

Ⓔ

E——Changchun yuan, Garden of Glorious Spring.
Detailed drawings dating from the twenty-ninth day of the third moon of the year xvi (1836) in the reign of Emperor Daoguang. Source: Ancient Palace Museum. © Wang Qiheng
F——Yuanmingyuan, Garden of Perfect Clarity. Scenery Wanfang anhe, Peace and concord with ten thousand horizons. Source: National Library of China. © Wang Qiheng

9——Son of Zhang Nanyuan 张南垣, a famous master stone carver. Cao Xun, "Qingdai zaoyuan dishan yishujia Zhang Ran he Beijing de 'shanshi Zhang'", *Jianzhu lishi yu lilun*, No. 2 (1981), Nanjing, Jiangsu Renmin chubanshe, 1982, pp. 116-125.
10——A painter of *shanshui* 山水画, literally "mountains and water", the term used for landscape.
11——This famous garden is also called Li yuan 李园. It belonged to Li Wei 李伟, marquis Wuqing 武清侯, a relative of the Ming Emperor Wanli (1563-1620, r. 1573-1620). The name Qinghua was given to the famous Beijing University created at the beginning of the 20th century, Tsinghua University.
12——*Nanmu*: a hardwood tree from southern China, prized because it does not expand, contract or rot, releases a subtle aroma, and naturally repels parasites, sometimes called white cedar. *Nanmu*, a rare and precious essence, is used in joinery and decorative panels, and less often for construction timbers.
13——The Office of Internal Affairs, in charge of day-to-day life in the imperial household.

The highly talented master builder remembered by the Emperor Kangxi in a poem must undoubtedly be Lei Jinyu.

Later on, during the work undertaken at Yuanmingyuan 圆明园, for the Gardens of Perfect Clarity Ⓕ, the new Emperor's favourite residence, Yongzheng (雍 正, r. 1723-1735), Lei Jinyu again distinguished himself. In recognition of services rendered, on the orders of the Emperor, an Imperial prince honoured him at the celebration of his 70th birthday with a calligraphic plate bearing the two characters *guxi* 古稀, "venerable". Then on his death, the Emperor granted the dead man's family a hundred taels of silver to cover the cost of returning the body for burial in his home town.[14]

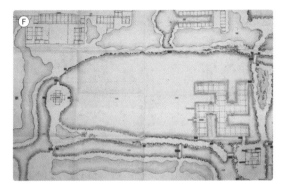

For the genealogical record, Lei Jinyu is considered to be the founding father of the Beijing branch of the Lei clan. Tableau des Yangshi Lei.

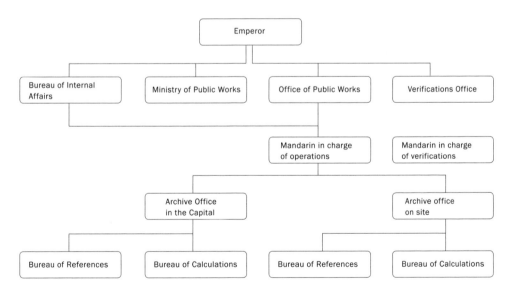

Once fame is established, the surname Yangshi Lei spreads!

14——The tomb of Lei Jinyu, which lies next to his father Lei Fada, is in the district of Jiangning 江宁县, outside the Ande 安德门 Gate, at the place called Xishan qiao 西善桥. A stele has been erected to commemorate Lei Jinyu's life and work.

Rise and fall of an exceptional line of master builders

Of his five sons, only the youngest, Lei Shengcheng (雷声澂, 1729-1792), followed in Lei Jinyu's footsteps.[15] However, there is little biographical information on this craftsman, which is all the more regrettable in that his career coincided with the era of the great building campaigns conducted by Qianlong (乾隆, 1711-1799, r. 1736-1796). The following fact is related: the father's position having been allocated to other functionaries, Shengcheng's mother went with a nurse and Shengcheng to complain at the Ministry of Public Works. As an adult, he was able to continue working at the Yangshi fang. A study of the text of the stele raised to the memory of Shengcheng's mother suggests that the episode is apocryphal, and it is likely that it was the action of three of Shengcheng's children that resulted in the recovery of the position of *zhangan*. Of these children, the eldest, Lei Jiawei (雷家玮, 1758-1845) spent his life in court service. Under Qianlong, he was dispatched to the provinces to inspect the *xinggong* 行宫, the Emperor's travelling palaces, and the dikes. He was also given the task of drafting reports on merchants who held the monopoly in salt selling, in cases of illegal use of State land, which suggests that Jiawei's integrity was recognized at the highest level of imperial government. The second son, Lei Jiaxi (雷家玺, 1764-1825) also worked for the court, in particular in the gardens of Wanshou shan, of Yuquan shan and of Xiang shan,[16] as well as in the hamlet of Chengde 承德.[17] He was also charged with the building of Chang ling 昌陵, the mausoleum of Emperor Jiaqing (嘉庆, 1760-1820, r. 1796-1821) Ⓖ . His attributions include the provision of the lanterns and fireworks for court festivals Ⓗ, and the construction of stage sets, temporary buildings and theatre stages for Qianlong's 80th birthday. The youngest brother, Lei Jiarui (雷家瑞, 1770-1830), was also active at court. He replaced his brother Jiaxi at the Design Bureau when the latter travelled to the Chang ling mausoleum construction site, and eventually became head of the Yangshi fang. Under Jiaqing, he was put in charge of decorating the interior of the Nan yuan 南苑, the imperial garden of the South, with *nanmu* wood. He also travelled to Nanjing to select hardwoods,[18] opened a sculpture studio there, and took advantage of this stay in the South to visit the family seat at Jianchang and update the family's genealogical record.

It is probable that it was the perfect cooperation between the three brothers that enabled the Lei family to retrieve the post of head of the Yangshi fang that their grandfather had acquired under Kangxi.

15—Lei Jinyu died three months after the birth of Lei Shengcheng. The latter's four brothers followed their father's coffin to his burial place, then remained in the south.
16—The three gardens of Qingyi yuan (清漪园, Pure Wave Garden) at Wanshou shan (万寿山, Mountain of the Ten Thousand Longevities), of Jingming yuan (静明园, Garden of Serene Clarity) at Yuquan shan (玉泉山, Mountain of the Jade Fountain), and of Jingyi yuan (静宜园, Garden of Serene Aptitude) at the Xiangshan (香山, Perfumed Hills) are the three Mountains of the Sanshan wuyuan complex (三山五园, three Mountains and five Gardens) under the reign of the Emperor Qianlong.
17—This is Bishu shanzhuan (避暑山庄, the hamlet of the Mountain to avoid the summer heat), the biggest imperial garden of the Qing dynasty (564 ha.), located at Chengde (Hebei province).
18—Mainly rosewood and sandalwood.

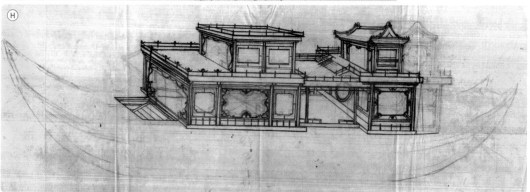

G——General plan of the Wannian jidi, a propitious site for eternity. In the centre, with black lines, Tai ling, mausoleum of the Emperor Yongzheng, to the left, with red lines, the future mausoleum: Chang ling, mausoleum of the Emperor Jiaqing. The document bears the seal of the collection of the Franco-Chinese University.
Source: Ancient Palace Museum. © Wang Qiheng
H——Plan of a vessel designed to sail on the lakes of the imperial gardens.
Source: National Library of China. © Wang Qiheng

Lei Jingxiu (雷景修, 1803-1866) ①, the third son of Lei Jiaxi, entered into an apprenticeship at the age of 16. He was 22 when his father died, and in obedience to a recommendation in his father's will, he gave up the post of head of the Yangshi fang in favour of an old friend of his father, Guo Jiu 郭九, whose assistant he became. At Guo Jiu's death, Lei Jingxiu recovered the post in 1849, twenty-four years after giving it up, at the end of a long procedural battle. He retained it until the sacking of the Summer Palace in 1860.[19] The family home in Haidian was pillaged by western soldiers, but fortunately not burned. The Yangshi fang beyond the wall of the imperial garden was not damaged. Lei Jingxiu retrieved all the archives and took them to Beijing, near Dong Guanyin si 东观音寺[20], where the family settled. The drawings and models filled three rooms in the new residence. Lei Jingxiu did not have the luck of his predecessors, since large construction projects were scarce in the reign of the Emperor Xianfeng (咸丰, 1831-1861, r. 1851-1862). For a long time, he stagnated at the ninth level of the Mandarin hierarchy and it was only with the work on the emperor's tomb at Pingan yu 平安峪, at the Ding ling 定陵 mausoleum, that he was really able to show his abilities. ①

19——The sacking and burning of the Yanming yuan by the British and French soldiers was the tragic denouement of the second Opium War.
20——The Eastern Temple of the Goddess of Mercy, inside the walls of Xizhi men 西直门.

In the village of Jushan cun 聚善村, on a plot granted by the emperor at the foot of the Xiang shan, Lei Jingxiu built the family tomb of the Lei, so that "they could all rest in the harmony of a single hall, and the light blaze on a thousand generations". He also raised a stele, in his own name and the name of his children, in memory of their ancestor, Lei Jinyu, and another to his father Lei Jiaxi. Ⓚ

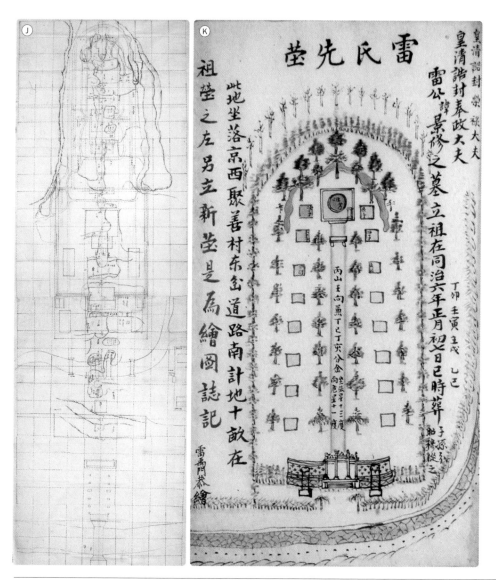

I——Portrait of Lei Jingxiu (1803-1866). Document taken from the genealogical record of the Lei clan. Source: Chinese Heritage Research Institute. © Wang Qiheng
J——Plan for Ding ling, mausoleum of the Emperor Xianfeng.
Sketch forming *pingge*. Source: National Library of China. © Wang Qiheng
K——Family tomb of the Lei at Jushan cun.
In the front part of the tomb, we see a portico with three bays, preceded by two steles.
The layout is planned by Lei Yumen (*hao* of Lei Siqi) [*hao* is an honorific title, a nickname or a name adopted by a scholar].
Text on the left: "The plot is situated to the west of the capital, to the east of the village of the assembly of virtuous, to the south of the division in the road. The surface area is ten *mu* […]"
Document taken from the genealogical record of the Lei clan.
Source: Chinese Heritage Research Institute. © Wang Qiheng

On this site with its reportedly lucky *fengshui*, the tomb occupies a plot of 30 *mu* [21], watered on the southern, western and northern sides by a stream running from the Futian si 福田寺, the monastery of the Fields of Felicities, and opening on its western side onto a stretch of farmland. The shape represents a ship angled south-west/north-west, pointing to the family's place of origin. The vessel symbolises the souls being carried to Yongxiu, source of the family line, for eternal rest.

Lei Siqi (雷思起, 1826-1876) Ⓛ, the third son of Lei Jingxiu, assisted his father with the building of the Xianfeng mausoleum, and with the restoration of the gardens burned in 1860 by the Westerners. In 1873, when the emperor Tongzhi took up the reins of power, at the instigation of Cixi 慈禧 and on the pretext of celebrating the Dowager Empress's 40th birthday, the restoration of the Yuanmingyuan was decreed. The general plan of the gardens of Yuanmingyuan, Changchun yuan 长春园 and Qichun yuan 绮春园 as presented by Lei Siqi received the full approval of the emperor and of Cixi, who rewarded the master builder with a second level mandarin's rank in 1875. He declined it in favour of his father Jingxiu. Shortly after, during the planning of the mausoleum for the Dowager Empress, Lei Siqi died.

21——Unit of area corresponding to 1/15th of a hectare.

The eldest son, Lei Tingchang (雷廷昌, 1845-1907), completed the work begun by Lei Siqi on the Ding ling site. The acknowledged expertise he gained in the design of the imperial tomb brought him the task of designing the Hui ling 惠陵, the mausoleum of the Emperor Tongzhi. His luck enabled him to acquire second level mandarin honours for his parents and grandparents. During the work on the mausoleum of Cixi at Putuo yu 普陀峪 and of Cian at Puxiang yu 普祥峪 Ⓜ, and the work for the celebration of the Dowager Empress's birthday at Wanshou shan, members of the aristocracy and senior state functionaries attended im on account of his position, in order to obtain honours in exchange for donations to finance the imperial construction projects.

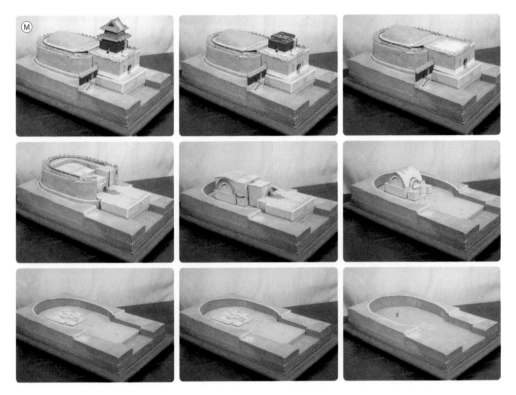

Under these last two members, Siqi and Tingchang, the Lei family reached the summit of its renown, but it was also the object of powerful hostility from certain senior functionaries.

Lei Xiancai (雷献彩, 1877- ?), Lei Tingchang's oldest son, was scarcely 20 years old when he took up the post of office supervisor at the Gardens of Perfect Clarity. He directed reconstruction work on the Hall of Sacrifice and annexes to Cixi's

L——Portrait of Lei Siqi (1826-1876).
Illustration taken from the special issue on the Yangshi Lei in the illustrated journal *Beichen huabao*
Source: *Beichen huabao*, volume vi-No. 9, October 1935. All rights reserved.
M——Collapsible model showing the different parties of the complex forming the *fangchen* (square citadel, providing access to the *minglou* and the orbital road around the *baoding*), the *minglou* (hall of brightness, housing the stele), the *baoding* (precious hill, burial barrow) and the *digong* (underground palace, sepulchre)
Tomb of Cixi (Putuo yu), to the east of Ding ling.
Source: School of Architecture archive apartment (Tsinghua University). © Wang Qiheng

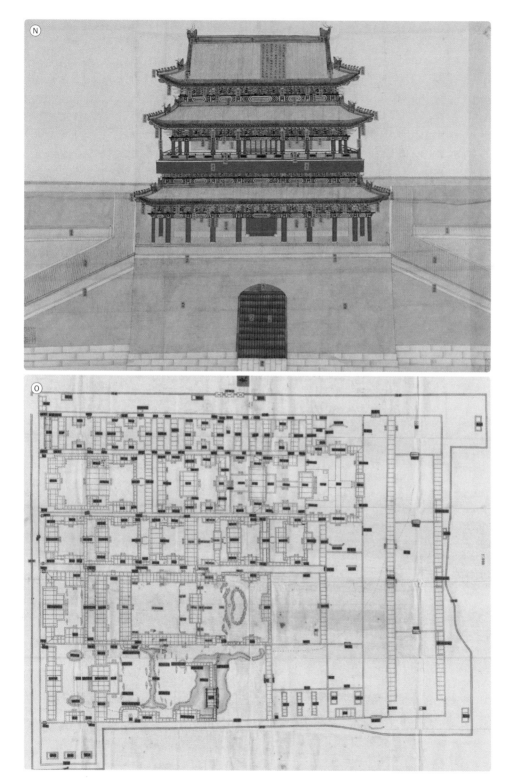

N——Restoration project for Zhengyang men, South Facing Gate, Beijing. *jianlou* (spire), axonometric view; *jianlou* (spire), longitudinal cross-section; *chenglou* (gate pavilion), elevation. Source: Ancient Palace Museum. © Wang Qiheng
O——Plan for the Print Regent's residence, Beijing.
Source: National Library of China. © Wang Qiheng

mausoleum at Putuo yu,[22] and construction work on the Chong ling 崇陵, the mausoleum of the Emperor Guangxu (光绪, 1871-1908, r. 1875-1909). He also headed the restoration work on the architectural structures vandalised during the Yihe quan insurrection 义和拳, the Fists of Justice and of Concord.[23] Ⓝ Ⓞ

The fall of the Qing empire and the Bureau of References archives

The fall of the imperial house of Aisin Gioro in 1911 ended the Lei family's role. The descendants tried to participate in the construction projects of the new emerging China Ⓟ, but there was tough competition with Western architects and contractors, and with Chinese architects returning to the country after training in European and American university architecture departments. This inability to anticipate and keep pace with the technological development of a fast changing nation, combined with a process of degeneration arising from the use of opium, gambling and bad company. Decline was inevitable.

P——Plan for the Navy Ministry, Beijing. Frontal perspective. Source: National Library of China.
© Wang Qiheng

22——The initial plan was to build two identical tombs for the two Dowager Empresses, Cian and Cixi. After completion of the work, Cixi managed to have the ground level buildings of the mausoleum demolished, on the grounds of "obsolescence", and to have the halls rebuilt with a luxury that makes Putuo yu the most sumptuous tomb complex of the Qing dynasty.
23——Yihe quan, a xenophobic movement better known in the West as the Boxers. The besieged Legations District was relieved by an expeditionary force sent by the Western and Japanese powers. The capital was pillaged and sacked, in particular the Forbidden City and the West Imperial Garden.

The Lei descendants[24] began by selling off the family real estate assets, stores, shops, houses, land, and once these ran out, they sought to sell objects from the archives, drawings, plans and models. The appearance of these items on the market drew the attention of both Chinese and foreign collectors, all in search of pieces of the heritage of a collapsing empire. Zhu Qiqian 朱启钤, who had just created the Zhongguo Yingzao xueshe 中国营造学社[25] became concerned. Rightly, he feared that the archive would be dispersed and managed to persuade a cultural action foundation to release the money necessary for the National Library of Beijing 国立北平图书馆 to purchase the items still available in 1930.[26] This acquisition was followed by a purchase by the Franco-Chinese University 中法大学.[27]

Most of the holdings consist of collections acquired by these two institutions, now the National Library of China 中国国家图书馆 and the Ancient Palace Museum 故宫博物院.

Other institutions, the National Museum of China 中国国家博物院, the Library of the Capital 首都图书馆, the documentation department of Tsinghua University's School of Architecture, 清华大学建筑学院资料室[28] the libraries of the University of Beijing and of the Chinese Academy of Social Sciences, China's No. 1 Historical Archives 中国第一历史档案馆,[29] the Taipei Ancient Palace Museum, hold some of the collection.

Abroad, items can be found in Japan,[30] in the US,[31]… In France, the Guimet Museum has a document of great value, a layout plan of the Yuanmingyuan on slightly colour enhanced paper. It shows the network of artificial mountains, lakes and rivers. There are ground views of the buildings with details on the number of bays and with captions. However, the drawing has no date or title. When we compare the Jiuzhou qingyan complex 九州清晏, where certain features are drawn in red ink to show planned modifications, with other plans, in particular the two plans in the National Library dated September-October 1873, which coincide with an operation to restore the Gardens of Perfect Clarity, we can conclude that the plan held in Paris must be one of the drawings made for the purpose of this same operation under Tongzhi.

24——There are still descendants of Lei Tingchang living in Beijing. Lei Zhangbao 雷章宝, great-grandson of Lei Tingchang and grandson of Lei Xianrui, is a teacher of physical education and lives at Xihuang cun, in Haidian.
25——Politician (1872-1964), Minister of Public Works then of Internal Affairs from 1912 to 1916.
The founding of the Chinese Buildings Research Society marked the start of research into traditional Chinese architecture by the Chinese themselves.
26——The archive consists of some 12,000 documents. Lei Zhangbao records that the transaction took place in June 1930. For a sum of 4,500 yinyuan 银元, the library removed ten lorry loads of drawings, written documents and models. "Guanyu wode xianzu Yangshi Lei" 关于我的先祖样式雷, Jianzhu shijia Yangshi Lei, Pékin, Beijing chubanshe, 2003, p. 402.
27——The institution was created in 1920 and closed in 1950. The collections were transferred to the Forbidden City Museum. The museum has 2,435 documents, 2,148 from the transfer, and 287 acquired separately or donated.
28——During the Cultural Revolution, when they were moved to repositories, many items were thrown out of the windows and used as missiles during pitched battles between opposing factions of the Red Guards. Today, the department retains 315 items, including the model of the minglou and the baoding of the mausoleum of the Dowager Empress Cian.
29——This institution, housed within the Forbidden City, possesses some 1000 drawings and written documents.
30——A collection acquired in 1931, consisting of 53 plans and several hundred written documents, is held at Tokyo University's East Asian Cultural Research Institute 东京大学东洋文化研究所.
31——Cornell University hold 2 drawings of the Tianjin xinggong, the US Library of Congress has a collection of fascicles of the rules on the work carried out at the Yuanmingyuan.

Yangshi Lei's operational scope covers every kind of building, from the emperor's palace to temples and monasteries, from gardens to imperial tombs, from infrastructures to the houses of princes and rich merchants.

The Yangshi Lei collection comes from two distinct sources: the Imperial archives, consisting of documents and items submitted to the emperor by the *yangshi fang*, and the private collection of the Lei family.

When work was approved by the emperor, the order was passed by the head eunuch 总管太监 to the functionaries of the Neiwu fu, the "Bureau of Internal Affairs", which notified the *zhangan* of the Yangshi fang. Once draft plans and, where applicable, a model had been prepared, they were submitted to the emperor for a decision. If the project was approved, the decree of implementation again passed through the hierarchy.

The *Gongcheng zuofa zeli* 工程做法则例,[32] jointly written by the Ministry of Works and the Bureau of Internal Affairs, and published in year xii (1734) of the reign of the emperor Yongzheng, establishes and standardises construction methods, making it unnecessary for builders to produce construction drawings for most work. The *yangshi fang*, with the assistance of the *suanfang*, drafted the *gongcheng zuofa* 工程做法 of the work to be done in the construction phase, which in most cases was sufficient for the workmen to do their job. Drawings were only necessary for structures not covered by the *Gongcheng zuofa zeli*, or when the complexity required explanation through detailed drawings or descriptions.

The graphic documents kept in the Lei archive contain both project sketches and working drawings. Different documents were produced at different stages of the project. There are surveys made when choosing the site, detailed site drawings for the project development phase, layout drawings and building drawings, detailed drawings, corrective drawings, progress drawings… which include ground plans, cross sections, elevations, layout plans and details. The scales used are the *yifen yang* (1:1000 scale, 一分样), *erfen yang* (1:500 scale, 二分样), *wufen yang* (1:200 scale, 五分样), *cunyuan* (1 inch drawing, 寸样, 1:100), *ercun yang* (two inch drawing, 二寸样, 1:50) and the *sicun yang* (four inch drawing, 四寸样, 1:25). The biggest is more than one *zhang* 丈[33] long and the smallest fits in the palm of the hand.

32——The 74 *juan* of the *Rules of Building* deal, as its name suggests, with rules and standards for all types of project, and with the standardisation and accounts for the construction process in the building phase.
33——Unit of measure equivalent under the Qing to approximately 3.10 m.

Some of them are only *cutu* 粗图, sketches, background drawings, ongoing surveys... others *xitu* 细图, detailed project drawings for submission to the emperor, with yellow presentation files. Few of the documents are dated, or datable from their content.

There are also perspective drawings ⓠ, both Chinese—cavalier or axonometric—and also western-style, frontal or vanishing point perspective.[34] For certain decorative projects, full-scale drawings were produced.

These drawings are on paper, mainly *xuanzhi* [35] 宣纸, but also on Korean paper, and more rarely on *daolin* [36] 道林纸 paper, silk or cotton. The drawing tools were mainly brushes, using the *jiehua* 界画[37] boundary painting technique. However, a few rare later documents contain drawings made with drawing pens or lead pencils, under the influence of techniques imported from the West following the arrival of foreign builders. The ink used is Chinese ink, and the colours are mineral-based. There are also some *caotu* 糙图, charcoal sketches.

Q——Plan for the Haiyan tang (Calm Sea Palace), in the Zhonghai, West Imperial Garden, Beijing.
The building resembles the edifice designed by the Jesuit Giuseppe Castiglione, the European style palaces of the Changchun yuan (Garden of Eternal Spring). The part to the front of the building is a clepsydra, a copy of the one made by the Jesuit Michel Benoist. Source: National Library of China. © Wang Qiheng

34——The Lei were in close contact with the Jesuit artists working at the Ruyi guan 如意馆, pavillon the Hall of the Granted Wish. Giuseppe Castglione (Chinese name Lang Shining 郎世宁, 1688-1766), a pupil of Andrea Pozzo (1642-1709), together with Nian Xiyao (年希尧, ?-1738) translated his master's treatise *Perspectiva pictorum et architectorum*, which was published in 1729 under the title *Shixue* 视学. The European palaces, erected in the Garden of Eternal Spring, were built under the supervision of Giuseppe Castiglione, with the collaboration of the Yangshi fang.
35——Rice paper made in Xuancheng (a province in Anhui), used for painting and calligraphy.
36——Phonetic transcription of Dowling Paper, imported glossy or satin paper.
37——Che Bing Chiu-Carolyne Gyss-Vermande, "*Jiehua-wenrenhua*. Formes et esprits: le jardin en perspectives", *Jardin du lettré*, musée Albert-Kahn, Boulogne-Billancourt, 2004, pp. 131-138.

Some documents in the archives have a regular grid. These are often detailed drawings or project outlines. This stage of the process is called *chao pinggezi* 抄平格子, transcribing onto a grid. It is done by drawing a grid centred around the site reference point, the *xuezhong* 穴中, the centre of the lair. The size of of the grid cells varies according to the requirements of the project. The level of the *xuezhong* is the reference level, positive values are called *shangping* 上平 and negative values *xiaping* 下平. Drawings of this kind are called *pingge* 平格, or square grid drawings.

This system is used equally for territorial projects—imperial Gardens, mausoleums—and for objects– statue, pedestal, decorative item.Ⓡ Ⓢ According to a statistical study of the Lei drawings, the size of the grid cell varies from 3 to 10 *zhang*. Altitude information can be recorded where the lines intersect.Ⓣ For the imperial tomb projects, the Lei applied the principle of *baichi wei xing, qiangchi wei shi* 百尺为形£ <千尺为势 where "a hundred *chi* [38] give the shape, and a thousand *chi* the configuration", based on *fengshui* theory. The *pingge* of the mausoleums of the two Dowager Empresses at Ding ling adopts a cell size of 50 *chi*, and the distance between the bridges on the sacred road, the width of the main hall, the square courtyard in front of the *fangcheng* 方城明楼, the square citadel and hall of brightness, all these elements measure exactly two cells, i.e. 100 *chi*. Whereas the overall depth is twenty cells, 1000 *chi*. [39]

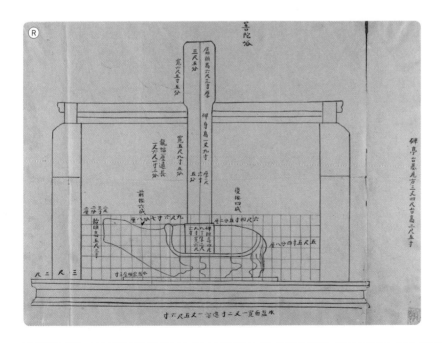

R—Designs for the pedestal carrying the beiting stele, stele hall, on the Ame Road, at Putuo yu.
Source: National Library of China. © Wang Qiheng

38—Unit of measure equivalent under the Qing to approximately 0.31 m.
39—*Op.cit.*, pp. 175-176.

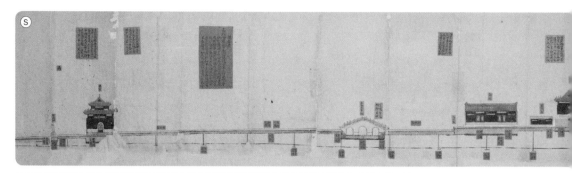

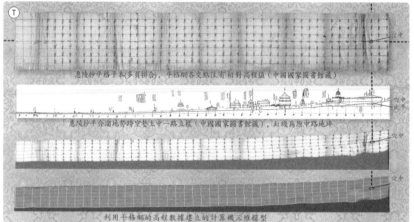

The model phase was important in the development of the project and in obtaining the emperor's approval. The models are essentially made of paper and wood. The walls and partitions are made of pasted paper or cardboard, depending on their thickness. The pieces are cut to the required dimensions, and the colour and decorative patterns applied before assembly. For large models, the gable walls are made of wood for greater stiffness. The structural and frame elements are made of sorghum straw and wood. The roofs are first moulded out of paper on pre-shaped clay, which forms the "skeleton" of the roof. The tile covering is made either from a plaster-based preparation or by wetting and reshaping incense sticks. Once the "rows of tiles" are in position, glued and dried, a sheet of Korean paper is placed on them, flattened and heat-shaped using an iron, hence the term *tangyang* 烫样, a model shaped with an iron. The roof is often detachable, so that the interior partitions can be seen.[U]

S——Plans for the mausoleums of Cian and Cixi, located to the east of Ding ling (mausoleum of the Emperor Xianfeng) on the sites of Tuxiang yu and Putuo yu. Longitudinal cross-section of Putuo yu, tomb of Cixi. Source: National Library of China. © Wang Qiheng

T——Hui ling, mausoleum of the Emperor Tongzhi: the detailed drawings transcribed onto sheets of the *pinggezi* notebook (here continuous) where the level information is recorded at the intersection of the lines. The red spot on the right is the *xuezhong*; the longitudinal cross-section on the axis through *xuezhong*; 3-4. digital reconstitution of the *pingge*. Source: National Library of China. © Wang Qiheng

U——Yuanmingyuan, Garden of Perfect Clarity. Scenery Wanfang anhe, Peace and concord with ten thousand horizons. *tangyang* of the Wanfang anhe building; internal view of the building (without roof) showing the partitions. Source: Ancient Palace Museum. © Wang Qiheng

Certain models depict a single building, others an entire scenery, with its buildings, artificial mountains, lakes, rivers, canals and plants.

The scales used are *wufen yang* (five thousandths model, 五分样, 1:200), *cunyuan* (one inch model, 寸样, 1:100), *ercun yang* (two inch model, 二寸样, 1:50), *sicun yang* (four inch model, 四寸样, 1:25) and *wucun yang* (five inch model, 五寸样, 1:20).

The first studies of the Lei family archives were conducted at the Society for Research on Chinese Architecture (SRCA) initiated in 1930 by Zhu Qiqian, or by its members. Realising that war would not leave the monuments and sites unscathed, and convinced of the need to protect the imperial China's building heritage and to preserve the expertise of the master builders, Zhu Qiqian took on the self-appointed task of preserving the memory and skills before they disappeared, by "visiting the master builders, famous craftsmen from the different trades, functionaries from the departments of works, specialists from the Bureau of Design and Calculation".[40]

It was in spring 1933 that the brothers Lei Xianrui 雷献瑞 and Lei Xianhua 雷献华 went to the premises of the SRCA to show the family's genealogical record, and the various documents and letters. Zhu Qiqian was able to use these elements to carry out the first study on Yangshi Lei.[41]

Following the study by Zhu Qiqian, Liu Dunzhen 刘敦桢[42] undertook research on the Yuanmingyuan in order to try to understand the organisation and operation of building management at the Qing court. The results of his work are recorded in a major article focusing on the campaign to restore the Yuanmingyuan in the reign of the Emperor Tongzhi.[43]

Shan Shiyuan 单士元,[44] an employee in the archives of the Forbidden City, was also in charge of the office established within the National Library of Beijing for the use of SRCA members, where they had special access to rare works. He helped Liu Dunzhen to examine the Lei archives, and he used his access to the archives of the Forbidden City to provide important historical documents. He is the author of an article on Yangshi Lei which expresses the first doubts on the truth of the story regarding the fitting of the beam in the Taihe dian, at a ceremony before the Emperor Kangxi.[45]

Jin Xun 金勋[46] developed a very early interest in the Imperial Gardens and managed to enter the enclosures to visit the architectural and landscape complexes. The reconstructed plan for the three Yuanmingyuan [47] gardens, which he produced in 1924, is the first drawing to show all the gardens before the sacking of 1860. Employed in the reading room of the department of engineering texts at the National Library of Beijing, he examined the documents in the Yangshi Lei archive and established the first registers of drawings and models. He assisted Liu Dunzhen in his research and provided Maurice Adam with many documents and much information for the writing and illustration of his work.[48]

41——Lei Fada entry, "Collected Bibliographies of Master Craftsmen" 哲匠录·雷发达, BSRCA, vol. 4, No. 1 (1933), pp. 84-89.
42——Architect (1897-1968) trained in Japan, Director of the Texts and Documents Department at the SRCA.
43——"Tongzhi chongxiu Yuanmingyuan shiliao" 同治重修圆明园史料, BSRCA, vol. 4, No. 2, pp. 100-155, and No. 3-4, pp. 271-339.
44——Historian (1907-1998) and architectural historian. He joined the SRCA's Sources and References Department in 1931 and became a Society member in 1933
45——"Jianzhu qiaojiang Yangshe Li" 建筑巧匠样式雷, Jianzhu xuebao (建筑学报, Architectural Journal), No. 2-1963.
46——Archivist (1883-1976). Jin Xun was born in Haidian to a family of entrepreneurs is ancestors had been involved in the building of the palaces and gardens of the emperor, princes and senior functionaries. He is the author of several articles on the Lei archives.
47——The work on Yuanmingyuan, Changchun yuan and Qichun yuan was all supervised by a single mandarin 圆明园总管大臣. The three gardens were given the generic name Yuanming sanyuan 圆明三园.
48——Yuen Ming Yuen. L'Œuvre Architecturale des Anciens Jésuites au xviiie Siècle, Pei-p'ing, Imprimerie des Lazaristes, 1936.

More recently, the government has granted a subsidy to the School of Architecture of the University of Tianjin 天津大学建筑学院, under Professor Wang Qiheng 王其亨 [49] for the research project [50] on Yangshi Lei's archives. The architecture department of Tsinghua University 清华大学建筑学院, under Professor Guo Daiheng 郭黛姮,[51] is also examining this archive. An exhibition [52] was mounted in Beijing in the summer of 2004. It is the first time that an exhibition has been produced around documents from the Lei family archive.

On June 20, 2007, Unesco placed the Yangshi Lei archives on the Memory of the World Register.

49——Mr. Wang Qiheng is a Professor and Director of Studies at Tianjin University's School of architecture, one of the greatest experts on the Lei archive, and one of the co-organisers of the exhibition.
50——Research programme on the dynasty's Yangshi Lei Drawing Archives, project No. 59978027 of the National Natural Science Archive Programme.
51——Mrs. Guo Daiheng is a professor and Director of Studies at Qinghua University's School of Architecture, specialising in Song architecture. She has specialised in the study of Qing architecture and the former imperial garden, the Yuanmingyuan, since the 1990s.
52——*Exhibition of drawings from the Yangshi Lei archive of the Qing dynasty*, jointly produced by the National Library of China, the Forbidden City Museum, Historical Archives No. 1 of China and the School of Architecture of the University of Tianjin. This exhibition was shown in France in May 2006 at the Paris-La-Villette National School of Architecture.

Bibliography

Chiu, Che Bing 邱治平, "The Master Builders", *Yuanmingyuan. Le jardin de la Clarté parfaite*, Besançon, Éditions de l'Imprimeur, 2000, pp. 96-98.

He, Beijie 何蓓洁, *Yangshi Lei shijia yanjiu* 样式雷世家研究 ("studies of the dynasty of the master builders, the Yangshi Lei"), Masters Dissertation at the School of Architecture, Tianjin University, 2007.
Jianzhu shijia Yangshi Lei 建筑世家—样式雷 ("The dynasty of the Yangshi Lei, master builders"), Beijing, Beijing chubanshe, 2003.

Jin, Xun 金勋, «Beiping tushu guancang Yangshi Lei zhi Yuanmingyuan ji qita gechu tangyang» 北平图书馆藏样式雷制圆明园及其它各处烫样 ("The models of the Yuanmingyuan and other sites, made by the Yangshi Lei, kept at the library of Beiping"), *Guoli Beiping tushuguan guankan* 国立北平图书馆馆刊, vol. vii, No. 3-4 ; "Beiping tushu guancang Yangshi Lei zhi Yuanmingyuan ji neiting linqin fudi tuji zongmu" 北平图书馆藏样式雷藏圆明园及内庭陵寝府第图籍总目 ("General record of drawings and written documents on the Yuanmingyun and the mausoleums and residences, kept by the Yangshi, in the collections of the Library of Beiping"), *Guoli Beiping tushu guan guankan* 国立北平图书馆馆刊, vol. vii, No. 3-4.

Liu, Chang 刘畅, « Cong xiancun wentu dangan kan wanQing Suanfang he Yangshi fang de guanxi » 从现存文图档案看晚清算房和样式房的关系 ("The relation between the *yangshi fang* and the *suanfang* at the end of the Qing Dynasty, according to currently available written documents and drawings"), *Jianzhu shi lunwen ji* 建筑史论文集, No. 15 (2002), Beijing, Qinghua University Press, pp. 93-98.

Liu, Dunzhen 刘敦祯, «Tongzi chongxiu Yuanmingyuan shiliao» 同治重修圆明园史料 ("Historical documents on the campaign to restore the Yuanmingyuan in the reign of the Emperor Tongzhi"), *Zhongguo Yingzao xueshe huikan* 营造学社汇刊, vol. iv, No. 2, pp. 100-155, No. 3-4, pp. 271-339.

Shan, Shiyuan 单士元, «Gongting jianzhu qiaojiang: Yangshi Lei» 宫廷建筑巧匠—样式雷 ("On talented master builders at the Imperial Court, the Yangshi Lei"), *Jianzhu xuebao* 建筑学报, No. 2-1963.

Su, Pinhong 苏品红, "Yangshi Lei ji Yangshi Lei tu" 样式雷及样式雷图 ("Yangshi Lei and the drawings made by Yangshi Lei"), *Wenxian* 文献, No. 2-1993.

Wang, Qiheng 王其亨, «Lei Fada Taihe dian shangliang chuanshuo de zhenxiang» 雷发达太和殿上梁传说的真相 ("The truth on the adjustment of the beam at the Taihe dian by Lei Fada"), *Xin jianzhu* 新建筑, No. 4-1988.

Wang, Qiheng 王其亨 – Xiang, Huiquan 项惠泉, "'Yangshi Lei' shijia xinzheng" 样式雷世家新证 ("New evidence on the Yangshi Lei dynasty"), *Gugong bowuyuan yuankan* 故宫博物院院刊, No. 2-1988.

圆明园资料集 ("Collection of documents on the Yuanmingyuan"), Beijing, Shumu wenxian chubanshe, 1984

Zhang, Wei 张威, *Tongzhi Guangxu chao Xiyuan yu Yihe yuan gongcheng sheji yanjiu* 同治光绪朝西苑与颐和园工程设计研究 ("study of the design of the work on the Yihe yuan and Xiyuan in the reigns of the Emperors Tongzhi and Guangxu"), doctoral thesis at the School of Architecture, Tianjin University, 2005.

Zhu, Qiqian 朱启钤, "Yangshi Lei kao" 样式雷考 ("Research on Yangshi Lei"), *Zhongguo Yingzao xuzshe huikan* 营造学社汇刊, vol iv, No. 1 (1933), pp. 86-89.

Zhu, Qiqian 朱启钤 – Liang, Qixiong, 梁启雄, "Zhejiang lu – Lei Fada" 哲匠录—雷发达 ("The master craftsmen – Yangshi Fada"), *Zhongguo Yingzao xuzshe huikan* 营造学社汇刊, vol iv, No. 1 (1933), pp. 84-86.

Family

Family structures in China long remained as immutable as house designs, reflecting a social order in which all structures focused on the person of the emperor, the intercessor between human beings and heaven. The primary element of this structure was the ancestors, who were the object of simple religious worship in every household, rich or poor. This system of ancestor worship, which also entailed strict obedience to funerary rights, is what guarantees the happiness and well-being of each household.

The Han conception of the family also seems inseparable from male preeminence, in other words patriarchy, even if women were sometimes able to play an eminent role in the structure of the clan. Veneration of the ancestors was matched by the respect owed by parents to grandparents and by children to parents. This vertical hierarchy extended to the respect paid by younger sons or daughters to older sons, every family connection being codified and each person given a position within the clan and within physical space. Uncles, aunts, brothers-in-law, sons-in-law, the position in the family could also vary according to whether kinship came through the female or male line.
The Confucian relationship is dual, respect towards one's elders being matched by a duty of protection towards the weakest, and children, a favourite subject in Chinese painting, are also respected for the intrinsic qualities attributed to childhood.

The ideal of the family clan, threatened by the failure to marry or to produce a son, was challenged by the violence of reality. Damaged by the sudden increase in population and then by family dispersal during the Maoist era, the model was overturned by the attempts at population control culminating in 1979 in the single child policy which, strictly applied in the cities, would have the effect of inverting family structure. Suddenly, the attention of the older generations was totally focused on the single child, who could thus become a caricature of the tyrannical little emperor.

Today, the essential community links maintained by the old family structure survive in some cases, have been lost in others. Grandparents are abandoned or cherished, as dictated by the ordinary laws of a globalised society.

Ren Xihai 任锡海
Qingdao Courtyard house n. 10, Mrs Wang the anniversary day of her death: her children come back to her old house to honour her memory, 2004. © Ren Xihai

Family structure

Dora Chesnes

Four generations under a single roof?

Today's Chinese family seems far from the traditional ideal Ⓑ of the multigenerational family and several households combined under a single roof, sons living with their parents after marriage. The myth survives, both in popular aspirations and reflected in history. It is kept alive through literary masterpieces such as *A Dream of Red Mansions*, by Cao Xueqin (1715-1763), which tells the story of an upper-class 18th-century family of four hundred and forty-eight characters, including a hundred or so masters, and their servants. In the 20th century, the joys and torments of large families were also brought to life by the pens of the great writers Ba Jin (1904-2005) and Lao She (1899-1966).

The multi-nuclear family (several married brothers and sisters living under the authority of elderly parents) was in a minority in ancient China. It was primarily a prerogative of relatively well-off families Ⓒ. Its extension to wider levels of society was linked with certain local cultures, with a limited geographical spread. Historically, the dominant arrangements in China were the nuclear family (couple with or without children) and the extended or multigenerational family, generally based on grandparents, parents and children living together. Nevertheless, there were significant variations between regions, and between town and country. In particular, as almost everywhere in the world, the cities generally contained more nuclear families than the countryside.

Ⓑ

A—Portait of ancestors, late 19th century, Shanxi. 230 cm x 100 cm. Frédéric Edelmann, Dominique Delaunay, private collection
B—Mingqi (funerary model) depicting a pig farm (Clay, green glaze). This object evokes the character for "family" 家 *jia* which consists of two elements: a roof covering a pig.
23 cm x 17 cm x 12 cm. Musée national des Arts asiatiques-Guimet (Paris), inv.: n MA 5133. RMN

C

The nuclearisation of the family

Until the late 1970s and the start of the country's economic takeoff, China was an essentially rural nation. Industrialisation developed relatively slowly. From the 1950s onward, urbanisation was limited by strict government control of migratory flows. Short-term travel required authorisation and the place where people lived and worked was defined by a permit, the *hukou*, which was virtually impossible to modify.

In the aftermath of the Communist takeover in 1949, the collectivisation of the land broke the link between the family and the unit of production Ⓔ Ⓕ and, by removing the peasantry's traditional reluctance to sacrifice arable land for the construction of new housing, indirectly fostered the breakup of the extended family. As a result, the nuclear family became the predominant family arrangement in China.

The 1982 census, the first after the Maoist era and the first to collect national data on family structures, shows that 68% of rural families were then nuclear in kind, 23% extended and less than 1% multi-nuclear.

Convergent urban and rural trend until the end of the 1990s

In the cities as in the countryside, the political and economic upheavals that accompanied the introduction of a new regime in 1949 acted as a significant catalyst to the nuclearisation of the family. The nationalisation of production turned the urban population into a society of employees. The multinuclear family was virtually eradicated by the elimination of the old ruling elites and wealthy merchant classes. Against this historic backdrop, a profound change in attitudes took

place: the ideal of the couple-centred family, which emerged between the 1920s and 1940s in big "modern" cities such as Shanghai, finally replaced the traditional large family ideal, and the preference for independent living after marriage became dominant.

The urban trend towards family nuclearisation from the 1950s onwards was nevertheless inhibited by the shortage of housing in the 1960s. Young couples had to wait several years to be allocated a home by their labour unit (an organisation which, before the liberalisation of the 1980s, managed the working and private lives of urban employees, are proving marriage or divorce, providing housing, childcare, healthcare). So whatever their feelings, they were obliged to live with one or other sets of parents (traditionally, the man's).

D—Portraits of a family from Anhui, late 1970s. © Lily Yang

According to the 1982 census, 69% of urban families were nuclear, 19% extended and a little over 1% multi-nuclear.

The move towards economic liberalisation initiated by the regime in 1979 had no significant impact on family structure until the late 1990s. In the countryside, the decollectivisation of the land did not reverse the trend towards family nuclearisation (the proportion of nuclear families was up at the time of the 1990 national census, at 70.5% for rural families; the proportion of extended families in the countryside had fallen slightly to 22.5%). In the cities, the easing

E, F——Lü Guangwei 吕光伟. "Corridor" dwelling, 2002, Luoyang, Henan. In China, the majority of "corridor" dwellings were bbuilt during the 1950s. They were used as offices or dormitories for the workers from the units of production.
© Lü Guangwei
G——Wang Jingsong王劲松. The standard family. © Wang Jingsong

of housing constraints boosted the trend towards a simplified family structure. The gradual liberalisation of the property market in the 1990s, alongside the policy of encouraging people to buy their place of residence, gave further impetus to the drop in the proportion of extended families (18.5% of urban families in the 1990 census, with the proportion of nuclear families continuing to rise at 71.5%).

Diversification of family structures since the end of the 1990s

The most recent national census, carried out in 2000, shows that 90% of today's Chinese families are nuclear (parents, unmarried child), or extended (grandparents, parents, child). Behind this global stability, however, several significant changes are happening which reflect the diversification of family structure in China. Families made up of grandparents living with their grandchild(ren) have increased markedly in recent years. Moreover, the relative proportion of traditional nuclear families, consisting of parents and unmarried children, is falling.

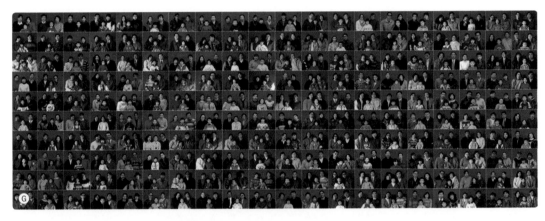

This shift coincides with the rise in two-person nuclear families (childless couples) and single person households, comprising a young person who has left the parental home or older people whose spouse has died. It also appears to be linked with the growing number of single parents.

On this latter point, the existence of single-parent and blended families (in which at least one parent is separated or divorced, with children who may have come from a previous relationship) is not documented in existing national censuses. However, despite the absence of statistics on these families, and in the light of their growing representation in the media, it may be assumed that they are on the increase as a result of the significant rise in divorce (five times more people in China divorce than 30 years ago, and 18.2% more in 2007 and 2006).

Urban families and rural families at the dawn of the 21st century: a broken mirror?

Beyond broad trends, the 2000 national census shows different urban and rural patterns in the recent changes to the morphology of Chinese families.

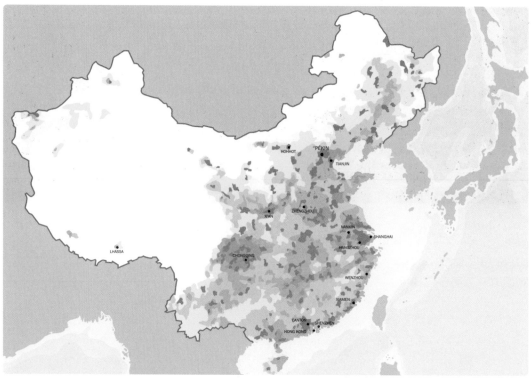

Population density: number of inhabitants by km²

- ■ More than 800
- ■ 800 to 400
- ■ 400 to 200
- ☐ 200 to 100
- ☐ 100 to 50
- ☐ 50 to 10
- ☐ Less than 10

0   500   1000 km

Effects of the single child policy and of changing attitudes on the rise of the two-person family

The single child policy introduced in 1979 to limit the birthrate had a significant impact on the rise of the two-person family from the 1990s onward, resulting in a fall in the relative role of the traditional nuclear family. Young people born since the early 1980s are old enough to leave the parental home.

The single child policy had a particularly marked effect in the cities, where it was strictly applied. Indeed, the punishment for non-compliance with the regulations varies depending on locality (a fine which, if not paid in time, can result in confiscation of assets, sacking, loss of social protection, withholding of healthcare for the child and significantly higher school fees). In the urban environment, the two-person family essentially concerns the 45-65 age bracket.

In the countryside, the single child policy did not fully achieve its goal and had to be adjusted. Given the traditional importance attributed to sons, a second child was authorised when the firstborn was a girl. The quotas are commonly exceeded, either because families pay the fines, or because they do not declare births (making life very awkward in terms of civil status for these "underground children", in particular as regards schooling).

Nonetheless, the single child policy has led to a reduction in the number of children per household in the countryside. So it has had a real but delayed impact on the growth of the two-person family. Because of the differences in the application of the single child policy in urban and rural environments, two-person families in the countryside are more concentrated amongst the over 50s, whilst in the city, parents from the single child generation become empty nesters sooner.

The development of late parenthood, promoted by family planning which encourages people to delay marriage and procreation, is the second factor behind the rise of the two-person family in China in recent years. This increase affects the 25-35 age bracket, with young couples choosing not to have children. This phenomenon is less pronounced in the countryside, where the first child is generally born quite soon after marriage. Couples who have decided not to have children belong to a higher socio-professional category. The choice by both members of the couple to focus on their careers has given rise to the so-called "DINK" ("Double Income No Kids") family.

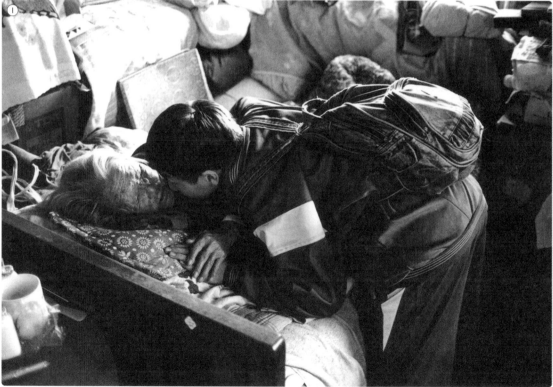

H——Ren Xihai 任锡海. Qingdao Courtyard house n . 10, Shandong. A young girl from the courtyard is getting married, 2001. © Ren Xihai
I——Ren Xihai 任锡海. Qingdao Courtyard house n. 10, Shandong. My son Yuanyuan kisses his grandmother before going to school, 1993. © Ren Xihai

Soaring real estate prices in the big cities in recent years, and the difficulties of young couples—particularly the poorest—in obtaining access to housing, has had no significant impact on the rising trend in two-person families. At most, it has reduced the rate by delaying the date when young people marry or leave the parental home.(H)

Urbanisation and the multiplication of families of grandparents and children (i)

The development of the two-generation family (grandparents, grandchildren) is an essentially rural phenomenon. It is linked with changes in the nature of the countryside exodus in the last 25 years. The economic liberalisation of the 1980s prompted the emergence of a so-called floating population (estimated today at between 150 and 200 million people). Rural migrants tried to get round the problem of unemployment in the countryside by seeking work in the cities on a more or less temporary basis, meeting the labour needs of the fast expanding coastal regions. Officially, however, they continue to be domiciled in their place of origin.

The first wave of migration, dating from the 1980s, consisted of young single women, mostly recruited as servants by the new emerging urban middle class. This was followed by a second wave in the early 1990s, mainly consisting of men going to work on construction sites. Certain rural areas, therefore, saw the emergence of families in which mothers remained alone with their children and the village elders.

A third wave of migration developed in the second half of the 1990s, characterised by couples going to the city and leaving their children with grandparents or relations. The living conditions of rural migrants are often precarious. Access to schooling, healthcare and the various social services depends on a local residence permit. It is therefore common for parents to choose to leave their children back home, so that they retain access to school and healthcare.

Because of its nature, it is this latest wave that has had a significant impact on Chinese family structure. In the countryside, it has prompted the development of extended two-generation families. This shift has not taken place without inflicting damage on the quality of children's emotional and education environment. "Children without parents" (liushou ertong), officially assessed at 23 million, have become a new social phenomenon, generating debate on the Chinese development model and its social cost. In the cities, this trend has been accompanied by a de facto increase in the proportion of two-person families, but there are no statistics on these, since the parents' residence permit is still recorded in their place of origin.

The two-generation family structure is a marginal phenomenon in the urban environment. However, it is worth noting the effects on this phenomenon of the rapid pace of China's urbanisation. It arises from the new strategies adopted by certain parents to deal with the schooling issue in the ever-growing suburbs. The educational structures in the new emerging suburbs are not always attractive in terms of teaching quality and reputation. Some parents who themselves have parents living in older neighbourhoods, with better local schooling, therefore choose to have their children brought up by grandparents.

Extended three-generation families

According to the 2000 census, the number of extended families is falling slightly in the cities, but rising markedly in the countryside. Whilst the effects on the overall status of this type of family is cancelled out by the opposing trends, with the total remaining relatively stable, the gap between town and country reflects distinct lines of evolution between urban and rural populations.

In the city, the retreat of the extended family is linked with the development of a family culture that emphasises independence between family members. Children leave the parental home earlier and earlier, and at latest when they marry. For elderly couples or elderly single people, intergenerational support comes less and less through living with their children. The maintenance of separate living arrangements is fostered by the existence of a system of social protection, however unequal its distribution in the urban population, and by the gradual—although still largely embryonic—introduction of support services for the elderly. Changing attitudes, together with the development of social services, are therefore fostering the development of the two-person family and the single person household in China's cities, to the detriment of the three-generation family.

In the countryside, the increase in extended families reflects the forced reduction in the number of children, in a context marked by the maintenance of a degree of traditional family culture. According to this tradition, it is assumed that parents continue to live with the only son (or one of the sons, generally the oldest). The effect of the reduction in the number of children is that fewer young people leave the parental home to start their families, and therefore a fall in the relative proportion of nuclear families. At the same time, it has fostered the relative increase in three-generation families.

Nonetheless, the way the rural extended family functions has changed: resources are no longer pooled and placed under the control of the older generation. In addition, the different generations usually have independent living conditions.

Moreover, the growth of the extended family in the countryside reflects the shortcomings of social protection. By contrast with the cities, healthcare and pension services are virtually non-existent there. This means that the extended family plays an important role in looking after the elderly.

Family structures in modern China are marked by a trend towards simplification and diversification, which has accompanied the reduction in the size of households (an average of 3.13 people in 2006, compared with 3.44 in 2000). However, there is less uniformity in their evolution in the urban and rural environments than 10 years ago. Differences in the application of the single child policy, structural inequalities between city and countryside, and the acceleration of the exodus of rural migrants to the city, are the main factors that explain these disparities between town and country.

Urbanisation is likely to result in greater similarities between rural and urban families. According to official statistics, cities accounted for 44.8% of the population in 2006, up by 8.7% compared with the previous census. Improvements in rural living standards, the development of a universal social security system and the reform of the residence permit rules should, if the measures announced by the government on the subject become a reality, contribute to reducing the gap.

The city moulded by its social classes

Jean-Louis Rocca

The transformation of China's great cities is not just a matter of urban planning, public policy or strategic decision-making—demolition of old neighbourhoods, creation of new roads, real estate market explosion. It is also a consequence of the social changes that have totally transformed the population's living conditions and lifestyles—rising standards of living, geographical and social mobility, increase in job opportunities and access to leisure activities. Not forgetting the considerable impact that the desires, demands and hopes of the "new" Chinese can have on urban space. In all these areas, the pace and depth of the change are transforming not only the appearance of the city, but also the social regulation of space.

New populations

One of the profoundly impactful phenomena that China's great cities have undergone is the emergence of new populations. Before the reforms, socialist society was marked by the desire to limit the visibility of differences—real as they were—and to divide them, almost by diktat, into three categories (peasants, workers, cadres). Individuals spent most of their lives in a constricted space, that of the work unit (government department, school, company), which generally provided housing and social services, or within the space of their district. Apart from the few residences set aside for party cadres and government officials, the urban world was characterised by uniformity, a repeated pattern of traditional housing, worker estates and a few "rare" State stores. Today, economic growth, price liberalisation and access to property ownership have generated a high degree of visible segmentation, with little State control.

A new category of the "rich" has emerged. Businessmen with political contacts, high officials with business interests, young graduates with influential parents, small traders who have made it big, together constitute a group of "new rich" (*baofahu*) with substantial spending power, who have contributed to the survival of luxury stores in the big cities. Ⓐ Ⓑ Ⓒ

Another category is the so-called "intermediate" (*zhongjian jieceng*), "middle-class" (*zhongjian jieji*) or "middle income" (*zhongdeng shouru*) social stratum. In official language, these are all those who have achieved "modest means" (*xiaokang*), who are not only able to feed themselves comfortably but have the means to buy themselves a small car, an apartment, to travel a little, etc. This is the group that is driving the quasi exponential growth of the property market. Attempts to evaluate this population have produced contradictory results, but it probably accounts for the great majority of the inhabitants of big cities who have urban resident status.

A——Zhongshan shipyard park. Zhongshan, Guangdong. © Yu Kongjian
B——Canton, 2006. © Research Observatory of Architecture in Contemporary China
C——Hu Yang 胡杨. Series "Shanghai families", apartment of an employee of a foreign business company, 2005. © Hu Yang

A third group is the migrants. They are the outcome of the continuing State control of geographical mobility. Since the 1950s, every Chinese citizen has been linked to his or her birthplace or workplace, which they cannot change without official authorisation. The 100 to 150 million peasants who come to work in the cities have, at best, no more than "temporary resident" status. They can be sent home at any time, and have no social protection in the city. Their children have no access to schools in the cities where they work, they are not allowed to benefit from social housing programmes, and cannot afford to keep up with the explosion in urban rents.

The final stratum is the city dwellers in a situation of "poverty", i.e. members of the socialist era working class who have failed to get aboard the "modest means" train: the unemployed, workers in early retirement, widows without means, retired people on low pensions, etc. Nevertheless, as town dwellers, they do have access to a basic social safety net, which "keeps them afloat": provision of housing, various benefits, even minimum income.

New areas

These sometimes violent transformations have had the effect of substantially remoulding the urban space. The upper and middle strata have made a significant contribution to the success of the automobile industry and therefore to the "all car" principle which dominates transport policy. For most urbanites, private car ownership is the most concrete symbol of the end of socialist penury and the beginning of an era of comfort. This has nothing to do with practical need: in China's cities, the considerable number of taxis makes the private car pointless for day-to-day transport. The power of this symbol of "freedom", which is associated with major economic stakes—the automobile industry is expanding fast and all the big manufacturers are heading for China—has led, especially in Beijing, to dramatic underinvestment in public transport. In cities that have grown very large, any kind of travel is a problem.

At the same time, the proliferation of shopping malls reflects the consumer culture that has developed in these same social strata. The increase in the number of spas, restaurants, bars, gyms, is explained entirely by the emergence of new lifestyles where the primary focus is leisure. However, it is undoubtedly in housing that the changes are most spectacular. Recent years have seen the appearance of a multitude of residential complexes, surrounded by high walls, protected by a host of guards and security systems. Everything is available in situ: shops, restaurants, gyms, sometimes banks. It is the effect of a combination of two influences. First, the media driven influence of the American smalltown dream; and secondly, the influence of the socialist system of residence-based social control, which restricted individual lives within very small bounds.Ⓓ It is no longer clear whether the inhabitants of these compounds are primarily protected from the outside or under internal surveillance. In some of them, for example, the management company's permission is required to remove furniture from one's own apartment.

The main consequence of migrations has been the emergence of urban wastelands, both in the centre and outskirts of cities, areas where traditional housing has been deserted by urbanites, who sublet their dwellings to migrant workers. These sorts of urban villages of single storey buildings are ripe for demolition.Ⓔ Ⓕ
They are found everywhere in the urban space outside the inner city, and cover most of the suburbs.

D—Lü Guangwei 吕光伟, Series "Corridor dwelling".
Housing building for workers built during the 1950s, Luoyang, Henan, 2002. © Lu Guangwei
E—Hutong, Beijing, January 2006. © Research Observatory of Architecture in Contemporary China
F—Hutong, Beijing, January 2006. © Research Observatory of Architecture in Contemporary China

E

F

The "unclassified" stratum of the urban population sometimes occupies the same areas as the migrants. Usually, however, they still live in the old worker estates of the socialist years. Wide blocks a few storeys high ⓖ where the apartments, often in an appalling state, were given or sold cheap to their occupants when the work unit system ended. From that point on, employers were no longer obliged to consider their employees' social well-being or construct or allocate them housing.

These estates too have been overtaken by real estate fever, and the inhabitants are often dehoused to make way for new shopping centres, leisure amenities or residential sites. The compensation provided, calculated with strict parsimony, is scarcely enough for their occupants to buy an apartment way out in the suburbs. Living a long way from their workplace, with the concomitant problems of transport, they join the streams of millions of workers stuck in inextricable traffic jams or in public transport systems that are inadequate to meet the commuting needs created by urban growth. They also suffer from the break with their old homes, where they may often have lived for several decades.

G——Lü Guangwei 吕光伟, Series "Corridor dwelling".
Housing building for workers built during the 1950s, Luoyang, Henan, 2002. © Lü Guangwei

Social relations and urban space

The Chinese city now seems to have been divided up into socially determined islands, linked by constantly increasing mobility imposed by patterns of consumption and work. However, this fragmented fabric is irrigated from another source: That source is "primary sociality", a factor that continues to play a determinant role. The relations with family, friends, colleagues, sporting partners, are central to the lives of the different social strata.

The multiplication of actors is redefining the way social structures are regulated within those islands. Apartments now belong to individuals rather than companies or the State. These property owners are keen to maintain the value of their assets and the quality of the services (expensive) provided by the operators of residential estates. They organise into associations to defend their interests. As for the old socialist residents' committees or the new "district communities" (shequ), they must adapt to the new status quo. Privacy rules, and they can no longer monitor what people say and do. Their functions are now restricted to relaying government recommendations and providing "services": small jobs, basic health care, leisure activities, information on social policy, funding of emergency benefits. The coexistence of this public institution with property owners—armed with their new legitimacy—and the real estate management companies—hungry for profits and often with local political connections—is often conflictual. Part of the stability of urban space will depend on the outcome of those conflicts.

Qingming shanghe tu

The magic realism of the scrolls from Kaifeng

Patrick Doan, François Pourcelet, sister Qiao Bian yun

This scroll, called *Qingming shanghe tu* comes from the brush of Zhang Zeduan, an official painter who specialised in the depiction of bridges and boats. Starting out as a military official in his birthplace Shandong Province (town of Dongwu, now Wucheng), between 1120 and 1127 he studied at the the Imperial Palace painting school in Bianjing (or Bianliang, capital of the Northern Song, now Kaifeng, in Henan).

The scroll probably dates from the period when Zhang was studying, so before 1127, when the Northern Song, driven by the Jurchen, fled the North to take refuge in Hangzhou. It is a silk wash painting in Indian ink with a few colours, which measures 525 cm long and 25.2 cm high.

At the end of the Song Dynasty (1279), the scroll was brought back to northern China, to the Imperial Palace. It was fraudulently removed and sold to a rich family, passing from hand to hand until it was sold to Yan Gao, Minister of State in the Ming Dynasty (1368 - 1644). The Emperor punished Yan by confiscating all his goods and the scroll returned to the Imperial Palace. It was stolen in 1578 by Feng Bao, one of the Palace eunuchs. Between 1736 and 1795, we find traces of it with Lu Feixi, then Bi Yueyin. The Qing Dynasty (1644 - 1911) returned it to the Imperial Palace. In 1911, the last emperor, Pu Yi, inherited it. When he lost the protection of the Japanese in 1945, he tried to flee, but fearing that he might be searched, he got rid of the scroll, which was finally found by the army. Today, the original is kept in the Museum of the Forbidden City, in Beijing.

The subject of the scroll

The title, *Qingming shanghe tu* ("Above the river at the festival of the dead"? "Along the river Bian, in the prosperous capital in time of peace"?) could indicate that the event depicted is taking place on the day when the ancestors' tombs were visited (4th, 5th or 6th of the 4th lunar month, therefore in spring). According to the inscription at the top of the scroll, the city is Bian, the Northern Song capital, today's Kaifeng. However, the term *Qingming* ("pure light") can also refer to a period of prosperity brought about by good government. The official translation of the title (provided by the Museum of the Forbidden City in Beijing) is "On the River Bian, on the day of Qingming".

The scroll is "read" from right to left. It depicts in order: the city environs, the river (Bian), the quayside and a street leading to the city centre. Two main scenes are described: the city outskirts and the activity on the river. Hong Bridge (rainbow, so called because of its shape) represents the link between these two elements.

The 550 or so figures depicted represent all categories: peasants, shopkeepers, doctors, soothsayers, monks, scholars, children, old people, etc.

The religions, intellectual currents and trades we encounter are:

>—three religions: Confucianism, Taoism and Buddhism;

>—nine intellectual currents: Confucianism, Taoism, Yin and Yang school, legalism, logic, mohism, astronomy, eclecticism and pedagogy.

>—small temporary jobs (five flowers):
>>kumquat flower: women selling tea
>>kapok flower: street doctors
>>daffodil: female restaurant singers
>>pimento flower: acrobats
>>morning glory: porters

>—trades conducted without owning a shop (eight doors):
>>Flag door: soothsayers
>>bark door: herbalists
>>colours door: conjurors
>>hanging door: comedians
>>speech door: storytellers
>>group door: musicians
>>harmony door: artists
>>eighth door: hawkers

The buildings are of different styles, depending on their function: small open-air restaurants, which sell tea, wine, etc. There are around twenty boats, as many litters, some fifty animals: donkeys, cows, pigs, horses, camels, mules. The camel trains represent trade with distant countries (Silk Road, northern deserts).

The style adopted by the painter is the so-called "bird's eye" style. Near and far, simple and complex, stable and moving are admirably structured. Choosing a festival day allows the painter to put more movement into the scene.

Detailed description

The scroll is divided into four pictures (three, according to some analysts: the calm of the country, the agitation of the bridge, the joy of the celebrating city):

First part: environs of the city of Bian. In the silent dawn, wisps of mist, a few thatched cottages, a track where two young people are leading their donkeys (this gives the direction of motion in which the scroll should be read). Then bare trees (winter is ending) with paths meeting amongst them. People are approaching on a wider road, and also a litter (higher social status), topped with flowers and plants indicating that the people are on their way back from the graves (precise date: Festival of the dead).

People and buildings become increasingly numerous, activities diversify: some are working, others resting or watching the passers-by. The street is lined with stalls (restaurants, counters for tea or wine, etc.). Beyond the city, there is a glimpse of carefully cultivated fields surrounding a well. We move into the city, the spectacle is in the street and on the river, which contains several types of vessel (cargo ships, pleasure boats, floating restaurants). A few chair-men provide a contrast with the bar customers.

Second part: The great Rainbow Bridge. This wooden bridge over the River Bian was designed, according to one historical source, by a simple anonymous soldier working at the prison. It provides the link between the land and water scenes. It is the central point in the scroll and the activity taking place on it: the water level is high, an overloaded boat is about to go under the bridge, but will it succeed? All the sailors are working: some are taking soundings, others lowering the masts. On the bridge, lookers-on shout advice, try to help... but others carry on their way, unconcerned. Life goes on as normal, customers, the shouts of merchants, disputes.

Third part: Beyond the bridge, a restaurant with the words *jiao dian* (place to rest the feet) on the door, which offers a simple shelter to travellers for a glass of tea or wine before continuing on their way. On the first floor, the luxury increases with the wealth of the customers, whose numbers suggest that business is flourishing. Further on, the precarious shelters give way to more solid buildings, but the water gives an impression of lightness and the far background gives free rein to the viewer's imagination (idea of mass and void so common in Chinese painting). At the intersection of two roads, the scene is more varied: people coming and going, small trades (wheel mender, sellers of medicine and food, a soothsayer in his booth, etc.). At the next crossroads, the courthouse, with its justice workers sitting by the door, with time to rest, which shows that there are no cases to handle, and therefore the relative security in which the society lives. Along the channels, leaning on the balustrade, people whose clothes show that they are scholars, discuss their ideas in this open-air salon.

Fourth part: Together with the bridge, the gate is the scroll's second focus of interest. It is the link between the outside and inside of the city. The outgoing caravan indicates trade with distant countries. This monumental gate is depicted down to the slightest detail. Activity here is intense: public scribes, archery, advertisements to attract customers ("Here you can smell good perfumes"), butchers, storytellers... On the upper floor of the first building, people are gambling, reading, relaxing. After the crossroads, there are more shops: a silk shop ("Here many colours"); at the end, a hospital; under the sunshades, a bakery; a public well where young people are drawing water; the house of a high official named Zhao; a doctor's surgery with two parallel inscriptions ("Here, you will find specialists for men, women and children" and "Here, you will find remedies against alcohol, for the stomach and intestines"). The street is populated with traders, storytellers, monks, goods carriers, etc.

A——The bridge in the 12th-century version of the scroll and in the 18th-century version. © Dominique Delaunay for the 12th century scroll, and © National Palace Museum, Taipei

At the end of the scroll a man appears, his belongings on his back. Is he a foreigner asking the way, whose gaze takes us even further towards the centre of the city?

Some believe that the author intended to leave this unfinished impression, that he wants to give free rein to the viewer's imagination. Others think that the end of the scroll was not painted by Zhang Zeduan.

Translation of the calligraphy above the scroll

Qingming shanghe tu, executed by Zhang Zeduan, an academician from Hanlin, seems to be the work of a divine being. Zhang Zeduan is also called Zheng Dao ("right way, straight way"), of Dongwu. From childhood, he was scholarly and continued his studies in the capital before turning to painting. He is an excellent landscape artist: towns, countryside, boats, carts, bamboos, trees, birds, horses... His way of structuring the nearby and the distant is representative of his style.

At the centre of the Qingming shanghe tu *is the River Bian. It accurately depicts the different social groups, the economic situation of the time, the relations between cities and countryside, habits and customs, etc. It describes this grand tapestry with precision. The representation of the parts is very dense, but nevertheless remains light. The movement is so lively that it seems real. The people refer to the three religions and the nine currents: doctors, soothsayers, astrologers*

B——The gate in the 12th-century version of the scroll and in the 18th-century version. © Dominique Delaunay for the 12th century scroll, and © National Palace Museum, Taipei

by appearance, peasants, wandering pedlars, Taoist monks. The animals depicted are: donkeys, horses, cows, camels. The methods of transport represented are heavily laden carts pulled by several horses; other horses are used as individual mounts by travellers. There are also people on foot. In the streets of the city, shops, restaurants and stalls overlap, like the scales of a fish. Everything is here, including "wise sayings" (sentences of advice written on papyrus and sold). The city gate is solid, very high and very wide. The artistry of the summit is impressive. There are very large numbers of people, of all sizes. Their activities are conveyed so vividly that we imagine the movement to be even more intense than the painting depicts. Admiration! Imagination!

Let us follow in their footsteps, walk with them. It expands the heart and refreshes the mind. It is truly a rare and precious work. Let us treasure it.

The 18th-century scroll

This work is a copy and update of Zhang Zeduan's 12th-century scroll. This popular theme has been copied countless times. The collections in the National Palace Museum contain seven versions, including this one, which is the work of painters from the Imperial Painting Academy in the reign of Emperor Qianlong (reigned, 1736-1795). In each version, the pictorial style and the depiction of everyday life are characteristic of the scroll's era.

Five court painters collaborated in this version, which was completed in 1736: Chen Mei, Sun Hu, Jin Kun, Dai Hong and Cheng Zhidao. This scroll combines the style of older versions with illustrations of everyday life under the Ming and Qing dynasties. The festival atmosphere is rendered by the depiction of a theatrical show, towers exhibiting monkeys, acrobats and martial arts performances.

The perfection of the lines and the beauty of the colours make this scroll a remarkable example of court painting under the Qing dynasty. This version makes no reference to the old Song dynasty, but provides many picturesque details on the end of the Ming and the beginning of the Qing eras. The style also reflects the influence of western pictorial techniques, which were then fashionable at court. The architecture and the streets, for example, are rendered in western perspective. There are even a few western-style buildings. The bridges and architecture have been drawn using a ruler. The characters are delicately depicted, with multiple details.

C——Scenes from the 18th-century scroll. © National Palace Museum, Taipei

蜀錦裝金璧吳工聚碎金謳歌弟
井富城闤九重涘盛事誅觀止遺蹤
惜探爲當時諺豫大川日欽徽欽
乾隆壬戌春三月御題

臣梁詩正敬書

繪乾臨瑤

拆

Destruction

Modernisation, destruction

Our view of China focuses on stereotypes of a country whose economic dynamism makes us forget the situation of the rural areas, of the poor, of minorities. The Olympic Games contributed to the neglect of these latent problems, until the Tibetan revolts in March of this year.

Whilst driven by other mechanisms, both the transformation of the big cities and the government commitment to modernisation express the same imbalances, or the same wish to impose a single order on the whole country.

Partly necessary, because of housing deterioration, modernisation took as its axiom the need to wipe out all traces of the past. Demolishing Beijing's *hutong* and old houses is the first task of the migrant workers (*mingong*), in theory seasonal, from whom the construction companies also recruit the militias responsible for imposing the new development order.

The demolition process follows precise rules, although they vary over time. Behind carefully constructed palisades, demolition begins in the areas where land values are highest, in other words those where the architectural heritage is most valuable and best maintained.

Preceded by the teams of *mingong*, which begin the work by hand, the bulldozers advance, from the richest areas to the poorest. This has the effect of convincing foreign visitors, who are only just arriving, of the necessity of a demolition process which now has little more than slums to work on. Displaced Chinese now have access, with their compensation packages, to brand new housing. However, speculation forces them to move to apartments a long way out, often a two-hour commute from their place of work, in suburbs where the urban fabric can often remain undeveloped for a long time.

The popular wisdom in the West is that the Chinese have never been interested in the material forms of their heritage. In Beijing, however, the inhabitants maintained the structure and shape of the city for six centuries, rebuilding in exactly the same way whenever a fire occurred. The only deliberate destruction took place in the Forbidden City, following two changes of Dynasty.

Wang Jinsong, 王劲松 One hundred sign of the demolition 1999. © Wang Jingsong

Destruction of Yuanmingyuan 1861

Victor Hugo

The second Opium War united the English and French troops who, on October 6, 1860, invaded, sacked and destroyed the Emperor Xianfeng's summer residence, a building of exceptional beauty. This act of destruction aroused the indignation of certain western witnesses. Victor Hugo was only familiar with this "wonder of the world" through the accounts of travellers, but he immediately took the side of the civilised Chinese against the Barbarians.

LETTER TO CAPTAIN BUTLER

Hauteville-House, 25 November, 1861

You ask my opinion, Sir, about the China expedition. You consider this expedition to be honourable and glorious, and you have the kindness to attach some consideration to my feelings; according to you, the China expedition, carried out jointly under the flags of Queen Victoria and the Emperor Napoleon, is a glory to be shared between France and England, and you wish to know how much approval I feel I can give to this English and French victory.

Since you wish to know my opinion, here it is:

There was, in a corner of the world, a wonder of the world; this wonder was called the Summer Palace. Art has two principles, the Idea, which produces European art, and the Chimera, which produces oriental art. The Summer Palace was to chimerical art what the Parthenon is to ideal art. All that can be begotten of the imagination of an almost extra-human people was there. It was not a single, unique work like the Parthenon. It was a kind of enormous model of the chimera, if the chimera can have a model. Imagine some inexpressible construction, something like a lunar building, and you will have the Summer Palace. Build a dream with marble, jade, bronze and porcelain, frame it with cedar wood, cover it with precious stones, drape it with silk, make it here a sanctuary, there a harem, elsewhere a citadel, put gods there, and monsters, varnish it, enamel it, gild it, paint it, have architects who are poets build the thousand and one dreams of the thousand and one nights, add gardens, basins, gushing water and foam, swans, ibis, peacocks, suppose in a word a sort of dazzling cavern of human fantasy with the face of a temple and palace, such was this building. The slow work of generations had been necessary to create it. This edifice, as gigantic as a city, had been built by the centuries, for whom? For the peoples. For the work of time belongs to man. Artists, poets and philosophers knew the Summer Palace; Voltaire talks of it. People spoke of the Parthenon in Greece, the pyramids in Egypt, the Coliseum in Rome, Notre-Dame in Paris, the Summer Palace in the Orient. If people did not see it they imagined it. It was a kind of tremendous unknown masterpiece, glimpsed from the distance in a kind of twilight, like a silhouette of the civilization of Asia on the horizon of the civilization of Europe.

This wonder has disappeared.

One day two bandits entered the Summer Palace. One plundered, the other burned. Victory can be a thieving woman, or so it seems. The devastation of the Summer Palace was accomplished by the two victors acting jointly. Mixed up in all this is the name of Elgin, which inevitably calls to mind the Parthenon. What was done to the Parthenon was done to the Summer Palace, more thoroughly and better, so that nothing of it should be left. All the treasures of all our cathedrals put together could not equal this formidable and splendid museum of the Orient. It contained not only masterpieces of art, but masses of jewelry. What a great exploit, what a windfall! One of the two victors filled his pockets; when the other saw this he filled his coffers. And back they came to Europe, arm in arm, laughing away. Such is the story of the two bandits.

We Europeans are the civilized ones, and for us the Chinese are the barbarians. This is what civilization has done to barbarism.

Victor Hugo
Actes et paroles II, " Pendant líexil "

Destruction and heritage

Frédéric Edelmann

The radical transformations taking place in most Chinese cities, officially legitimised by a drive for modernisation, but which entail a historically unprecedented process of deliberate destruction, largely elicit two types of reaction from foreign observers: dismayed stupefaction or smug acceptance. The same two responses are to be found amongst the Chinese.

How may such a phenomenon be analysed? Curiously, the historical approach suggests an entirely different situation. When, in 2001, Jocelyne Fresnais published *La Protection du patrimoine en République populaire de Chine* [Heritage protection in the People's Republic of China], *1949-1999*, she was primarily interested in historic monuments (*wenhu*) which in fact receive some degree of attention today. However, this attention is subservient to the interests of tourism, which is supposed to be a factor of protection through the money it brings: this is apparent in the historic Chinese centre of Shanghai, unconcernedly transformed into a shopping centre, or in Nanjing, around the temple of Confucius.

The year 2003 saw the publication of Zhang Liang's book *Birth of the Concept of Heritage in China,* a sober work which is more about analysing Chinese attitudes to the forms bequeathed by History, the institutional aspects and the reactions of professionals to a concept that he extends to whole cities, while failing perhaps to realise or record that these are in the process of being permanently erased. With a few exceptions, such as the listing of 27 km^2 of Shanghai, which represents more of a freeze in development than protection as we currently understand it in Europe. Similarly, hesitations about several theoretically preserved sectors are as likely to lead to their destruction as to a temporary halt in poorly planned operations, or, of course, to their conversion to pastiche (Nanchizi, Qianmen, Beijing, etc.). The wavering between the terms heritage and historical monuments is in any case a source of confusion, with consequences that are accidentally or deliberately damaging.

In its existing definition, the French word for heritage—patrimoine—(which becomes *baohu* in Chinese) only appeared in France in the late 1970s. It was a "cultural corruption" of a primarily legal concept (legacy) which was used to escape from the "Historical Monument" notion inherited from Mérimée. In 1992, Françoise Choay wrote in *L'Allégorie du Patrimoine* [The allegory of Heritage]: "the paradox of the semantic shift that the word has undergone alerts one to the intricacy and opacity of the thing. A historical legacy and the practices associated with it are held within layers of meaning where the ambiguities and contradictions create connections and divisions between two worlds and two visions of the world." "At the end of the 1970s", explains the historian Jean-Michel Leniaud, "it was understood that adopting the word "heritage" was a way of emphasising the collective dimension of legacy: it gradually became common to speak of "European heritage", then of "world heritage" in referring to monuments, objects and places. [...] The word "heritage" then became very convenient: referring to the most varied of human productions, it has an inclusive quality that crosses disciplines; by bringing art and artefacts of all kinds under a single umbrella, it provided a way of avoiding the trap of a hierarchical vision restricted exclusively to artistic masterpieces." [1] This "convenience" has led to an anachronistic use of the word, and to a tendency to see all the objects linked by the term heritage in terms of criteria of respect and value, or conversely in certain cases, in terms of rejection, when in fact those objects may have appeared only very recently, and been shared by many countries in an era that is actually quite recent in historical terms.

A——Old temple abandoned in Liulichang area, Beijing. © OACC

1——Article on "Heritage, art", Encyclopaedia Universalis, 1997.

The word and the thing

Like its English equivalent Heritage, the French word *patrimoine* became widespread in France from 1980 onwards, encompassing first the fundamental dimension of urban structures, then subsequently a whole category of skills. The boundaries between the words heritage and culture would thus eventually become blurred, the two forming a vast territory that is more identifiable by what threatens it than by what protects or engenders it.

If we are to take a position on the destruction, the protection and more generally on all the manipulations (pastiches, identical reconstructions, etc.), visited on China's cities, we need to give equal attention to the origins of words, concepts and sentiments in our own climes. It should be noted here that there are similar problems with the emergence of the word *architect* or *architecture* in China. The conclusion in both cases is that the reality precedes its definition and eventually places in the hands of academics alone knowledge which, before them, was, shared at least differently if not more widely. Europe's cathedrals do not have architects, they have master builders, but were nevertheless erected in accordance with rules and techniques of dazzling ingenuity and formal genius.

The appearance of Renaissance treatises in Europe (close in time to their Chinese equivalents, whether popular like the *luban jing* or learned like the *yinzao fashi*) perhaps formalised the "architectural object", but it was not until the 17th century that the nobility and grand financiers began to turn to the profession of *architect* for their construction projects. The French title of Architect of Historical Monuments finally appeared roughly at the time of the invention of photography, which coincided with the moment when the West discovered the architectural riches of the Far East. This provides a valuable tool of inventory and compilation, but tells us nothing (as do certain photographic series recording the work of western engineers) about the nature and the activity that—beyond the picture—underlie the reality of buildings or heritage structures.

In the matter of heritage, the transmission of skills should receive as much attention as dismay at the transformation of the cities. In Europe, the primary channel for the transmission of building knowledge was the oral tradition, the guilds. It is a tradition which also feeds on secrecy, the secrecy that would give rise to freemasonry but which also served to maintain specific crafts within the profession. In China too, the mason or master builder and the carpenter precede the architect.

Since then, builders, carpenters, architects, and eventually engineers, have continued to coexist, and with them all the specialists in restoration and in the historical aspects of urban planning. Is it so different in China where the mason learned the craft of joining, stone cutting, building walls of clay or brick, perhaps with the assistance of the *Luban Jing* and then the *Yinzao fashi*, but primarily by learning on the job.

No doubt, there are essential structural differences in constructional codes and methods, but it is just as important to look beyond cultural divergences for the similarities, or indeed differences, in the organisation of the different building trades. If any work has been done on the relations between the noble and popular aspects of the building trades, it has not become common knowledge. Similarly, there does not seem to be much interest in a comparative study of the western and far-eastern world (including Japan and Korea). Yet the factors that underlie the emergence of palaces and hovels, of cities and villages, need to be better understood if we are to look at the other side of the coin: the destruction and disappearance of heritage (whatever it may be), and what it means for citizens. Which would again require that no prejudices, no hasty conclusions, should cloud the way we perceive the instinctive response of the less educated categories of the population compared with the culture of the more privileged classes.

The question of heritage cannot be reduced to the history of knowledge, nor to that of trades, and even less to the descriptions of travellers and diplomats alone. That could insidiously lead to a distorted perception of that heritage, in the West and Far East alike, or indeed in the Islamic countries. Or allow the development and survival of misinterpretations whose consequences might prove damaging. Thus, to say of a nation that it has neither attachment nor respect for the buildings or cities bequeathed to it by History, can play into the hands of those who wish them gone (deliberate intention to eradicate a culture or pure financial speculation) and justify their actual destruction, whether by occupying armies or by the populations themselves: all it takes, indeed, is a cultural fracture caused by wars, colonisations, revolutions, economic upheavals... Although the causes and the scales vary, comparable phenomena can be observed in Romania, in Lebanon, in China.

Protecting and renovating

Two or even three authorised references finally give reality to presuppositions that might be missed by a simple and untutored vision. In her *Dictionnaire des idées reçues* [2] [Dictionary of received ideas] on China, Stéphanie Balme cites Simon Leys (Pierre Ryckmans) on the subject of heritage to produce one of those ideas on which she seeks—very brilliantly, it should be added—to cast doubt. We retain here the argument and terms of her text. Following, according to her, Frederick W. Mote's work on Chinese architecture, Simon Leys explains the Chinese paradox: the past is everywhere although few traces of it remain, to the point that the author wonders whether, at the time of the Cultural Revolution, "there was that much to destroy". In China, writes Leys, although "the presence of the past can be felt everywhere", that past is curiously elusive "because the past inhabits people rather than stones, the architect rather than architecture".

However, the internalisation of a culture anchored in the past does not exclude the possibility of an attachment to what we today call heritage: the house, the village, the city, the landscape, a bridge, a temple. The destruction of the Maoist period seems to have been focused primarily on religious, political and cultural symbols: destruction of statues, imperial systems of defence (the Beijing wall), prohibition

---

B——Restoration of Toshodaji Temple in Nara, Japan. © Frédéric Edelmann

2——Stéphanie Balme, *Dictionnaire des idées reçues*, éditions le Cavalier Bleu, 2008

or destruction of certain works. Another form of attack is to convert temples into factories, schools or barracks, which damages them but does not destroy them physically, or to cram the population into houses not designed for such a purpose, which then inevitably deteriorate. However, the real destruction occurs after Mao and the Cultural Revolution, under the combined impact of the demand for comfort, a fascination with modernity and unbridled real estate speculation. It follows Deng Xiaoping's famous injunction to "Get rich!", which calls on the forces of individualism to rebuild the financial resources of a deeply depleted nation. It is possible that the "deculturation" of the country played a major role here, which explains the sentiment expressed by Simon Leys, who seems, when he proposes this hypothesis (almost universally adopted by sinology), not to see, not to look at the physical reality of Chinese "heritage", the multiplicity of cases and the diversity of situations with which it is confronted during the Maoist era.

In this respect, the case of Japan provides an example and a striking shortcut for the gap that has grown between reality and theoretical knowledge. Although certain cities, like Nara and Kyoto, were spared at the end of the Second World War, at the prompting of prestigious academics, most of the historic sites were destroyed by American bombing, a counterpoint to the destruction and atrocities committed by the Japanese at Chongqing and more cruelly still at Nanjing (to speak only of China).

Even before the war, but especially after, the idea was that the Japanese had no respect for their heritage. Better still: the story went that the demolition of cities and temples was a ritual act, as if this strange pastime could constitute a cultural "virtue" in itself. Where did this widely held idea come from? [3] There is in Nara, which was briefly the capital before the birth of Kyoto (two cities themselves based on the layout of Chang'An), a very important heritage research centre focusing on wooden construction and chronodendrology (dating by the study of wood). It is located near the demolished, but recently excavated, site of the Imperial Palace. It has a simple but educational museum. Here, we discover the value attributed to each fragment of wood, mainly in monumental construction (temples and palaces). It shows the great threat of fire to buildings whose value was also associated with the survival of a myriad technical secrets, then shared like the most precious of cultures. And through this realisation, we understand the importance of the past, beyond the simple desire for permanence. The population's attachment to its universe is not only about form, but also the materials that constitute that form.

3——It also applies to the USA: the permanent conflict between speculation and heritage does not preclude a system of protection that might be called liberal (sustained by foundations and private initiative) compared with the stricter national system, with its burden on the public finances, found in countries such as France.

Three Shinto temples (there are others on the list, but our contacts in Nara do not seem to agree) in the two former capitals were destined for a more ephemeral—but finally relatively painless—fate. Every twenty years, they had to be dismantled, which does not mean destroyed, and then rebuilt in identical form, with new wooden frames, a few yards from their initial site. Parts of the dismantled temple were then reused for other sacred buildings, a process of transmission that itself had a religious element. To prepare for the ritual rebuilding of these temples and of the other sanctuaries, entire forests of cypress trees were planted in a special configuration relative to the sun, a few decades before they were used (the purpose of this process is primarily technical). Once cut and sawn, the main columns were transported and arranged in a new temple, in such a way that the same side was always turned towards the sun.

The way that westerners often interpret this patrimonial vision of Japan, founded on the sacred, on a sense of unity with the nature and spirit of the trees, came to be strangely inverted. It was imagined that the Japanese joyously and ritually destroyed the totality of their cultural assets simply in order to rebuild them exactly the same. In reality, only one of the three Shinto temples, specifically part of the Temple in Ise, near Nara, continues this practice of religious transhumance. One of the two others was burned. The third has reverted to common Buddhist temple practice.

C—Restoration of the Confucius temple in Beijing, 2003. © OACC

The desire for permanence

Historic China was neither more spendthrift in the management of its forests, nor more unconcerned at the disappearance of its monuments, nor less worried about the natural human disasters that threatened its cities. We need to distinguish between several types of attitude. The use of "scorched earth" tactics, the destruction of enemy cities, ended with the stabilisation of the empire. The shift from one dynasty to another may have caused upheavals in the capitals. However, these transformations primarily affected the Imperial Palace, as was the case with the Forbidden City in 1416 (the earth removed during construction was used to build the coal hill in Jingshan Park north of the Palace and especially in 1664 when the Manchus burned down the Palace and founded the Qin dynasty). Otherwise, however, the cities lived mainly in fear of fire, flood and earthquake. From the Yuan dynasty onwards, the focus was largely on maintenance, with differences between regions and construction methods.

Whether we call this the desire for permanence or the maintenance of ancestral heritage, what in reality are the differences between the development of Europe's and China's cities? Why should we congratulate ourselves here, in Europe, for our constant concern with the maintenance of buildings, when the transformation of our cities is a recurrent and evident process. To the point that, in Paris itself, as in many other cities, the oldest house is identified and dated (1407). Which parts of this smart vestige are original, and which restored? This question also applies to Notre-Dame, as to many of the cathedrals restored but also redesigned by Viollet-le-Duc and his emulators. Can this permanent transformation of most of the great western cities be compared with that of their Chinese counterparts?

At the beginning of the 20th century, Beijing, the archetype in this sphere, had hardly changed since the Yuan dynasty, when the city's layout, streets and levels were established. The concern for the physical and spatial continuity of urban features, as manifested in the Chinese capital, cannot seriously be seen simply as a spiritual attitude, a desire for "permanence". It is a more sacralized form of the conservation imperative that characterises the western approach, equally or even more pragmatic in its desire to maintain or renew, depending on epochs and needs. In China, as in the West, certain buildings are repaired or rebuilt, because the materials they are made of deteriorate, or occasionally here and there to combat an evil spirit or correct a bad *fengshui*. From the largely baseless idea that the materiality of the past has no value, it has been inferred that there was less feeling, less respect for heritage than in Mérimée's France, which, it is true, became its theoretician and spokesman.

D and E——Qu Yuan village, moved and rebuilt near the Three Gorges Dam. © OACC

The Maoist period and the cultural Revolution themselves did not profoundly alter the apparent immutability of Beijing, which prompted many travellers to describe it as the world's most beautiful city. During this period, no doubt, several factors contributed to the deterioration in the buildings, whether in the capital or in provincial cities. The phenomenal growth in population, which was to rise to almost a billion at the beginning of the Deng Xiaoping era, was in itself a crucial factor. Maoism exacerbated the consequences, forcing families to live together in the old courtyard houses (siheyuan), installing factories or garrisons in temples and some of the palaces, thereby preventing the minimum level of maintenance that buildings anywhere require.

The great model built in 1999 by the Bureau of Town Planning shows how the original city continued to survive, although the walls have gone together with most of the gates, replaced by the second orbital road. Chang'an Avenue, Tian'anmen Square and the two big shopping streets of Wang Fujing and Xidan are the most visible features of a transformation that primarily affects the periphery of the old town. Nonetheless, in China as a whole, the years 1980-2000 represent a pivotal time, since it was in this period that the 21st-century urban future took shape, both mentally and politically. A million miles from the discomfort of overpopulated houses and their courtyards full of parasitic shacks. To the point of fencing in, but not felling, the hosts of "regulation" trees which covered the capital with an astonishing canopy of leaves.

F, G and H——Destruction in Suzhou, 1992. © OACC

In Shixing hutong, awaiting the expulsion

Lily Eclimont

The Li family lives in the Qianmen district. Situated southeast of Tian'anmen Square, right in the heart of the Chinese capital, this historic district has been almost flattened in the last two years. All that remains is a few alleyways (*hutong*), with their traditional quadrangle courtyard houses (*siheyuan*). Today, around 5000 families live in these old houses, and the many buildings that have been added to it over the last five decades, in what is classified as a "protected sector". The government's plan is to build high status housing here. The Li family and their neighbours have been offered financial compensation, but have all refused. There has been a stand-off for two years. The inhabitants get by in the ruins as they await their imminent expulsion.

In the little Shixing *hutong*, news often travels by word of mouth. One evening in December 2005, when Mrs Li is cleaning her coal stove, Mr Wang comes rushing in, interrupting her favourite TV soap about eunuch conspiracies in the Ming era. While out walking his dog a few minutes before, this neighbour and friend has seen a poster attached to the wall of a house at the end of the alley. Signed by the Bureau responsible for land management in the Chongwen district, the big printed characters announce that: "All the houses within the area linking the eastern side of Qianmen Avenue as far as Xinge Street from west to east, and the back of Heyan Street to the east of Zhushikoudong Street from north to south, are to be demolished". A notice of this kind has been hung in every *hutong* in the district. The neighbours congregate in front of the brick wall. In a few seconds, anxiety and anger spread. Mr Li's face, marked by years of work in one of the capital's construction firms, remains impassive, as ever. He is not entirely surprised. A few days earlier, when his son had briefly relinquished the computer which he uses to play online football every day, Mr Li had seen a pop-up on the Sina website announcing the information. He hadn't wanted to believe it. Apparently, real estate promoters had obtained permission from the authorities in Chongwen (the "Respect for Culture" district, southeast of the Forbidden City), confirmed by the Beijing city council, to buy the *hutong* area. As is his habit, old Li doesn't say a word. He returns calmly to his wife, who is waiting for him with his dinner of smoking cucumber pancakes.

A strategic neighbourhood

Situated a kilometre from Tian'anmen Square, the little Shixing *hutong* is part of the Qianmen district. Bounded to the north by the avenue that runs along the old Ming city to Qianmen Gate, and to the south by the street bordering the Temple of Heaven (Tiantan), this district covers approximately 25 hectares. Made up of traditional alleyways lined with connecting houses, it is one of the Chinese capital's historic areas.

Since 1990, the city has been undergoing major reconstruction and renovation programmes. The most ambitious of these was initiated by three Frenchmen, the entrepreneur Alexandre Allard, the company boss Anthony Béchu and the architect Jacques Jobard, who in 2006 had proposed to develop the 25 hectares of the Qianmen district for the "Dazhalan Project": more than 100,000 square metres of luxury shops together with art galleries and a branch of the Maeght foundation or of the Georges Pompidou Centre.

The project is still ongoing, but in March 2007 it was transferred from the French developers to the Soho China group, which is required to fulfil the same heritage protection criteria that Beijing's Urban Planning Bureau had demanded of Alexandre Allard.

The Qianmen district is now classified as a "protection area" ("保留地区"). This status does not prevent demolition, but requires the architects to design new buildings in a so-called "neotraditional" style. This means that the design of all the planned shops and luxury malls, including those in Qianmen Street, which are scheduled to open for the Olympic Games, must be based on Qing style (early 20th century). A number of fine residences situated in the hutong east and west of Qianmen Avenue will be kept and restored (the restoration being done in record time, largely for the Olympic deadline, with the help of Italian architects).

Once the work is done, it will cost 20 to 30 million yuan (2 to 3 million euros) to buy these properties, an amount that the Li family will never be able to put together with their monthly pension of 1,500 yuan (150 euros). At the moment, the couple only pay rent of 20 yuan (2 euros) a month to occupy the western side of an old courtyard house, where Mr Li's parents moved back in 1949.

Previously, this *siheyuan* had belonged to a single family, a corporation of shopkeepers from Jiangxi province (southeast China). In 1949, the houses became the property of the State: the courtyard houses were rearranged to house several families and a bureau responsible for allocating the apartments was created. To rent one of them required a Beijing residence permit (*hukou*), a criterion that Mr Li's parents were able to meet, as they were natives of the capital and worked in one of the city's State enterprises.

Of the 15,000 dwellings originally scheduled for demolition, around 5000 are now left. In the last three years, two thirds of the families have been exiled beyond the fifth orbital, more than 15 kilometres away, and their houses have been demolished. Hosts of government representatives, ordinary people employed by the Chongwen authorities, regularly turn up at the doors of the few remaining recalcitrants. They are offering financial compensation of 8,020 yuan per square metre (764 euros; 1 euro = 10.49 yuan), based on the floor area of the original house. This means that the various extensions added by the occupants are not included in the compensation package.

The Li are refusing to leave. As are their neighbours. But for how much longer? In China, land remains the property of the State; in other words, private property covers only the right to use one's house, limited to a maximum of 70 years, a right that can be sold or transferred and is guaranteed by law.

A——Another Li family (a very popular surname in China) from Shixing *hutong*. © Lily Eclimont
B——Xiao Wa, their employee. This young girl, originary from the poor province of Gansu, helps Mr Li take care of his handicapped wife for a few hundred yuan a month. © Lily Eclimont

"An arm cannot twist a leg" "胳膊拧不过大腿"

Mrs Li is retired and spends days idle in front of her television, waiting for meal times which are her time of activity. Once the meal is over, she immerses herself passionately in the soap *"Golden Wedding"* ("金婚") which retraces the history of a couple from their marriage, in 1956, to the present day. She becomes immersed in this sentimental story, which deals successively with the famine of the Great Leap Forward, the Cultural Revolution and the economic reforms of the 1980s, all periods that Mrs Li remembers well. Then comes the time to walk the dog.

Mrs Li walks amidst the debris of the wide street under construction at the end of her alley, the same street where only yesterday stood the house on which the poster announcing the destruction of the *hutong* had hung two years before. Today, that long street is nothing more than a great swathe of ruins, soon to disappear under tons of concrete. Here, in this desolate landscape that still bears the traces of the desertion of whole families, neighbours have brought their little folding chairs. At nightfall, they sit in the dust and speculate about their uncertain future, to the distant sound of the concrete mixers which continue to work, despite the late hour, near Qianmen Avenue.

C——Destroyed alley next to Li's house. © Lily Eclimont
D——A washing machine abandoned by an exiled family in the 5th periphery. © Lily Eclimont

"They came again this morning", complains an angry neighbour. "But what do you expect, an arm cannot twist a leg" (胳膊终归是拧不过大腿的) retorts another neighbour resignedly, quoting a local proverb expressing impotence; a leg is inherently stronger than an arm, the government will always be more powerful than the people. "Perhaps we should ask the US Army to come and save us", jokes a third.

Mr Li never takes part in these neighbourly conversations. He prefers to watch over his home. There have recently been thefts in the *hutong*. The neighbours blame workers employed to clear debris and dust out of the main alley. Rural migrant workers from the south of the country, these peasants stay in their hundreds in the old primary school at the end of the alley, now a giant hostel.

"We don't like these *waidiren*" (外地人: *outsiders*, a term used for income is who are not from the city), he exclaims. "Since they started coming, Beijing hasn't been as safe; they are people without education who take our jobs and steal our houses. Foreigners need a visa to come to China; the *waidiren* should be required to have a visa to come to Beijing."

In the *hutong*, no one talks to them. Once they finish work, the migrants congregate in makeshift tents erected on the work site. They play cards, cigarettes in their mouths and cans of Yanjing, a Beijing beer, in their hands, just a few metres from the folding chairs of Mrs Li and her neighbours.

On every tongue, the same subject of conversation, the derisory sums offered by the government. Mr Li rejects the whole idea. For him, this *hutong* is not for sale. He was born between its walls, like his son, and his parents died here. There is no important moment of his life that these dirty and badly insulated walls have not witnessed. In the evening, he often talked about it with Mr Wang. On the doorsteps where they stand guard, Liu challenges him. "Li, enough of your nostalgia! What's this *hutong* life you talk about? Do you find it normal in the 21st century that we're still living in these tumbledown houses dating back to the Qing era?"

"I participate, I am happy, I sacrifice myself" "我参与, 我快了, 我奉献"

Mr Wang is not fond of the cramped 9 square metres where he lives with his wife and two children. His daughter and son, respectively aged 28 and 26, take turns sleeping on a bed made of planks suspended between two chairs. Mr Wang escaped the single child policy. In 1969, right at the beginning of the cultural revolution, he was sent to Shanxi province, southeast of Beijing, to be re-educated because of his social background. His grandfather had owned land north of Beijing, making several generations of landowners in the family. In Shanxi, he met his future wife, a native of the province. The single child policy introduced in 1979 by Deng Xiaoping limited the size of urban families to one child and of rural families with an elder daughter, to two children, as in Wang's case.

In their cramped room, only the TV has anything that could be described as its own place: it stands on a high sideboard, so that every occupant, whether on the top bunk bed or the wooden planks, can follow the soaps or read the subtitles of the karaoke DVDs that old Wang likes to play after supper. In the courtyard that they share with three other families, the Wang have built themselves a little shed that they use as a kitchen. This is where they keep the piles of woks, saucepans and greasy pans.

E——Wang's courtyard. © Lily Eclimont
F——Mr. Li's courtyard. © Lily Eclimont
G——Wang's Kitchen. © Lily Eclimont

To wash, the Wang use the hutong's public showers, summer and winter. The Wang do have running water, but no bathroom. Mr Wang, for his part, is lucky enough to live in a larger courtyard. In summer, he showers in the small private yard he built himself. Mr Wang would be happy to swap his makeshift shelter for a heated, well insulated apartment, with an indoor bathroom and kitchen.

He is angry with the government. When he reads in the papers about the almost daily corruption stories that shake his country, Mr Wang is disgusted. All that money being pocketed by certain Party cadres or unscrupulous businessmen. The creation in September 2007 of a National Anticorruption Bureau responsible for analysing information from sources like banks, the land registry, medical facilities and telecommunications, and passing it on to the courts and police, leaves him cynical.

"It's all smoke and mirrors. The decisions are taken in Beijing, but after that, in the provinces, local officials can do what they want. They are so far from the capital... so an anticorruption bureau in the heart of the capital, it's just completely pointless!", he exclaims, his voice rising. "These days, we live in "a society that drinks our blood" ("喝血社会" he xue shehui), embellishes Mr Wang, in a subtle pun on the slogans of the "harmonious society" ("和谐社会" he xie shehui) promulgated by President Hu Jintao. "What is this system that sucks the blood of the people to develop and grow."

Mr Wang feels left behind. His pension of 1200 yuan (120 euros) is hardly enough to live on and the 70 yuan (7 euros) a day or so that his wife earns as a street trader, selling cards and caps stamped "Beijing 2008" to tourists on Tian'anmen Square, hardly gives them a decent standard of living.

Mr Wang and Mr Li would like their sons, both aged 26, to be married. Except that, in China, the groom's family is supposed to provide accommodation for the new couple, a luxury that is not open to the Wang at present. In the meantime, his son's girlfriend comes regularly to the house. They wait patiently for his parents to look the other way to snatch a furtive kiss.

Opposite Mr Wang's house, a long banner hangs from the metal sheeting that partly hides the work on the main street. On it is written the welcome slogan for the Beijing Olympics. "I take part, I am happy, I sacrifice myself" ("我参与, 我快乐, 我奉献"). As he leaves home, in the morning, he comments bitterly "Take part? In what? I am happy? They're taking my home. Sacrifice myself? I wasn't given any choice!"

Mr Wang lives with a poster of the great leader hanging above his dining table. These days, he is almost nostalgic for that era. Long gone is the exile in Shanxi during the cultural revolution and the 25 years he spent there, and at least the leaders then had principles and cared about the people. "Sure, he cheated us with his class warfare, he comments glancing at the portrait, but today's leaders are much worse."

"In old Mao's day, perhaps all we ate was dumplings, adds Mr Li, but at least he was a leader with integrity. He tried to reduce the differences between rich and poor, not like nowadays", explains the man who spent 10 years of his life digging the fields in the Beijing suburbs in the 1960s and 70s.

A painful era, certainly, but one in which, for them, the phrase "I take part, I am happy, I sacrifice myself" actually meant something.

H——Mr Wang's living room.

城

The photographs used to illustrate this article are all taken from short films in the "5x18" collection made for the *In the Chinese City* Exhibition. These films are presented in the article "On filmmakers and cities" by Jordi Balló, which appears on page 30 of this catalogue. With the exception of the photograph of Wei Lai, page 278.

10

Cities

Geneviève Imbot-Bichet

"When we hear tell of remote things, they always seem more extraordinary than they are in reality. However, here it is quite the opposite: China is more extraordinary even than one can recount."

Gaspar da Cruz, Portuguese Dominican friar (? – 1570), taken from his *Treatise, the first European book entirely dedicated to China since the mediaeval accounts.*

Since Marco Polo, a young 13th century Venetian merchant who lived 24 years under the reign of Kublai Khan, China has continued to fascinate, and numerous personal accounts, travel notes and letters describe those marvels that first excited the merchants—those bold explorers—and then the missionaries and ambassadors of European courts, and finally curious travellers of more recent times. Over time, these writings describe the China's glorious civilisation, its imperial past, its slow and painful movement towards modernity. Our theme is a literary promenade glancing at eight cities from Beijing to Shenzhen, taking in Xi'an, Chongqing, Hangzhou, Suzhou, Shanghai and finally Canton, listening to the words of authors who have at different times described the Middle Kingdom. Testimonies in which China emerges both as reality and dream, made up of impressions and sensations. Fragments of texts that reflect the metamorphosis of these cities under the impact of the great reforms and that bear witness to the immense change of direction announced by Deng Xiaoping, a change to a modern China, a new giant in the world order. The urban landscape, a symbol of this economic awakening, has altered more in ten years than in ten centuries, and this transformation and the concomitant deconstruction, gives third-millennium China its place in the evolution of the modern world. It should be remembered that the population has increased threefold and that formerly rural China is in the process of becoming a primarily urban nation.

北京 Beijing, Imperious Capital

Beijing, capital of the North, whose vestiges date back to the 12th century, has a long history. In 1261, Kubilay made it his capital under the name of Dadu and Marco Polo describes this city of the great Khan as a "city of straight lines, with roads straight as an "I" from one end to the other". Long held by "barbarian" dynasties, Beijing only became capital of the Chinese empire in the reign of Yongle,

Wei Lai 魏来, Shanghai 2004. © Wei Lai

the third emperor of the Ming dynasty (1368-1644). In *The Last Days of Peking* Pierre Loti writes of a city "designed with unity and daring, regular as a geometrical figure". Victor Segalen sees this capital as an architectural masterpiece:

"*Pei-king, 28 February 1911.* Better than a tale of imagination, it seemed to have, at each of its leaps into the real, the power of all magic enclosed in these walls..., where I will not enter. It cannot be contested that Pei-king is a masterpiece of mysterious construction. And first of all, the triple disposition of these cities does not answer to the laws of land registries nor the accommodation needs of people who eat and populate. The capital of the greatest Empire under heaven was thus desired for itself; designed like a chessboard at the extreme north of the yellow plain; surrounded by geometrical walls; woven with avenues, a grid of straight alleys and then raised in a single monumental act...—inhabited, then, and finally overflowed in its interloper suburbs by those Chinese parasites.—But the principal square, the Tartar-Manchu city, still provides a good home for conquerors—and for this dream: in the middle, in the depths of the middle of the Palace, a face: a child-man, and Emperor, master of the Earth and Son of Heaven.[1]"

For the writer, novelist and dramatist Lao She, born in Beijing in 1899, "Peiping, [is] a peaceful city par excellence, with its lakes and its hills, its imperial palace, its terraces and altars, its temples and its monasteries, its mansions and its parks... Peiping with its white marble bridges, its plants and its flowers in all seasons."[2] In his novels, he brings to life the Beijing of the 1930s and its timeless beauties: "At that moment, the winds scattered the clouds and unveiled the moon. They arrived at the north end of the street. The red wall of the Forbidden City—the imperial city— was reflected on the frozen and slightly shining canal. Within the Forbidden City reigned absolute silence: the roofs with their richly decorated corners, the panels with their green and gold inscriptions, the purple gate, the pavilions on King-chan Hill seemed to hold their breath to listen to a strange song. A breeze, a plaintive whisper, as if charged with ancient memories, wafted through the multiple towers and temples of the palaces. Tigress walked towards Golden Dolphin Bridge to the west. [...] In the distance, the silhouettes of the pagodas and halls rose, darkly, above the lake; only their yellow roof tiles shone palely. The White Tower touched the clouds; its pallor rendered the landscape even more desolate. All this district of San-hai, asleep and as if crushed by the splendour of the past, symbolised the solitude of the North."[3]

1——Victor Segalen, *René Leys*, L'Imaginaire Gallimard, 1971.
2——Lao She, Four generations under a single roof, 1996.
3——Lao She, *Le Pousse-pousse*, translated into French by François Cheng, Robert Laffont, 1973.

However, whilst for centuries no one dared disturb the traditional and quasi sacred arrangement of this imperial city, dating back to the era of the Yuan dynasty, the new masters of Communist China began the first transformations in the 1950s for a new urban plan. They decided to open up Chang'an Avenue, which crosses the city from east to west, cutting across the imperial road that led from the Forbidden City to the Temple of Heaven in the south. In 1959, Tian'anmen Square was designed as the new centre of power: a rectangular area of 40 ha, capable of accommodating thousands of people, framed to the east by the People's Assembly and to the west by the Museum of the History of the Revolution. Then in 1977, Mao's mausoleum was built right opposite Tiananmen Gate, disrupting a major symbolic north-south counterpoint around which Beijing was structured, the final challenge to the forces of ancient China. Since 2000, Beijing's development has been stunning and the demolitions have followed each other at headlong pace. The shady little 13th-century alleyways are disappearing day by day, taking with them the low old houses with their square courtyards to be replaced by wide avenues lined with glass buildings; probably a quarter of the *hutong* and tens of thousands of *siheyuan* have been swallowed up and a whole way of life is disappearing. "Tabula rasa. Beijing. They emerged from the belly of Beijing without warning. In the space of a few weeks, the new buildings hatched, swelled their glass flanks, unfurled their steel curves. An astonishing architectural blitz has just struck Changan jie, the avenue that divides Tian'anmen from east to west. The road is no more than a set of mirrors, a boulevard of ice that irritates the eyes as it reflects the blaze of the autumn sun. Perpendicular to it, Wangfujing Street is the epicentre of the crush. The road has become a wide pedestrian alleyway ornamented with fountains and lined with shopping centres, the most recent destination for citizens of Beijing, visibly full of pride at the explosion of such "modernity". Whole families rush here. Few take any notice of the discriminatory sign at the entrance to a department store—"Access forbidden to anyone improperly dressed"—since they are all properly dressed in this new middle-class paradise. The "improperly dressed" are the scruffy and sometimes smelly *mingong*, intruders despised by the refined urbanites."[4]

A few islands, fragments scattered here and there north of the Forbidden City between Coal Hill and the Belltower, still retained their former charm and, to quote Saint-John Perse in a letter to his friend André Gide: "You will like this anonymous and lunar city, where the notion of space has its own value, like that of time. Above all, you will like Peking, the astronomical capital of the world, out of place and out of time, struck by the absolute."

4——Frédéric Bobin, *Voyage au centre de la Chine*, Éditions Piquier, 2007.

Xi'an, the heritage paradox 西安

Capital of the country in Antiquity and in the Middle Ages, between the first millennium BCE and the 8th century, Xi'an is today capital of the province of Shaanxi. "Western city of peace", Xi'an was from the 3rd century BCE the departure point for the Silk Route, linking China to Central Asia. In 221 BCE, after unifying the Empire, the emperor of the Qin established his capital at Xianyang, near today's Xi'an. Then under the Han, it became Chang'an, the city of "Eternal Peace", a prosperous city, described in detail by the researcher Liu Xujie: "At the end of the Qin dynasty, Liu Bang, who took the name Gaozu when he became the first emperor of the Western Han, built a new capital called Chang'an. The city was practically rectangular in design and was surrounded by a wall 22.7 km long enclosing an area of 35 square kilometres, with three gates on each of its sides. The main arteries of the city led to two gates: Heng Gate which pointed to the north and the River Wei, and Xuanping Gate which opened to the east, towards Luoyang. Once through Heng Gate, the visitor arriving in Chang'an took a road which was no less than 50 m wide and 5.5 km long, in other words running almost the whole length of the city from north to south. In all, eight major roads crossed the capital of the Western Han from north to south, and nine from west to east, linking the different districts of a conurbation with a population of some 240,000 by the end of the Western Han dynasty."[5]

Xi'an became China's leading tourist site in 1974, following the discovery of the first Qin Emperor's terracotta army. Has Xi'an eradicated its prestigious past? What remains of the architectural vestiges of Antiquity and the Middle Ages, of the greatness of its former glory? A city on China's Loess plateau surrounded by countryside polluted by a battalion of heavy industries.

A——*Outside Xi'an*, Chen Tao. © X-stream/CCCB/Cité de l'architecture & du patrimoine

5——Liu Xujie, "The Qin and Han dynasties", in *L'Architecture chinoise*, Piquiers, 2005. (Liu Xujie teaches architecture at the University of the South-West in Nanjing, where he is also a researcher).

The only "vestiges" of that now vanished historical and cultural splendour are the descriptions by Jia Pingwa, a great novelist who drew endless inspiration from his native city Xi'an: "Zhuang Zhijie found the number on the plate, 37 Street of the Four Residences. The architecture of the entrance gate was finely wrought, covered with rounded and varnished ridge tiles, and the top of the walls decorated with small sculpted scenes; only one of the boards of the frame was missing; the black lacquer of the two great doors was flaking and six of the great round nails had fallen out. The imposing granite columns were decorated with a pair of carved unicorns. Steel rings were set into the brick walls on either side of the gate and, just below, was a long reddish stone. Zhao Jingwu noticed the interest with which his friend was examining everything [...] Zhuang Zhijie indeed admired their refinement and commented that all the fine examples of architecture in Xijing [Xi'an] had now disappeared and that no one, alas, was any longer interested in these sculpted pillars. He would have liked to make a rubbing of them for his collection."[6]

Chongqing, by force of arms 重庆

Formerly the capital of Sichuan province, since 1997 Chongqing has been an autonomous municipality like Beijing, Tianjin and Shanghai, under the direct authority of central government. It is a new city which occupies the territory of the municipality of Chongqing—"it is the built-up area plus its rural environment and the neighbouring countryside"—and has twice as many rural as urban inhabitants. What distinguishes this riverside city is that it is made entirely of curves. Clinging to a craggy landscape, Chongqing was made of an inextricable tangle of alleyways interspersed with staircases. And it is above all this craggy landscape that strikes travellers of different times: "The position of Tchoung-King is incomparable.

6—Jia Pingwa, La Capitale déchue, translated into French by G. Imbot-Bichet, Stock, 1997.

On the slopes of a long crescent-shaped peninsula, the commercial metropolis of the Sé-Tchouan stacks up its overlapping buildings, the whimsical silhouettes of its temples, its white walled yamens, its "hongs" bursting with merchandise. At the summit of the high cliff stand old ramparts run through with semicircular arched gates, whence staircases of four or five hundred steps descend to the beach. On these steps, a whole host of sailors, porters, chair-men hustle and bustle, whilst hundreds of junks disgorge the contents of their hulls onto the stones, balls of wool from Tibet, cotton from Hou-Pé, crates of opium and tea, bags of salt, wax cakes from Kia-Ting. Opposite, on the right bank, cheerful countryside, terraces of crops, gardens, rice paddies, fields of corn and poppies, cottages nestling amongst the mandarin trees, occasional hamlets amidst the pale greenery. Further off, towards the southwest, stands the screen of mountains rising 700 to 800 metres, punctuated with pagoda towers, oratories, monasteries, charming buildings half temple, half cottage."[7]

Lucien Bodard describes a peninsula at the confluence of two rivers in *Monsieur le consul*: "A town on the rock emerging from the tremendous waters of the Yangtze and its tributary the Jialing. Palace above, below hovels clinging to the precipice. On the steep side, gigantic stairways, stone steps worn by human feet, by the constant movement of beings in search of food or pleasure."

François Cheng describes a "swarm of hills of different shapes" which form "a panorama of audacious harmony": "Tchoungking (Double Celebration). (...) The site is superb, framed by two rivers—the Jialing to the north and the Yangtze to the south. Dominating them from above, Tchoungking resembles a peninsula formed of a sequence of flat-peaked hills, and at the end, where the two rivers join, an immense rocky spur. At the summit and on the sides of the sloping cliffs, descending in multiple layers, is a mass of overlapping low cottages and high buildings, like a multitude of shells tightly encrusted in the rocks. Everywhere, the streets and alleyways are linked by innumerable steps.

On the heights stretch avenues, wide or narrow depending on the nature of the terrain, which converge into crossroads engorged with shops, restaurants, theatres and cinemas, dance halls and tea rooms, American-style bars.

Certain places, full of trees and rocks, are laid out as public gardens with terraces offering grandiose views, as only long-scrolled Chinese painting could show."[8]

7—— Marcel Monnier, *Le Tour d Asie—L'Empire du Milieu*, Plon, 1899, p. 203-204
8——François Cheng, *Le dit de Tianyi*, Albin Michel, 1998, p.104-105

From 1938 to 1945, Chongqing was the capital of Chinese resistance, of "nationalist" China, the only period when the Guomingdang, Chiang Kai-shek's Nationalist party, and Mao Zedong's Communist Party presented a united front to the Japanese invader. The bombing did not spare the city, and turned it into an immense brazier, destroying its ramparts and temples. Lao She lived here during these war years and depicts the atmosphere of the city as it was assailed by summer heat and enemy shells: "The heat was intolerable, as there was not the slightest breeze. The sea in miniature was like an oven; everyone sweated and found it hard to breathe. The blinding sun reflecting on the water set the yellow sand and the rocks ablaze. Above the river, the city seemed stifled under a cloud of greyish mist, between the water that stretching at its feet and the rocks dominating it. If the sea was an oven, the city was a steam room. [...] The foggy season ended in April but a layer of mist still hung above Chongqing every morning. White, cottony and icy, it covered the city like a shroud until the sun managed to eliminate it. The red globe of the sun was a bad omen. Sinister and bellicose, it announced clear weather, in other words the resumption of bombing. Chongqing's climate was divided into two seasons: winter with cold and fog, summer with heat, without fog but with... danger. Everyone knew: as soon as the sky cleared, we would hear the rumbling of the planes again." [9]

Returning from his trip to China in 1955, Michel Leiris notes his impressions in his *Chinese Journal*: "Tuesday 25th October [1955] 4:25 p.m.: arrival at Tchong K'ing, which was Tchang Kai-Chek's retreat in the final period of the war .

The city—more than two million people—grew up during the war. The terrain is very uneven. The descent to it was almost a feat of mountaineering. It is not beautiful, but lively and appealing. You feel much further away here than in Beijing or Shanghai.

We were shown the confluence of the Yang Tsé Kiang and its tributary, a grandiose site, where we saw large numbers of junks, and even a small passenger boat, motorised or steam driven. On the bank opposite us, an industrial district. A little later, returning, we would see it all sparkling with light. An enormous staircase leads to the port and the quay for the boat to Nanjing.

9——Lao She, *The Drum Singers*, 1952.

At 8 p.m., our hosts—who also showed us the Sino-Soviet hall (with a Chinese style portico in its outer entrance, and a central part that imitates the Temple of Heaven in Beijing)—take us for supper in a place near the hotel, frequented by Soviets."[10]

"Many times destroyed and many times rebuilt" Chongqing has continued to expand "like an excrescence which takes on monstrous dimensions". Today, this city in the centre-west is still the departure point for the descent of the Yangtze: "with 31 million inhabitants, this gigantic municipality of cities, towns and villages, has become the planet's largest centre of conurbation. Pollution and damp rising from the Yangtze (the blue river) which irrigates its banks, makes Chongqing a city where the sun rarely rises". Chongqing, China's fourth largest city, has become the economic and financial powerhouse at the heart of the country, a significant driving force for the Yangtze valley, which will have to absorb some of the populations displaced by the opening of the Three Gorges Dam. The government's ambition is to use it to create a centre of growth for the Chinese interior.

Hangzhou, a new paradise 杭州

The high point of this city came under the Southern Song, when the court decided to move its capital there in 1138. In the 12th century, Hangzhou was, with Suzhou, a highly prosperous city, which acquired its beauty from water, in particular from Xihu—the Western Lake.

Marco Polo describes its riches and beauties and calls it a "most noble and magnificent city" when he travels there on an official mission on behalf of Kubilay Khan in 1283: "It was said first of all in this writing that the city of Hangzhou is so large that it is one hundred miles around and that there are twelve thousand stone bridges, most of them big enough for a ship to pass under. Let no one be surprised that there are so many bridges, for I tell you that the city is entirely built upon water, is entirely surrounded by water, which is why there must be so many bridges to move around it. In this city, there are twelve mills, each trade having twelve thousand shops. Know further that the great masters of these shops and their wives did nothing with their hands, but retained a bearing as impeccable and magnificent as if they were kings. [...] In the south of the city, but within it, there is a great lake which measures some three hundred miles around, and around the lake, there are very fine palaces and houses so magnificent that they could not be more so; they belong to the nobles and grandees of the city."[11]

C—*Wait*, Peng Tao. © X-stream/CCCB/Cité de l'architecture & du patrimoine

10——Michel Leiris, *Journal de Chine*, Gallimard, 1994.
11——Marco Polo, *Description of the World*.

Hangzhou reflects the art and pleasure of life characteristic of the Song dynasty at its economic height in the 12th century. After the Manchu invasion, it became the refuge of scholars who enjoyed the charms of its peaceful gardens. Ruined and hostile to the new Qing dynasty, Zhang Dai (1597-1684), the great prose writer of his time, wrote to preserve the memory of his region, Hangzhou, and of the Western Lake: "The Garden of the Happy was the vacation retreat of the Imperial Censor Han Wuyun. It is situated on the side of Dragon Mountain: as the mountain becomes flatter at this point, the boundary is not too abrupt, and because the water flows in all directions, nothing has a fixed appearance. In the house, in which the doors opened onto the mountain and the windows onto the water, it was as if one was unrolling a painting showing a sequence of Chinese views. In front stretched a fertile garden divided into sections and mainly planted with fruit trees. While Gongdan was alive, bamboo shoots, oranges, plums, apricots, pears, azarole, cabbages and pumpkins supplied a market within the doors; a lake covering ten *mu* fed fat fish; there were also a hundred mulberry trees and dozens of peach trees. In a single day, it brought the equivalent of a "relief from punishment". In the spring, the boiled bamboo shoots were a delight; the fruits combined with silk; everything came in its time and in its place."[12]

Simone de Beauvoir, for her part, remembers it as a provincial town from her visit in 1955: "Since my arrival in China, everyone has boasted of the beauties of Hang-tcheou. It was the capital of the Song dynasty, whose reign coincided with the finest moment of Chinese civilisation, and it is considered to be the Athens of China. Its lake, the "Western Sea" Lake, has inspired many painters and poets. [...] The city of Hang-tcheou strikes me as provincial and a bit dull. It is an "average little" town, which has 600,000 inhabitants. Open-air traders, sitting in the shade of small trees, sell sweets, walnuts, sugared peanuts, water chestnuts, combs, soaps, cheap jewellery. There are still a few rickshaws in the streets and I find it uncomfortable to see men running barefoot between the forks. The city's only luxury is the silks with which the shops are full. Mrs Cheng invited me to take tea at her home. Her house—formerly occupied by a Kuomingtang official who fled—belongs to the State, which rents it out."[13]

The capital of Zhejiang province, Hangzhou, which now has more than six million inhabitants, is ranked number one for its quality of life. It is one of the richest cities, full of tourists when the osmanthus blooms in autumn, renowned for its dikes and its lake, and also for its chic shops. Whilst the vestiges of the scholars have been preserved, this little "Paradise on earth", although it has not escaped the rush to modernisation, has managed to retain a certain control over its development.

12——Zhang Dai, The Garden of the Happy , in *Les Paradis naturels, jardin chinois en prose*, translated by M. Valette-Hémery, Picquier, 2001.
13——Simone de Beauvoir, *La longue marche et la Chine*, Gallimard, 1957.

Suzhou, the past reconstructed 苏州

Suzhou was the capital of the kingdom of Wu in the 6th century BCE, but it was under the Southern Song, in the 12th century, when the court moved its capital to Hangzhou, that it reached its apogee. The city was then a vast citadel embedded in a quadrilateral with a double network of canals and streets, with bridges above them, crossing it and linking it to the Grand Canal. The growth and manufacture of silk developed here and under the Ming and Qing the mandarins and scholars used it as a favourite holiday retreat, because of its gardens and residences.

In 1932, the Jesuit priest Joseph de Reviers de Mauny gave his first impressions of Suzhou: "On 21st December, through the triple gate of the city, we take the circular canal, a waterway some 100 metres wide. The bridge is very old, 53 arches. A city on the water, on the grand canal, Suzhou is surrounded by moats, with a network of 40 kilometres of canals and waterways straddled by 163 bridges. It is called the Chinese Venice, which is to do it much honour. But Suzhou remains an attractive city. Square in design, surrounded by high crenellated walls that are reflected in the blue water of the wide canal, Suzhou has a proud appearance. Inside, the chequerboard of its districts is divided up by narrow little canals, encased into the houses. The barges move through it with difficulty and float on water black with oil and littered with paper, orange peel, cabbage leaves, tin cans. The streets are narrow, except the one that follows the consul of the Americans, who are numerous in this city. It has been widened. So it is the street of the merchants, the street of the banks and of the magic poppy shops. Suzhou also has old pagodas, topped with green or orange tiles, fantastic gardens where the little paths surrounded by rocks force you to follow a maze which constantly offers you new views on the same garden."[14]

Lu Wenfu, a writer born in 1928 near Suzhou, describes the grandeur of his city and the transformation it experiences in the early 30s and 40s, when the traditional residences were redistributed, then in the 1960s when they became proletarian squats: "At that time, the city had few inhabitants. Where there were the fewest was not the little out-of-the-way alleys, but the city walls which were completely deserted. (...) From Hulong Street, we went as far as Sanyuanfang. Arriving at the Temple of Confucius, we turned left and, walking along the river from Blue Wave Pavilion, we entered the garden from the south. (...) In the moonlight, the pavilion offered a vague and mysterious landscape. When we looked to the south beyond the green water, there was on one side an old park in the Chinese style, and on the other side a Roman building. Asia and Europe telescoped, Rome met Suzhou, the two great systems, hidden by the moon and the water, were in harmony, formed

14—— Christine Cornet & François Verdier, *Carnet de Chine, 1932. Le voyage insensé du père Jo,* Actes Sud- Bleu de Chine, 2004.

a single whole, providing a glimpse of a vague beauty, both familiar and strange. (...) The Grand Canal, impetuous with the water collected from the north and south, flowed eastwards, surrounding Suzhou in its own way. Its wide white edge clasped the wall, even more ancient than itself."[15]

No account of Suzhou would be complete without mention of the refinement of its cuisine, both streetside snacks and gourmet restaurants, which adds an extra dimension to its reputation. And it is with a poetic and humourous pen that Lu Wenfu describes the importance of the culinary arts in Suzhou, a city for which he felt tenderness and passion all his life: "Heaven houses Paradise; the Earth, Suzhou and Hangzhou." We do not know who invented this saying, who dared place Suzhou before Hangzhou. But it is also said that this order has its reasons. Because it was not until the era of the Northern Song that Hangzhou was made capital. But already at the time of the Tang dynasty, Suzhou had "One hundred thousand taxpaying families, five thousand soldiers guarding the borders" (verse by the poet Bai Juyi, 772-846). With Shanghai's development over the centuries, men who had become achieved their mettle through competition in that foreigner-infested metropolis, became masters of the residences and industries of Suzhou: a place favourable to initiative, a place without losers. Suzhou was in no way a political or economic centre. It had never been the prize in a serious battle over the previous two millennia. Pleasant climate, varied products, splendid site, Suzhou lacked none of these advantages. [...]. Merchants, former brigands, failed scholars and prostitutes of some renown had always sought to end their days here. So the gardens of Suzhou had become the most famous in the world. The art of the table also reached its apogee. For in the long run, landscapes become insipid fare. If Suzhou held the best place in "paradise", it probably owed it to the superiority of its cuisine and its people were proud of it. [16]

Suzhou has come to an accommodation with its past, and although the city has been truncated, we still find in its gardens that alternation of space and content associated with painting, a concept intended to engender a subtle harmony that Shen Fu, an 18th-century scholar and native of Suzhou, describes in his *Six records of a floating life*: "As for gardens, it is important to make the empty spaces dense by giving reality to illusion, and to open up dense spaces by creating illusion in reality." That is the interpretation given by P. Ryckmans; another translation of the same lines goes: "In laying out gardens, try to show the large in the small and the small in the large, and to reveal fullness in emptiness and emptiness in the full."

15——Lu Wenfu, *Nid d'hommes*, translated from Chinese to French by Chantol Chen-Andro, le Seuil, 2002.
16—— Lu Wenfu, *Vie et passion d'un gastronome chinois*, translated into French by A. Curien and F. Chen, Picquier, 1998.

In 1998, Unesco placed four of its gardens on the world heritage list and this recognition supports the city's own moves to honour its heritage. It is a stated objective to focus strongly on the development of tourism in Suzhou, a city of 2.7 million inhabitants, whereas Nanjing, the capital of Jiangsu province, some 200 km to the north, has become a seething industrial centre of the lower Yangtze.

Shanghai, siren of the Yangtze 上海

In Imperial China, under the Southern Song dynasty, Shanghai was a prosperous city of secondary importance. It was under the Ming dynasty (1368-1644), however, that Shanghai would develop significantly as a result of its commercial activities and extensive resources. "Shanghai is not a European city created by applying a simple colonial graft to the land of the Yangtze Delta. Even if it clearly shows the legacy of the Nanjing Treaty of 1842, it was already by then part of Jiangnan's network of merchant cities. Apart from the original Chinese quarter, it is true that most of Shanghai's urban fabric up to the end of the 1980s emerged from the buildings and extension of the French and international concessions and no longer showed the spatial design and architecture typical of a Chinese city. However, the street network was based on the lacework of canals that formerly structured the west bank of the Hangpu River."[17]

D——*Being and Nothingless*, Han Jie. © X-stream/CCCB/Cité de l'architecture & du patrimoine

17—— Thierry Sanjuan, Beijing, Shanghai, Hong Kong, Three destinies of cities in within China, Big-city geopolitics, Hérodote, 2001.

In 1842, the ratification of the Treaty of Nanjing ended the Opium War and opened five ports to foreign trade, one of them Shanghai. The city's cosmopolitan and unusual features immediately proved attractive and in 1850 foreigners set up concessions there which made the city—previously round in shape, of timber construction and surrounded by walls—overflow its boundaries. The maritime city rediscovered its lost growth, making its commercial and cultural exchanges the paradox of its prosperity. This prosperity continued and the Shanghai grew with the land conceded to foreigners along the Huangpu, as described by Albert Londres: "Shanghai, a city that is American, English, French, Russian, German, Japanese, and all the same slightly Chinese, is a phenomenon unique in the world. To explain it, a picture maker would have to depict it as a goddess with twenty heads and one hundred and forty-four arms, with eager eyes, and fingers caressing dollars." And he adds: "A word on the concessions. First the French concession. It starts at the River Whangpoo, on the Bund, and this base of its quadrilateral is called quai de France. It is not long, but the quadrilateral extends back twelve kilometres. On the left side, a creek, and what a creek! separates us from Chinese territory. On the right side, contact with the international concession. The fourth side of our possession, the side which is twelve kilometres from the quay, merges with the countryside and its coffins. Now take a duck's egg and place it in the quadrilateral not far from the quay: that is the Chinese city of Nantao. Within our walls, apart from the 1300 French we have a swarm, alas! without a queen, of 400,000 Chinese. Our concession is entirely surrounded by barbed wire, Nantao also." Shanghai was at this time characterised by its dynamism and above all its architectural originality, when Sassoon, in particular, opposed the development of the Bund, but also when the American architect Henry K. Murphy held the post of adviser to the Nationalist government. A modern city with new ideas, a great rival to the prudish Beijing, capital of the North, Shanghai was simultaneously a paradise for adventurers, the seat of power of the Nationalist regime, the nucleus of protest in intellectual movements and political literature, and the birthplace of the Chinese Communist party on July 1, 1921. It is this diversity, this blend of cultural and social singularities that gives Shanghai its rich pluralism. It is also this that generates Shanghai's ambiguity: "expressing an international modernity which is actually rooted firmly in a specifically Chinese identity." In 1949, Shanghai became Asia's biggest metropolis as a result of economic success based partly on a powerful class of Chinese entrepreneurs, but also on the foreign settlements and their international contacts.

After a period of stagnation during the dark years of Maoism, when the coastal areas were neglected in favour of the provinces of the interior, in the 1990s Shanghai rediscovered its vitality, its dynamism and the architectural originality that had characterised it since the 1930s, when Jiang Zemin and Zhu Rongji, both former mayors of Shanghai, became respectively President of the Republic and Deputy Prime Minister. Loans granted by the municipality and the influx of foreign investment contributed to its development.

The city began its transformation and major construction projects were launched, often carried out by the *mingong*, that floating population of country folk, peasants or workers, temporarily allowed into the city to work. This new sub-proletariat, the spearhead of the blinding burst of urban development, represents a population of 6 million in the city of Shanghai alone. In *La Promesse de Shanghai*, Stéphane Fière, a French writer living in China, casts a lucid eye on this marginal population: "Since the mid-1990s, my father had complained of the deterioration in our living conditions; the central government had decided to promote the development of the coastal provinces to the detriment of the countryside. [...] As we waited for better times, the cyclone propelled us here. Here in Shanghai, a sad December morning. [...] My father and I remained six days and five nights on the station concourse amongst thousands of other peasants waiting interminably, either to buy a train ticket when the station managers decided to sell them, or to find a job somewhere in the city. For here, on the Shanghai station concourse, was the real job market where bosses and foremen of all kinds came to hire labour."[18]

The official short-term objective is to make Shanghai one of the leading cities in Asia. As China's financial capital, Shanghai is a locus of every challenge. Its "urban alchemy" generates a magical atmosphere between the Shanghai of Pudong, a 21st-century Manhattan, and the narrow, winding alleyways of the old town, here called *lilong*, which are also disappearing but still retain their mystery, which the Shanghai writer Wang Anyi describes so beautifully: "The alleys of Shanghai are sensual, intimate like the touch of skin; both cool and warm to the touch, they keep their feelings secret. The greasy windows of the kitchens, at the backs of the houses, allow the maids to gossip, one inside, the other outside; the rear doors provide passage for young ladies going to school, satchel in hand, or for amorous appointments; the great front doors are only opened for important events. (...) The terraces and balconies are a safe place for confidences; at night, here and there, knocks can be heard on the doors. It is best to choose a place that overlooks

18——Stéphane Fière, *La Promesse de Shanghai*, Bleu de Chine, 2006.

the city to see it from the right perspective: the drying linen, hung on intersecting bamboo poles, reveals the intimacy of beings, as do the balsams, houseleeks, spring onions and green garlic in their pots; the empty pigeon cages on the roofs are like waiting hearts; the broken and disordered tiles are all symbols of hearts and bodies. Like ravines, the rear depths of the alleys are sometimes concreted, sometimes paved with tiles."[19]

A living architecture museum with its attractive mix of art deco buildings on the left bank and futuristic tower blocks on the right, Shanghai will be ready to host the 2010 universal exhibition, all with a focus on sustainable development, exemplified in Jacques Ferrier's plan to design the French hall around the concept of "evoking nature in the city .

Canton and the pearl river delta 广洲

Canton is situated on the Pearl River estuary in China s most southerly province. Its period of most striking success was under the Tang dynasty, in the 8th century, when the port was declared open to foreigners. This was the time of China s opening to the South Seas. A large community of foreign merchants lived there and the Muslim community quickly built mosques. The most ancient dates back to 627: In the evening, we stopped in another village and so on, until we arrived at Sîn Kalân, also called Sîn as-Sîn [now Canton]. In this city, they make porcelain as they do in Zaytûn. It is here that the river Âb al-Hâya emerges, a place that is called the confluence of the Two-Mothers. Sîn as-Sîn is a big city with very beautiful

19—Wang Anyi, "Ruelles", in *Shanghai, fantômes sans concession*, Autrement, 2004.

markets, including the porcelain market, which is one of the largest. It is from this city that porcelain is exported to the whole of China, India and the Yemen. At Sîn as-Sîn, there is a great temple with nine gates [the 10th century Temple of the Six Banians], in each of which is a roofed gallery and benches where those who live in the temple sit. (...) It is a king who erected this temple, establishing its dependent villages and orchards as a pious foundation for the benefit of the temple, where can be seen the King s portrait, which the Chinese come to worship. In one part of the city is situated the Muslim district, where stands the mosque built in the 7th century by an uncle of the Prophet, Abû Wanku, the *zâwiya* and the market. The Muslims have their cadi and their sheik. Indeed, in every Chinese city, the Muslims have their sheik who settles disputes between them and their cadi who renders judgement between them. [20]

Under the Ming dynasty, Canton experienced a time of prosperity and was the meeting point between China and the West. This was the period when merchants and missionaries arrived. It became a major urban centre, overflowing into suburbs south of the walled city. This expansion continued under the Qing. At the age of 19, Count Ludovic de Beauvoir made a world tour between 1865 and 1867, coming, amongst other places, to Canton, which he describes as follows: Canton extends on both banks of its wide river, and consists of two cities, the floating city and the terrestrial city. We navigate left and right amid thousands of barges where whole families live. A roof of bamboo and dry leaves protects each of these house-boats: at the back, the altar to the ancestors is lit by small perfumed torches. (...) We climb the ladders that lead to the top of the famous five-storey pagoda, which is at the centre of a group of twelve forts, and stands at the north end above the whole city. From its summit, we can clearly see the rounded triangle formed by the old land city, with its walls more than ten kilometres long, its sixteen bizarre bastion gates, its pagodas, its mosques and its *yamouns*. Here, on our left, the breach where the allies mounted their assault in 1857; alongside, in the shade of some poplar trees, at the very foot of the wall, is the cemetery of our brave dead. [21]

Effervescent capital of Guangdong province, China's third ranked economic metropolis, Canton has administrative control of the Pearl River Delta. Thierry Sanjuan, a specialist on geopolitical and urban issues in China, explains its development as follows: "The Pearl River Delta is in fact made up of three nested deltas, those of the Xijiang, Beijiang and Dongjiang rivers. In the 1980s, this region experienced exceptional rates of economic growth. Until the mid-1990s, most of the development of the delta took place in the central rural areas.

20—— Ibn Battûta, *Voyages et Périples, Présent à ceux qui aiment à réfléchir sur les curiosités des villes et les merveilles des voyages*, Gallimard, 1995.
21——Ludovic de Beauvoir, taken from *Voyage autour du monde : Java, Siam, Canton*, Kailash, 1992. Description dated February 15, 1867.

The industries here made great use of migrant populations from the provincial outskirts or the interior of the country. The delta is now covered by a dense network of roads and motorways, making the innumerable ferries a thing of the past. However, this regional development has had its downside. The destruction of the landscape has been exacerbated by pollution, which a problematic joint regional development has failed to resolve. The rural landscape of the Pearl River Delta of the 1970s has thus given way to a dense fabric of towns and small cities, with ever expanding industrial and residential zones. Ambitious real estate and urban development projects have transformed many rural suburbs into new urban districts. Cities have been created (Shenzhen, Zhuhai, Nansha) and multiple tourist operations vaunt the tropical conditions." [22]

Mian Mian, a caustic young writer born in Shanghai, gives another view of Canton. In her novel *Candy*, a mix of black romanticism and social realism, she depicts the misadventures of her 20-year-old heroine, whose love plunges her into a world of sex and drugs: I had just left Shanghai for that little southern city, it was 1989. I can t even remember why I noticed that tall boy swaying in his corner. He asked me what I was doing in the city. I answered, like everyone, people came here to make money, and that was all that was left for me to do, since I didn t have any qualifications and couldn't find work in Shanghai. [...] I rented a dilapidated little apartment. My landlord was like all the guys around there, all the time giving me the eye, a rough leer. One day he even asked me if I was a whore. All the girls who came from the interior were whores. I said no, not me, I come from Shanghai. Ah, they're smart, the Shanghai girls, here they all find married men to keep them, they're even worse than the whores. Eventually, I found myself a job in a nightclub where I sang love songs in Cantonese wearing a really slutty evening dress: miniskirt, cleavage and stilettos. And one fine evening, this tall young guy I'll never understand anything about just materialised in front of my door. Hand in hand, we went for a walk, hand in hand like a couple of wounded friends. It was full of people who had made it in the city, and others who were there to try their luck, everyone was there for the money, it was a weird place, with its heavy and humid climate, its streets full of down-and-outs and whores, there were whores everywhere, all dressed in black. We ended up in the bar where we first met."[23]

22—— Thierry Sanjuan, in *Dictionnaire de la Chine contemporaine*, Armand Colin, 2006.
23—— Mian Mian, *Les Bonbons chinois*, French translation by S. Gentil, L Olivier, 2001.

Shenzhen, the capitalist 深圳

In the 1980's, just before Deng Xiaoping created the special economic areas of Shenzhen, Shantou, Zhuhai and Xiamen, created by Deng Xiaoping, the region didn't offer any interest to tourists nor to foreign investors. In fact, it is hard to find an old description of this new Eldorado, which until the 1980s was nothing more than: "Courtyard houses shared by six or eight families, pigs wandering along earth tracks, rice fields either side of the Canton-Hong Kong railway line: that was what could be seen in the village of Shenzhen in 1984. Now an entry point to the People's Republic of China, on the motorway linking Hong Kong to Canton, the city which has become the biggest of China's five special economic areas has nothing much to interest tourists. You can shop there, as prices are significantly lower than in Hong Kong." [24]

It was in 1979 that Deng Xiaoping began to turn this enclave concept into an experimental laboratory of capitalism: "In fact the special economic areas were primarily laboratories of reform kept within circumscribed zones along the southern coast, in provinces with a tradition of openness to foreign influence and sufficiently peripheral not to threaten the country itself. As experimental zones, the special economic areas naturally came to act as communication airlocks between China and the world economy. That is why many Hong Kongers now live in Shenzhen and commute to the Hong Kong special administrative region." [25]

Today, in this new golden triangle of liberalism, Shenzhen "is the leading and most concentrated of the special economic areas, the ultimate artificial city. It is a new, logical city, efficient and beautiful in its singularity. Urban planning is the main reason for its artificiality."

Shenzhen was planned for the very clear purpose of providing a production base near Hong Kong and therefore near the other industrialised countries of South-East Asia. It was devised with a remarkable practical sense of connections, expansion, time and economy. [...]

Within this set framework, Shenzhen has tried out various approaches to urban policy, property rights and financial systems. These experiments have given rise to a mosaic of lifestyles, of uses of space and social standings, and new intermediate relations have emerged from the interaction between shifting strata. This explains the irresistible development, in Shenzhen, of an optimistic, open and realistic mindset. [26]

24——*Chine de Pékin à Hong Kong*, Guides Bleus, Hachette mars 2007.

25——Thierry Sanjuan, in Dictionnaire de la Chine contemporaine, Armand Colin, 2006.

26——Ma Qingyun, Le Paradigme du delta dans l'urbanisme chinois , in *Alors, la Chine ?* Catalogue of the exhibition staged at the Centre Pompidou, October 2003.

He Jiahong, currently Professor of Criminals Law at the University of the People in Beijing, situates the plot of his thriller between Hong Kong and Shenzhen. The idea of making the province of Guangdong the location for his story came to him during a stay in Hong Kong as a guest of the law faculty. He provides a precise and lucid description of Shenzhen in the novel: "Leaving the airport, Hong Jun took a taxi to the Shengguo Hotel on Shengbei Avenue. After unpacking, he went down into the street. Although it was already early autumn, the southern sun was so hot that it burned. He followed the avenue westwards, walking in the shade of the trees. It was undoubtedly the pleasantest spot in Shengguo. Large, newly constructed buildings were laid out in zigzags, as tightly interlocked as the teeth of a comb or neatly spread. The avenue, very wide and very clean, and the palm trees along its edges, very elegant despite their small size, helped to fill the visitor with a magic of Southern landscapes. [...] As it was still very early, he walked southwards as far as Shengnan Avenue. It was neither as wide nor as beautiful as Shengbei, but the many shops along it and its bustling traffic justified its reputation as the city's liveliest shopping neighbourhood. Walking eastwards through the hubbub and crowds, Hong Jun soon arrived at the avenue's intersection with Shenzhong Road, the city's main north-south axis. This crossroads had naturally become the focal point of the city. The future Shengguo Square, which was under construction, will occupy the northeastern corner. According to the town plan, the square would consist of a set of buildings, the tallest in the city, containing a shopping mall, several restaurants, a leisure centre and offices. The demolition of the old neighbourhoods was almost complete. Hong Jun, standing to the west of the crossroads behind the fence, contemplated the remains of the past with a pang of sadness. How could the role of money in the modernisation of the cities be denied? It is money that knocks down the old houses and brings skyscrapers out of the ground; it is money that attracts investors and encourages the authorities to grant advantageous conditions".

Destruction! Watchword and slogan of third millennium China! Does one have to destroy to build better... The character 拆—chai—, which means demolition, appears everywhere. In this immense process of renewal, China's cities are being replaced by modern metropolises, urban agglomerations of the most contemporary kind. But at what cost? A cost to millions of people displaced all over China in just a few years. It is a high price to pay for the lightning-fast transformation of these ever-growing megacities. Once the wind of madness blowing across China has passed, what will remain of its heritage and of the architectural diversity that made this vast empire the splendour and glory of an incomparable civilisation? Is the urban quake that is shaking China and causing the spectacular metamorphosis and evolution of its cities, a necessary stage in the process of responding to new needs brought about by urban mixity, the rural exodus and the ensuing fragmentation of ancient frameworks. In any case, as an incredible reflection of this economic vitality, the grandiose character of its urban development offers China the luxury of entering the era of globalisation on the ground floor.

北京

Beijing

11

The Capital

Each of us has our own image of the world's most mysterious capital, of its most blinding city—blinding because always seen as the most dazzling, notwithstanding the grey walls of the vanished *hutong*—as today in the crushing brightness of the 2008 Olympic Games.

Beijing was always confusing to those who knew it when its rows of narrow streets nestled in the shadows of the Forbidden City, because every face, smiling or stern, carefully washed or steeped in grime, seemed to bear the wrinkles of 6000 years of civilisation. Beijing today continues to confuse: apart from its illustrious monuments, scarcely a brick has remained in place. The long legacy of the Yuan dynasty, founded by the Mongols and unchanging for almost seven centuries, has given way to the vertigo of a city whose characteristic imperiousness seems founded in the unceasing accumulation of urban freeways, and a succession of rarely identifiable constructions.

It is not a city without qualities, since its inhabitants are still those Pekinese whose imperishable portrait was painted by the historian Lao She. But it is now a city without identifying features, unless you count the new monuments to power, to sport, to finance and the media, which are almost invisible in this horizonless city, like the new lighthouses of the modern world.

More than ever, indeed, Beijing is the head of an empire that used to be called China, but whose true dimensions are now those defined by the country's considerable monetary reserves. The decisions that govern the world now come as much from Zhongnanhai, the capital's power centre, as from Washington or New-York. However, these decisions dramatically influence the future at a time when major ecological, economic and social imbalances are beginning to emerge, together with new tensions at the country's borders.

We were used to match our pace to that of the walkers of New York, be they rought cowboys or wealthy poets. Now we will need to try to understand whether or not the Beijing model, with its swirls of sand and smoke, its uneasy authority, its uncontrolled computerisation, can give way. Is today's China able to take up the baton, offer an ideal, and allow the return of a wisdom once deemed eternal.

If the city and architecture could speak, it is undoubtedly they that would show us the way.

Bell Tower, Beijing. © OACC

To the sources of the capital of the North

Chiu Che Bing

Rites and transformations for the capital under heaven

The city of Beijing (北京) has existed as a dynastic capital since 1260, the year when Kubilaï Khan[1] decided to build on the lands of Yan[2] a new citadel (大都) on the site of Zhongdu (中都, the former capital of the Jin (金). He dispatched his adviser Liu Bingzhong[3] to inspect the site and design the city plan. The latter chose to build the new citadel on a site with an abundant water system and a lake fed by the Gaoliang (高梁河), a river linked with the springs and waterways to the north of the city. The design was centred on today's Hibiscus Island, Qionghua dao (琼华岛), and includes the river transport terminus on the Grand Canal. The work was done in two successive phases. The first part covered the infrastructures, city walls and hydraulic projects,[4] and the major palace, administrative and cultural complexes, and lasted from 1267 to 1285. The second phase of operations, mainly covering the construction of the residential district, continued from 1285 to 1295. At this time, the city may be considered complete and in its final morphological form.

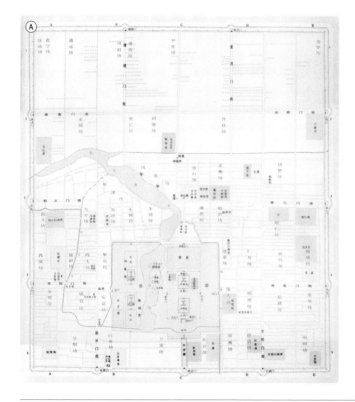

A——Dadu from Yuan dynasty. Source: *Beijing lishi dituji*

1——Kubilai Khan (忽必烈 1215-1294, r. 1260-1294), grandson of Gengis Khan, who succeeded his brother Mongke on the throne of the great khan.
2——燕 Monosyllabic name that traditionally refers to the Beijing region.
3——Liu Bingzhong (刘秉忠1216-1274), a man of great learning and a specialist of the divinatory arts, much trusted by Kubilai for whom he became an influential adviser. The *History of the Yuan* ("元史") attributes to him the idea of changing the dynastic name of the Mongol empire, Menggu (蒙古), to Yuan (元), a term taken from the *Yijing*. When Liu Bingzhong left to inspect the site of the future capital, he had already designed the plan of Shangdu (上都 Kaiping开平), the first capital of the Yuan Dynasty.
4——Hydraulic projects were always a major concern of the Yuan. Guo Shoujin (郭守敬 1231-1316), a hydraulic engineer, mathematician and astronomer, pupil of Liu Bingzhong and Minister of the Water Management Department, played an important role in the development of the Dadu system.

This city, built and designed solely under the experienced management of Liu Bingzhong,[5] may be seen as a complete expression of 2000 years of urban planning experience. The design, based on the main philosophical and cultural currents of ancient China, reflects the hierarchical order of Confucian practices and the traditional Chinese cosmological beliefs.

The description of the ideal royal city is contained in a document included in the *Zhouli* which replaces a lost text, known by the title *Kaogongji*, "考工记, Essay on Crafts". The passage describing the "construction of a royal capital by craftsmen" ("*jiangren yingguo*", 匠人营国), sets out the following principles: the city is square in shape, each side measures nine *li* and has three gates; across it run nine roads oriented south-north and nine roads oriented east-west, each wide enough for nine carts to pass; the Temple of the Ancestors is situated in the east, and the barrow of the spirits of the soil and of the earth to the west, to the south the palace of audiences and to the north the market, palace and market each occupying an area of one hundred paces square.[6]

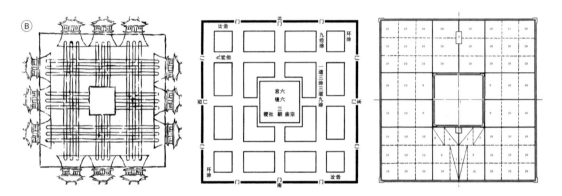

The city of Dadu was surrounded by three successive concentric walls: the *gongcheng* (宫城), the palace city in the centre, surrounded by the *huangcheng* (皇城), the imperial city, and finally the *dacheng* (大城), the greater city.

To calculate the dimensions of the city and the position of the ramparts, Professor Hou Renzhi, a geographer and academic at the University of Beijing has suggested that "the width of the Jishui tan lake from east to west was used as a measure equalling half the width of the city, and to establish the position of the two eastern and western walls of the city enclosures".

B——Diagram illustrating the "royal capital" according to *Kaogongji*.
Nie Chongyi, *Sanli tu*. Dai Zhen, *Kaogongji tu*. He Yeju, *Kaogongji yingguo zhidu yanjiu*.

5——The historical sources mention the assistance of the minister Duan Zhen, of the soldiers Zhang Ru and his son Zhang Honglüe, of the building foreman Yang Qiong, of Ikhtiyar-al-Din, a "man with eyes of colour" (a Muslim), the main supervisor at the Palace Office, of the Nepalese sculptor Anige. Other names appear, whose role we are ignorant of, such as the Mongol Yelu Buhua, or else the mention of a nationality, without further details: a *nüzhen* (Jurchen). After Liu Bingzhong, the design and management of the work were assigned to Yu Ji (1272-1348), also an aficionado of the *Yijing*.
6——This document, dating from the end of the so-called period of Springs and Autumns (770-476 BCE), has been much studied and commented, and a work from the Song period, the *Sanlitu* ("三礼图") , provides an illustration of this "ideal city".

In reality, geophysical constraints imposed some readjustments. The distance that separates the east wall from the geometrical centre is shorter than the distance from the west wall to the centre. This difference is explained by the presence at the time of a marshy area which made it necessary to move the outline of the east wall inwards. Similarly, the position of the south wall had to allow for the position of the north wall of the ramparts and moats of Zhongdu, and of the south wall of the existing *huangcheng* ramparts. The south wall of *dacheng* had to be built in this strip of land. Within these ramparts, the city is rectangular, almost square in shape.[7]

The wall was made of tamped earth, reinforced with posts and crossbeams, and as protection from the rain the sides were covered with layers of reeds, which gave the city the nickname *suocheng* (蓑城), the "city in a straw overcoat". There was a plan to cover the wall with stone and brick facing, but political will was lacking to implement it.

According to Beijing's oral tradition, Liu Bingzhong, the imperial Great Protector, based the plan of the city on the anatomy of a divine being, guided by the mystical figure of Nezha (哪吒).[8] The work *Nongtian yuhua*[9] reports that the city's eleven gates, a somewhat unusual number for a capital, "show the three heads, the six arms and the two feet" of the infant deity. If the angry figure of Nezha is destined to overthrow enemies of the faith, the city of Beijing is more interested in his ability to tame dragons, troublemakers responsible for floods and calamities of all kinds. And according to local tradition, there have always been widespread rumours of malignant dragons on Yan land.

But it is more likely that Liu Bingzhong drew inspiration once again from the *Yijing* in deciding the number of gates in the city. The canonical text specifies that "there are five numbers of Heaven, there are five numbers of earth". The numbers 1, 3, 5, 7 and 9 are *yang* numbers and refer to heaven, whereas 2, 4, 6, 8 and 10 are *yin* and refer to earth. The centre of these two series of numbers is 5 and 6, the sum of which gives the number 11, adopted by Liu Bingzhong to achieve balance between yin and yang. ©

The creation of three gates on the south wall and only two gates on the north wall reflects the correspondence between south for heaven, with odd numbers, and north for the earth, with even numbers. The positioning of the trigram *kan* (坎) at exact north, following the order established by the Zhou Dynasty's king of letters, undoubtedly explains the absence of the gate, since according to the *Yijing* this

---

7—6,730 m (E-W) x 7,600 m (S-N), making a surface area of almost 50 square kilometres.
8—Nezha is the phonetic transcription of Nata, the Sanskrit name of a character from basic Buddhist texts. The novel *The Investiture of the Gods* (封神榜) made him one of the great popular heroes. Whilst still a child, he overthrows the third prince of the Dragon King of the Eastern Seas and makes a lasso out of one of his tendons.
9—The *Talks from the Farm* ("农田余话") is signed by Changgu Zhenyi (长谷真逸), the true Hermit of the Long Valley, the pseudonym of an unknown author who lived at the end of the Yuan and beginning of the Ming dynasties. Chen Hok-lam (1996), p. 71.

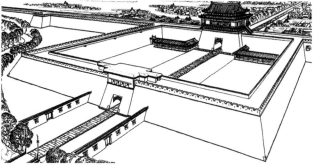

position represents concealment and ambush. It is still the custom in popular tradition to protect oneself from the north, a cardinal point always considered malign, by the erection of a blank wall.

An analysis of the city's urban structure reveals a highly regular grid. This network of straight lines is reinforced by the contrast with the sinuous curves of the Jishui tan lakes. The city is crisscrossed with wide roads ending at the city walls.

In his work *Xijing zhi*[10], Xiong Mengxiang (熊梦祥) describes the planning of Dadu's urban network:

"The roads are ordered as follows: those with a south-north orientation are called *jing* (经), those running east-west *wei* (纬). The width of the main roads is set at 24 *bu*[11] (步), that of the secondary roads at 12 *bu*. There were 384 *huoxiang* (火巷), 29 *longtong* (衖通)."

The Dadu network is therefore composed of four categories of regulated streets: the main road, the secondary road, the *huoxiang* and the *longtong*. The width of the first two is clearly specified, respectively measuring 24 and 12 *bu*, corresponding to 36.96 and 18.48 m. Xiong Mengxiang did not provide the width of the *huoxiang* and the *longtong*, but studies have suggested that they must be 6 and 3 paces, corresponding to 9.24 and 4.62 m.[12]

The second category roads, which Xiong Mengxiang refers to as *longtong*, are known today as *hutong* (胡同). This term *hutong*, according to the linguist Zhang Qingchang, is likely to be a phonetic transcription of the mongol *huddug*, or *hottog*, which refers to the notion of a watering point, or a settlement with a well.

C——Heyi men Gate.
The Yuan gate was walled up inside the Xizhi men gate when Beijing's city wall was rebuilt at the beginning of the Ming dynasty. Demolition work on this section of the ramparts in May 1969 uncovered the remains of Heyi men. Reconstruction of the gate. Source: Fu, Xinian, *Fu Xinian jianzhu shi lunwen ji*, Beijing, Wenwu chubanshe, 1998, p. 381. © Chiu Che Bing

10——The book, written at the end of the Yuan Dynasty, is lost. However, passages have been collected, in particular in the great Ming Encyclopaedia, the *Yongle dadian* (永乐大典), and the monograph compiled in the reign of the Emperor Qianlong, the *Rixia jiuwen kao* (日下旧闻考).

11——The *bu*, "pace", under the Yuan Dynasty, was equivalent to 1.54 m

12——In the Song era, in the capital Biangliang (today Kaifeng), the streets and alleys were called *huoxiang*, which means "fire-[break] tracks". By phonetic distortion, *longtong* would become *hutong*. *Xijing zhi jiyi* (*Collection of fragments from the Monograph of Xijing*, 析津志辑佚), Beijing, Guji chubanshe, 1983, p. 4.

Between the main roads that led to the gates of the two east and west enclosure walls are twenty-two parallel *hutong*, each 50 paces apart (77 m). The depth available for building, minus the width of a *hutong*, is 44 paces (67.76 m). An imperial edict of the 22nd year of the Zhiyuan era (1285) announces the mode of occupation:

"Let it be known to those who dwelt in the old city and plan to move to the capital city: people in possession of wealth or holding a position of functionary have priority. The regulations establish a plot with an area of 8 *mu* as a single unit."

A plot 44 paces square is equivalent to 8 *mu* (亩).[13] Surveys carried out at Dongsibei [14] (东四北) confirm these figures: the distance separating the east and west ends of the *hutong* is approximately 700 m, which corresponds to an estate of ten basic plots.Ⓓ

The excavations carried out on the Houying fang (后英房) site, near today's Xin jiekou (新街口), to the north of the Jishui tan (积水潭) lake, confirm this. The dwelling is approximately 70 metres wide, with a large main courtyard and a deep building with a south-north orientation. Ⓔ

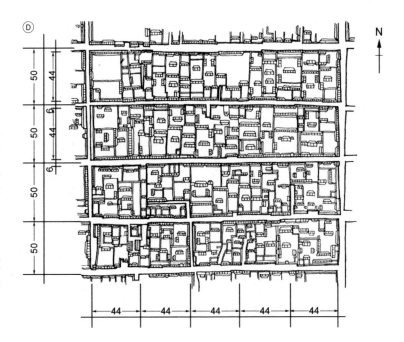

D—The plot divisions inherited from the urban development carried out under the Yuan dynasty are still perfectly visible on the plan of the city of Beijing drawn in 1750, under emperor Qianlong of the Qing dynasty. © Chiu Che Bing

13—Suggestion made by Wang Pin in *Beijing weiguan dili biji*, p. 65-67. The *hutong* in Dongsi are between 7 and 9 m wide, possibly corresponding to the 6 *bu* of the *huoxiang* under the Yuan, and the *hutong* in Xisi measure between 4 and 5 m, possibly corresponding to the 3 bu of the *longtong*. The average width of the only *hutong* remaining from Dadu, the Zhuanta hutong, Brick Pagoda Alley, is 4 m. Other hypotheses suggest widths of 9 and 6 bu, respectively corresponding to 13.86 and 9.24 m.

14—Unit of area corresponding to 1/15th of a hectare.

The wall, a ubiquitous feature, is the partition that organises and orders space, playing an essential role in defining specific spaces. It encloses the basic cell of Chinese society, the family, in its *sihe yuan* (四合院), in the same way as it protects the emperor's palace in the imperial city. The organisation of the social hierarchy is thus reflected in the perfect arrangement of the capital, and the city is divided

up like a great chequerboard of juxtaposed districts or squares, *fang*[15] (坊), overlapping and combining together, from the *sihe yuan* around their courtyards to the plot divisions precisely defined in the urban fabric.

Still according to Xiong Mengxiang, Liu Bingzhong set the number of districts by reference to the text of the great Commentary to the *Yijing*, which specifies that the number of "the great Transformation" is fifty, and the name given to many *fang* in the capital has its source in the *Book of Changes*.[16]

The *fang* delineated in this way are served by streets or alleyways, *hutong*, generally running from east to west. There are two categories of *fang*, those determined by the intersection of main roads and alleyways, and those situated on either side of a main road.

The depth of the first category of *fang* is determined by two parallel alleyways with a centre-to-centre distance of 50 paces, making a depth of 44 paces. This measurement of 44 places sets a limit on the depth of the houses. It sets the dimensions of dwellings as a three-courtyard type *sihe yuan*.

E——Reconstruction of residential complexes from the Yuan era at Houying fang. Source: Fu, Xinian, *Fu Xinian jianzhu shi lunwen ji*, Beijing, Wenwu chubanshe, 1998, p. 383.

15——This sector "to the north of the four [porticos] of the East" corresponds, under the Yuan, to the Juxian fang, the district of the Dwellings of the Eminent. The regularity of the original Yuan plot divisions is still very visible here.
16   System of administrative control which consists in placing walls around the residential districts bordered by roads. The Tang capital Changan had 110 *fang*, the biggest of which measure 1100 x 600 m. But already by the ninth century, the system had relaxed, the strict separation between market and residential district was disappearing, and stalls and inns were set up within the *fang*, with shops located along the roads. By the middle of the Northern Song era, in the capital Kaifeng, the wall enclosing the *fang* had disappeared but the name, *fang* "district", remained. At the end of the Northern Song era, Kaifeng had 121 districts, the city of Pingjiang (today's Suzhou) 65, and the the Beijing of the Ming and Qing dynasties, 36 districts.

When a larger dwelling was planned, for princes, high functionaries or rich merchants, it could only be done by joining adjacent plots, to the east or west, by attaching a second or third series of courtyards to the main axis, that of the first *sihe yuan*. This basic unit is also used in setting the dimensions of big building complexes such as palaces, government institutions, ministries, administrative departments and courts, and depending on the size of the complex, the footprint could extend up to five *hutong* depths, and over the width of four plots.

The depth of the *fang* situated on either side of the main roads was determined by the main road and the first parallel alley serving it, a distance of 70 paces (107.8 m). Subtracting half the width of the main road and of the alley, 12 paces and 3 paces, gives a depth of 55 paces (84.7 m.). This increased depth made it possible to build stores for commercial activities along the main roads.

After the capture of Dadu by General Xu Da (大都) in 1368, the northern wall of the city was moved further southward to improve the city's defences. However, the founding emperor of the Ming dynasty chose to found his capital in Nanking, and Dadu lost its status and was renamed Beiping (北平), Peace of the North. Zhu Di (朱棣), the fourth son of the emperor, was given fiefdom of this land and the title of King of Yan (燕王). He managed to seize the throne of China in 1402 and this era took the name reign of Yongle (永乐). The following year, Beiping was renamed Beijing, capital of the North. In 4006, the emperor decided to make his former fiefdom the new capital of the empire. After long and meticulous gestation, work began in 1417 and after the completion of the palace in 1420, the emperor moved to Beijing. ⒡

In this 18th year of the Yongle era, the city's physiognomy was once again similar to that of Dadu, with its three concentric enclosures, with the Forbidden Purple City in the centre, the *Zijin cheng* (紫禁城), the emperor's residence, surrounded by the imperial city, *huangcheng*, itself surrounded by the capital city, *ducheng* (都城).

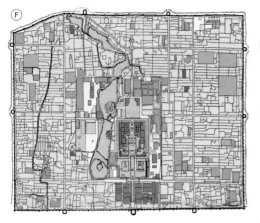

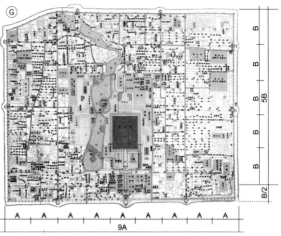

The dimensions of the Imperial Palace were based on those of the capital city. Placed along the city's south-north axis of symmetry, the palace is situated in the centre and covers a width representing one ninth of the distance separating the two east and west walls. In the south-north direction, it is slightly offset southwards, in a ratio of 1:3, and occupies a fifth of the length. These two figures nine and five, and more specifically the pair nine-five, designate the emperor and refer to the classical texts and particularly the *Yijing*.[17] The 9, an eminently *yang* number, is the symbol of Heaven itself. The *Luoshu*[18] places the 9 at the top and the 5 occupies the position of the centre. The diagram thus refers to the pair 9-5 with the Central Hall around which Time turns, and the four cardinal halls [19] symbolising the four seasons. Ⓖ

In 1419, the line of the southern wall of the city was moved southwards, which altered the arrangement of the space leading to the palace and its surroundings. This extension was probably intended to restore the concept of the Great Transformation introduced by Liu Bingzhong through the fifty districts of Dadu. However, the new concept refers to the practical use of this number, i.e. 49.[20] The surface area ratio between the palace and the capital city thus became 1:50. In this way, the set-aside part, the palace, allows the whole, the 49 acting parts, to undergo transformation and evolve in accordance with the fundamental principle of the *Yijing*.

In 1553, work began on a new enclosure which was to surround Yongle's *ducheng* and form a fourth enclosure. The state of the imperial treasury made it necessary to reduce its size, so that only the southern part of the city was included within the new wall. At the end of the operations, the outer line of the walls defined the final morphology of the city.Ⓗ The two parts, the old "inner city" and the new "outer city" combine to form a square set into a rectangle, a geometrical form suggesting the

---

17—The number fifty refers to the 50 yarrow stems required for the process of consulting an oracle. *Yijing*, Paris, Médicis, 1973, ch. IX "De l'oracle", p. 348.

18—In the *qian* hexagram, the Creator, number 9, the fifth place corresponds to the position of the "Dragon flying in the sky", and the commentary to the next: "The king occupies position 9-5, that of wealth and eminent rank". *Op.cit.*, pp. 25, 357 et 427.

19—According to tradition, the *Book of [the river] Luo* 洛书, a diagram formed by the first nine numbers arranged in a magic square appeared to the mythical Emperor Da Yu, Yu the Great, carried on the back of a tortoise emerging from the water.

20—The numbers of Heaven, 1, 3, 5, 7, 9 are arranged with the 5 at the centre of the magic square, and 1, 3, 7, 9, at the four cardinal points. Marcel Granet, *La Pensée chinoise*, Paris, Albin Michel, 1968, pp. 145-174.

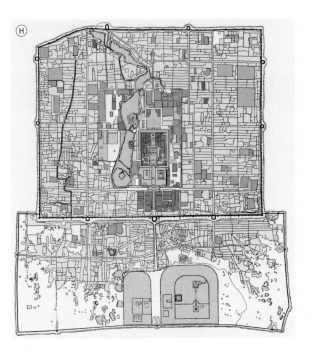

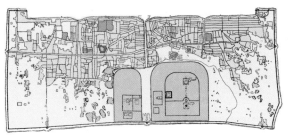

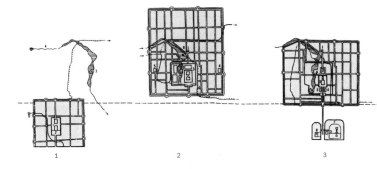

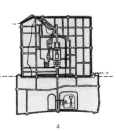

F——The city of Beijing at the beginning of the Ming dynasty. From *Beijing lishi dituji*© Chiu Che Bing
G——The nine : five ratio between the Forbidden City and the city of Beijing. From *Beijing lishi dituji*© Chiu Che Bing
H——The *waicheng*, the Outer City, after the addition of the surrounding wall under the reign of Emperor Jiajing.
The city of Beijing, with its two cities, *neicheng* and *waicheng*, in its final layout. The evolution of the capital cities through history:

    1 Zhongdu, capital of the Jin
    2 Dadu, capital of the Ming
    3 Beijing, at the beginning of the Ming dynasty
    4 Beijing, in the middle of the Ming dynasty and under the Qing. From *Beijing lishi dituji* © Chiu Che Bing

Chinese characters ao (凹) and tu (凸), "concave" and "convex", which resemble the assembly of a mortice and tenon joint in a timber construction frame. In accordance with its function as an imperial dwelling defined as a *yang* structure by its convex shape, the palace is embedded in the site, its concave shaped protective receptacle, which is *yin*. The stability of the city's "structural" form and of its embeddedness in the site combine, expressing the dynasty's solidity for the coming centuries. In addition, the city's external outline seems to reflect the recommendations of *fengshui* (风水): the convex part to the south corresponds to the position *qian* (乾), heaven, and depicts the roundness of the celestial vault; the oblique part in the north-west corner corresponds to the position *gen* (艮), the mountain, and depicts withdrawal on contact with it; the protuberance at the southeast corner corresponds to the position *dui* (兑), the marsh, and depicts forward movement to fill the space. ⓘ

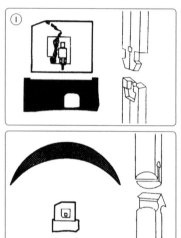

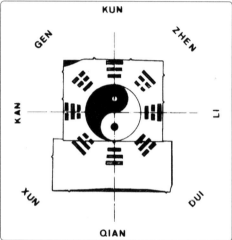

The arrival of the Manchu dynasty (Qing) on the Beijing throne did not disrupt the urban structure of the capital. The new rulers drove the Han Chinese [21] out of the Inner City, and divided the city within the walls into eight sectors under the control of banners.[22] The Inner City became "Tartar" whereas the Outer city, where the Chinese were relegated, became "Chinese". When the empire fell in 1911, Beijing retained the physiognomy of the 16th-century city, and a significant part of its structure was a legacy of the city laid out in the Yuan era. ⓙ

I—Assembly of the *neicheng* on the *waicheng*, like a mortice and tenon joint in a timber frame. The positioning of the capital within its site. A reading of the city of Beijing from figures in the *bagua*, the *eight trigrams*.

21—"The number of the Great Transformation is fifty, its use is forty-nine." *Op.cit.*, p. 348, slightly different translation.
22—At the beginning of the Manchu Qing dynasty, under the reign of the Emperor Shunzi, the outer city contained 37,000 households.

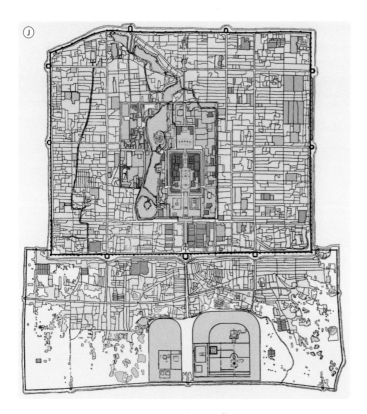

Professor Liang Sicheng[23] (梁思成) described the city of Beijing as *an unrivalled masterpiece of urban planning*.[24] Indeed, whilst the imperial capital contained within its walls an impressive number of historic monuments and remarkable cultural sites, the city itself, as a whole, may be seen as a work of art of exceptional and inestimable quality. It was with the aim of protecting the ancient capital that, in 1950, in collaboration with Chen Zhanxiang[25] (陈占祥), he developed the idea of building a new administrative city to the west of historic Beijing. This project, now known as the *Liang-Chen Proposal* (梁陈方案), was published under the title of the *Proposal on the Location of the Central People's Government Administrative Center*.

Given the uncontrolled urban development of recent decades and the destruction of the capital's building heritage in the last half-century,[26] it can only be regretted that Liang Sicheng's efforts to save Beijing's historic heritage came up against an inflexible commitment to indiscriminate modernisation.

J——Reconstruction plan for the city of Beijing based on the plan drawn in 1750, under the Qing emperor Qianlong. From *Beijing lishi dituji* © Chiu Che Bing.

23——A military and administrative system introduced by Nurhachi organise the Manchus.
24——Architect (1901-1972), trained in the Architecture Department of the University of Pennsylvania, a pupil of Paul Cret. On his return to China, he joined the Society for Research on Chinese Architecture and dedicated himself to the study of traditional Chinese architecture. He was one of the most ardent defenders of heritage protection in Beijing.
25——Title of an article published in April 1951 in Xin guancha (新观察), vol II, n. 7-8.
26——Urban planner (1916-2001), trained at the University of Liverpool, pupil of Sir Patrick Abercrombie (1879-1957). On his return to China, he was appointed Head of the Projects Department in the capital's Urban Planning Committee, and professor at the School of Architecture of Tsinghua University, specialising in the teaching of urban planning.

Today, uninterrupted streams of vehicles have replaced the imposing wall of the ancient centres, gigantic expressways have gutted the city and buried the *hutong*, and glittering buildings, covered with the external symbols of modernity, have wiped the *sihe yuan* off the map and out of mind...

The measures taken by Beijing city council in 2000 to list twenty-five sectors of old Beijing as "historical and cultural protection zones", and the recent declarations by official figures, Mr. Sun Jiazheng, Minister of Culture, in May 2006, and recently in June 2007, Mr. Qiu Baoxing, Vice-Minister of Construction, publicly regretting the destruction of the city's architectural and urban heritage, raise hopes of a genuine new awareness of the urgent need to protect the heritage of the ancient imperial capital. ⑪

However, it is to be feared that it is already too late for this *unrivalled masterpiece of urban planning* as a global structure.

Bibliography

Alexander, Andre-de Azevedo, Pimpim, & al., *Beijing Hutong Conservation Study*, Beijing, Guangbo xueyuan chubanshe, 2004.
Arlington, L.C.-Lewisohn, W., *In Search of Old Peking*, Peking, Henri Vetch, 1935.
Chen, Gaohua, Yuan Dadu (*Dadu des Yuan*), Beijing, Beijing chubanshe, 1982.
Chen Hok-lam, Liu Bowen yu Nezha cheng (*Liu Bowen et la cité de Nezha*), Taibei, Dadong tushu, 1996.
Chiu, Che Bing, "Pékin, espace sous influences", *Asies II-Aménager l'espace*, Paris, Presses de l'université de Paris-Sorbonne, 1993.
Fu, Xinian, Guanyu Mingdai gongdian tanmiao deng da jianzhuqun zhongti guihua shoufa de chubu tantao" (Preliminary study of construction processes for great palatial and cultural architectural complexes under the Ming dynasty), *Fu Xinian jianzhu shi lunwen ji* (*Recueil de textes sur l'histoire de l'architecture de Fu Xinian*), Beijing, Wenwu chubanshe, 1998, pp. 357-378.
He, Yeju, *Kaogongji yingguo zhidu yanjiu* (*Study on the development principles for a royal capital*), Beijing, Zhongguo jianzhu gongye chubanshe, 1985.
Hou, Renzhi (Ed.), *Beijing lishi dituji* (*Collection of Historic Plans of Beijing*), Beijing, Beijing chubanshe, 1985.
Liang, Sicheng, *Liang Sicheng wenji* (*Collection of Liang Sicheng's Writings*), 4 volumes, Beijing, Zhongguo jianzhu gongye chubanshe, 1984-1986.
Liang, Sicheng-Chen, Zhanxiang, *Liang Chen fangan yu Beijing* (*The Liang-Chen proposal and Beijing*), Shenyang, Laoning jiaoyu chubanshe, 2005.

Albert-Kahn Museum, *Chine. 1909-1934. Catalogue des photographies et des séquences filmées*, 2 volumes, Boulogne-Billancourt, Musée Albert-Kahn, 2001-2002.
Qianlong jingdu quantu (*Plan complet de la capitale sous Qianlong*), Beijing, Ditu chubanshe, 1986.
Shoudu bowuguan (Ed.), *Yuan Dadu*, Beijing, Yanshan chubanshe, 1989.
Sirén, Osvald, *The Walls and Gates of Peking*, London, John Lane, 1924.
Steinhardt, Nancy Shatzman, " The Plan of Khubilai Khan's Imperial City ", *Artibus Asiae*, 44/2-3 (1983).
Wang, Bin, *Beijing weiguan dili biji* (*Notes on microscale elements of the geography of Beijing*), Beijing), Sanlian chubanshe, 2007.
Weng, Li, *Beijing de hutong*, Beijing, Yanshan chubanshe, 1992.
Wang, Jun, *Chengji*, Beijing, Sanlian chubanshe, 2003.
Xiong, Mengxiang, *Xijing zhi jiyi*, Beijing, Guji chubanshe, 1983.
Yi King. Le Livre des Transformations, version allemande de Richard Wilhelm, traduction française d'Étienne Perrot, Paris, Librairie de Médicis, 1973.
Xu, Pingfang, *Ming Qing Beijing chengtu* (*Plans of the city of Beijing under the Ming and Qing*), Beijing, Ditu chubanshe, 1986.
Zhao, Zhengzhi, " Yuan Dadu pinmian guihua fuyuan de yanjiu ", *Kaogu*, n˚6, 1972.
Zhu, Zuxi, *Yingguo xiangyi* (*Principes d'aménagement d'une capitale royale*), Beijing, Zhonghua shuju, 2007.

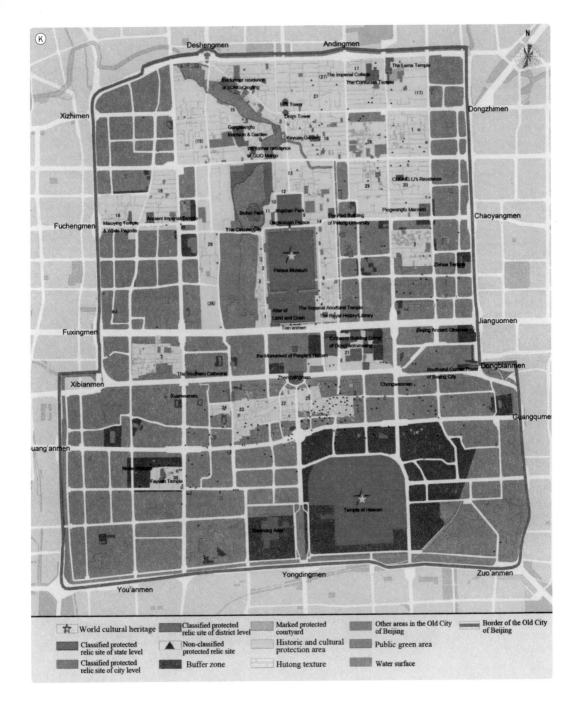

Deshengmen   Andingmen

N

Xizhimen

The former residence of SONG Qingling

17   The Imperial College
The Confucian Temple   The Lama Temple

(27)

27

(17)

Dongzhimen

19

Bell Tower

Drum Tower

Gongwangfu Mansion & Garden

(15)

Keyuan Garden   16

1

The former residence of GUO Moruo

28

19

13

CHONG Li's Residence

29   20

Chaoyangmen

12

10

Beihei Park   11   Jingshan Park

Pingwangfu Mansion

Fuchengmen

Miaoying Temple & White Pagoda

Ancient Imperial Temple

Daguodilan Palace   14   The Red Building of Peking University

The Curious City

26

Zhihua Temple

5

Palace Museum

3   6

Fuxingmen

(26)

Altar of Land and Grain   The Imperial Ancestral Temple
The Royal History Library

Beijing Ancient Observatory

Jianguomen

1

Tian'anmen

6

Embassy Building Group of Dongjiaomniuxing

3

21

Southeast Corner Tower of Beijing City

Dongbianmen

Xibianmen

The Southern Cathedral

the Monument of People's Heroes

Zhengyangmen

Chongwenmen

Xuanwumen

24   23   22   25

Guangqumen

uang'anmen

Niese Museum

Fayuan Temple

Temple of Heaven

Temple of Heaven

Xiannong Area

Zuo'anmen

You'anmen   Yongdingmen

☆	World cultural heritage		Classified protected relic site of district level		Marked protected courtyard		Other areas in the Old City of Beijing		Border of the Old City of Beijing
	Classified protected relic site of state level	▲	Non-classified protected relic site		Historic and cultural protection area		Public green area		
	Classified protected relic site of city level		Buffer zone		Hutong texture		Water surface		

K—Master development plan for the city of Beijing up to 2020, with the "historic and cultural protection zones".
© Chiu Che Bing.

Lao She's Beijing

Yves Kirchner
with the collaboration of Paul Bady

Lao She's life is intimately tied up with the city of Beijing,[1] where he was born on February 3, 1899, i.e. on the eve of the lunar New Year which in China is called "the Spring Festival", and where he died, probably from blows inflicted by the Red Guards, on August 24, 1966. Surprisingly,[2] Lao She has little to say about the political upheavals affecting China, like Zhang Dage, one of the characters in *The Half-Open Cage*, who, recalling the upheavals and revolutions at different times of his life, is surprised to realise that they had never really affected his personal existence. "Even a change as important as the transfer of the capital, in 1928, from Beijing to Nanjing, had had no impact on his life, he concludes." That is, of course, with no inkling of the sinister end that was to come...

Childhood in the Manchu city

By birth, Lao She belongs to the people of the banners, the Manchu ethnic group which, since 1644 under the name of the Qing, has held the destiny of the Empire in its hands. His father, however, a man of very modest condition—a guard in the Palace of the Forbidden City—is killed in August 1900, when the allied troops come to relieve the legations from the Boxer siege. Lao She would only refer to the reality of his family situation in a posthumously published novel, *Child of the New Year* (1980). In it, he describes a society in decline, where luxury and poverty, pride and shame, live shoulder to shoulder. Within a few years, the end of Empire would put a final stop to the refined and complacent existence of the capital's Manchu rulers. When the Empire fell, most of the Manchus in the Emperor's service found themselves moneyless and jobless.

Lao She was born in a house in Small Sheepfold Alley, near the Temple of National Salvation, in the city's western district. The design of the place, which bore no relation to the grid layout of Beijing's streets, suggests that it was a former sheepfold. The house itself seems badly designed. The east-west facing rooms, giving on to a narrow courtyard, have structural failings, in particular during the heavy autumn rains. The walls have collapsed several times and only the most northerly wall might have deserved any praise. At this time, on a moonlit night, the little Beijing *hutong* is plunged into frightening shadow, and anyone who ventures alone into the alleys, by the light of a lantern, is quickly afraid of getting lost. His youngest sister is sent to fetch the midwife. By good fortune, her route was lit up by New Year firecrackers, set off to drive away evil spirits.

A——Lao She's portrait. © Paul Bady

1——Lao She would go so far as to compare his attachment to his native city with his affection for his mother, in "I adore the new Beijing", a 1957 text.
2——"In general, writes Lao She, the day-to-day events we witness seem superficial and of little interest, accustomed as we are to reading newspapers. When you want to become a novelist, on the other hand, you must look at them very closely, like the lawyer who sees proofs of innocence or attenuating circumstances in every feeling, every reaction of the guilty man about to commit his crime." "The use of events", in *Lao niu po che* [*The Old Ox Cart*], a self-critical essay on the novel and humour, translated by Paul Bady, PUF, 1974, p. 111.

According to Beijing customs, the new year of the peasant calendar begins at the start of the 12th lunar month. This festival, which lasts almost four weeks, is a holiday period for children, and a holiday time for the peasants, whose work in the fields is interrupted by cold weather. However, this has no effect on the the effort put into celebrating the new year, mainly because spring is imminent.ⒹOn the eighth day of the month, the shops are crammed and the alleys echo with the cries of street sellers. The tradition is to prepare a broth made of several varieties of rice, beans and dried fruit. This preparation is accompanied by garlic marinated in vinegar and ravioli. The twenty-third day resembles a full-scale dress rehearsal, the "Little New Year". In olden times, this is the evening when the gods of the hearth were worshipped: people would first throw a handful of firecrackers, then burn an effigy of the gods. A few days before, the streets are full of people selling corn-based nougat and sticky rice cut into squares or watermelon shapes.Ⓔ According to the experts, these sweets dissuade the gods from telling the celestial Emperor about the misdeeds committed in the family. It is also the time for final preparation.

B——Lao She's birth place, Beijing. © Paul Bady
C——Huguosi (monastery of the protection of the country), 28 January 1909, Beijing. Albert Dutertre, © Albert Kahn Museum
D——Dong'an shishang (market of the Western Gate of Peace), during New Year's Eve, 25-28 January 1909, Beijing.
Albert Dutertre. © Albert Kahn Museum
E——Yongdingmen dajie (avenue of the gate the eternal stability), New Year Fair, January 1909, Beijing.
Albert Dutertre. © Albert Kahn Museum

The prints have been hung, the house cleaned, the food shopping done, as shops are closed until the sixth day of the next month. Some people claim that any cutting must be done before New Year's Eve, to avoid using a knife between the first and sixth day of the month.

The first modernisations of the capital

The Manchu dynasty is overthrown by the Xinhai revolution. On January 1, 1912, Sun Yat-sen announces the birth of the Chinese Republic. Lao She goes to teacher training college where "not only were the lessons free, but you were also given food, your uniform and books". A few years earlier, the foreign powers, whose presence in China had been reinforced by the signing of the "Boxer Protocol" in 1901, opened the first Beijing-Hankou and Beijing-Moukden railways, with the building of two stations on either side of Zhengyang Gate, one in 1902 by a Belgian firm in traditional Qing architectural style, the other in 1906 by an English firm in the Victorian style. New urban roads are built to facilitate access to the Tartar city, partially destroying several gates and walls. Qianmen Square is developed by the German architect Curt Rothkegel. In addition, the city opens a university, followed in in 1911 by a school of technology (Tsinghua) and in 1920 by the American University of Yenching (Yanjing). Graduating from Beijing teacher training college at the age of 17, Lao She is appointed to positions as a school director, then as an inspector. Perhaps in order to avoid compromising his career, he plays no part in the Reform Movement of May 4, 1919, which in any case "did not appeal to him". "It was the 4th May that cut me off from the student world", [3] he writes. Moreover, unlike many of his compatriots who are openly hostile to their country's domination by western culture, Lao She learns English in evening classes at the University of Yanjing, and establishes relations with the pastors of the London Missionary Society, who persuade him to leave for London in 1924.

On his return to China, in 1929, the teacher turned writer finds a profoundly altered situation, coloured by the Japanese threat. Lao She tries to express his anxieties and his bitterness in a satirical work of fantasy entitled *City of Cats*, in which a Chinese astronaut crashes on the planet Mars and finds a society of greedy, doubledealing, drugtaking cats, led by a puppet emperor. The persistent rumours of enemy invasion fail to change the situation. At the point when the cat people should close ranks to confront the threat, they remain riven by internal conflicts, playing into the hands of the invaders, who turn out to be dwarves.

Not long after the abdication of Emperor Puyi, the Forbidden City had hosted an exhibition of ancient art. A decade later, on October 10, 1925, on the occasion of the Republic of China's National Festival, the palace museum, which housed the former collection of the Qing emperors, opened its doors to the public for the first time.

3—*Lao niu po che*, self-critical essay on the novel and humour, translated by Paul Bady, PUF, 1974.

The reform policy initiated at the beginning of the 20th century by the Qing government had promoted an architectural renewal, based on the renewal underway in Europe and the US, characterised by rivalry between neo-Gothic and neoclassical, Art Nouveau and colonial: the new theatre on Qianmen Square, built by Shen Liyuan in 1915, was given a neoclassical facade of columns surmounted with capitals. However, a powerful revival of the national style took place in the 1920s and 1930s, characterised by pastiches of Qing architecture like those of Beijing's library and hospital.

While he regards political upheavals merely as blows of fate, Lao She is nevertheless very accurate in his account of their impact on the people. It is his characters' wanderings around Beijing in different seasons that tell us most about the transformations of the city. "That indeed is my native city, and all I need to

F——Between Chongwenmen (Letter Veneration Gate) or Hadamen, south-east corner of Tartar City, January 1909, Pékin. Albert Dutertre. © Musée Albert Kahn
G——In the Western Tartar City, January 1909, Beijing. Albert Dutertre. © Albert Kahn Museum
H——In the Eastern Tartar City, 1909 ?, Pékin. Jacques Gachet. © Albert Kahn Museum
I——Xiyuan (Western Imperial Garden), 3 July, 1912, Beijing. Stéphane Passet. © Albert Kahn Museum

do is think of those two characters 北京 in order immediately to see hundreds of metres of film showing the landscapes of the old capital." [4]

When he begins the writing of *La Cage entrebâillée*, in 1933, a law allowing Chinese women to divorce has just been added to the new Civil Code. The main character, Lao Li, is an official in the new Republican bureaucracy, "as loathsome as the old one". Beijing society provides a spectacle of dangerous decay, caused mainly by the compromises that damage public and private life. Unlike his work colleagues, Lao Li has decided to bring his family from the country, whereas others have no hesitation in buying a concubine or taking a mistress. One early morning, before sunrise, he is crossing part of the city. It is cold. Not far from the ramparts a camel train is approaching, clouds of steam rising from the animals' nostrils. Ⓕ At this early hour, Beijing seems to look different. As he moves through the streets, the electric bulbs that light the road are gradually transformed into "simple nets of gold". In the distance, the clatter of the first trams can be heard. Then, gradually, the street fills up, as if the sun's heat had finally convinced the inhabitants to come down. "A rag picker passed, carrying a on her back great empty basket, but still bent double. Unfortunate children, weighed down with sunshades, banners and other objects for a funeral procession, shuffled quickly along in their old slippers." Ⓖ His steps took him to the banks of Lake Zhonghai, west of the imperial city. Its surface was varnished with a thin layer of pale green ice that glistened in the first rays of the sun. However, his gaze is attracted by a sedan chair blazing with colours. Ⓗ Perhaps it is hurrying to meet a young country bride. "Lao Li looked at it, with a bewildered air: it felt as if he was seeing something mysterious, strange and slightly ridiculous. Yet nonetheless, that thing existed; otherwise, how could people have retained their respect for something that was, at bottom, nothing more than a big birdcage?" Then he reaches Xisipailou, the "Four triumphal Arches of the West", at the crossroads of Xuanwumen and Fuchengmen Avenues, in the western part of the Tartar city. Here there was a big market with all sorts of meats and dead or living fish laid out on stalls. "The ground was covered in puddles of pig's blood and onion peel that had frozen there. Eels and burbot, in innumerable quantities, wriggled in the bottom of a bucket, their heads crowned with ice cubes. The eyes of the burbot bulged, as if they were trying to hypnotise the passers-by. Everything was happening in the greatest disorder, amongst disgusting smells, in the midst of extraordinary agitation."

4——"How I wrote *The Divorce* ", in *Lao niu po che*, self-critical essay on the novel and humour, translated by Paul Bady, PUF, 1974, p. 52.

The house he has rented for his wife and children is situated in the Brick Pagoda hutong, in the western part of the Tartar city. It is close to a market and a tramline. In the courtyard stand three pavilions. Lao Li and his family are to live in the one on the northern side, which is five windows wide. Although freshly painted, the pavilion's roof leaks. And the window paper has not been changed. Only the mosquito nets have been mended. Nevertheless, the living-room has a western-style stove. From the outside, the entrance door was topped with a lintel with a lion cub on each side and in the middle the eight trigrams, the Taoist symbol of universal order.

Going in to the office early, Lao Li passes through the Western Gate of Peace and admires the cathedral, the Library, the Lakes of the Centre and North. The rain that has just stopped has dispersed the crowd and all the irritations of city life. Under the rain, the "city becomes an abstraction, a combination of architectural beauty and aesthetic pleasure. In contemplating it, he thought only of the artistic tastes of the Ancients and of his own present satisfaction; nothing else existed. Lao Li found himself before an immense picture with meticulous drawings: from the pavilions and pagodas to the lotus flowers, everything was accurately drawn. Beyond the upper storeys of the buildings, a chain of blue mountains could be seen, and close by, on a lily petal, a small dragonfly." Symbol of Beijing, the Imperial River bridge, situated between the lakes, covered on either side by flowering lotuses and already bearing intense traffic, represented a successful synthesis of art and nature: "Beijing was never as beautiful as after the rain!"

The city under Japanese occupation

Whilst Lao She was always reticent, even prudent, in regard to the revolutionary movements shaking China, he clearly took sides in the war with Japan, described in his preface to *The Incineration*, written on January 1, 1944. Indeed, he takes the view that: "If we did not discuss the war and its repercussions, it would be as if we were living with our eyes shut, pretending to be stupid."

In *Four Generations under One Roof*, a saga he began writing in Chongqing, the war itself plays a limited role: one event in particular that might have been developed, the fall of Beijing, is described as single sentence: "The summer was very hot, but every heart in the country had frozen: Peip'ing était had fallen into enemy hands."[5] The novel thus opens with the Marco Polo bridge incident, on July 7, 1937, and ends with the capitulation of Japan at the end of the Second World War on August 15, 1945, following the two atomic bombs dropped on Japan, of which Lao She

5——*Dread*, beginning of chapter 4, p. 77.

would say that it was "the greatest shame humanity had ever known".[6] Lao She was obliged to go into exile in Hangkou where, on March 27, 1937, he founded the Federation of Chinese Writers and Artists as a resistance force against the enemy. He was elected head of the association. However, even far from the city, as a novelist he continues to focus on life in Beijing, receiving news about the Japanese occupation from family and friends. One of his characters, Guan Xiaohe, a former official seeking a position in the government of the occupied city, rather effectively summarises the situation of the population, "whose happiness should have consisted in living in a great city with sumptuous gardens and a glorious cultural past, but now politically and militarily dependent on Tianjin. That, indeed, was where the Chinese figures most desirous or most willing to help Japan were to be found. Tianjin had the big show with violent combats and fine airs, but all that was playing in Peiping was the scene from "Stratagem of the empty city."[7]

The novel is almost always accurate in its facts, whether reporting on the "New People's Union", whose members favoured collaboration, and the events that it organises in the occupied city, on the system of communal informing which claims to maintain the safety of each hutong, on the settlement of Japanese immigrants in the capital,[8] on the difficulties between the puppet governments of Beijing and Nanjing,[9] or else on the participation of certain intellectuals in the Japanese installed government. Control of broadcasting,[10] censorship in education and collaborationist propaganda in the theatres,[11] suppression of local commerce [12] and confiscation,[13] the disappearance of fuel and ever increasing shortages,[14] arrests, imprisonments and searches, trafficking, widespread corruption, life under occupation is accurately described. Famine occurred, to the point that property owners, like the character Marquis Wen, are ready to plunder the princely palaces of Peiping, with their precious timber frames and varnished tiles, which are sold one after the other. Some property owners sell bricks and tiles individually to buy food. "The decline of this nobility was reminiscent of mushrooms after the rain, which initially look very fine, but are quickly reduced to dust and scattered by the wind."[15]

After moving to the United States in 1946, at the invitation of the US government, Lao She was hesitant and only returned to Beijing at the end of 1949, soon after the proclamation of the People's Republic of China on October 1, 1949, in Tiananmen Square.

6——*Famine*, vol. III, p. 394.
7——*Dread*, p. 125.
8——A pointless life, p. 97
9——A pointless life, p. 359
10——A pointless life, p. 50
11——*bid.*, 367-368
12——Cf. the suicide of the merchant Tianyou, *ibidem*, pp. 405 sq.
13——Cf. metal collection, *ibidem*, p. 374
14——Cf. the queues for distributions, in the third part, *Famine*, and the death of little Niu from malnutrition right at the end of the novel. On the lack of coal, cf. *Dread*, p. 358
15——*Dread*, p. 448.

The disappearance of a world

In Beijing, the beginning of spring coincides with a period of wind. And paradoxically, observes Lao She, his role is less to bring spring than to divert it temporarily with the strength of his squalls. At the time when he was writing *The Child of the New Year*, which coincided with the 1960s, Lao She regretted the fact that they were cutting down the trees on the heights of the city, without replacing them. The hills near the cemetery where his grandparents lay, in the north of the city, had "become bald". As a result, nothing could stop the violence of the gusts that swept the walls of the capital, however thick and solid. "It was an icy wind, an absolute devil of a gale which moaned and raised whirlwinds of sand and suddenly plunged earth and sky into complete darkness. The blue sky suddenly became a yellow, and a hailstorm of sand struck the city." In a single movement, the wind carries everything before it, lifting into the air all sorts of objects that are not riveted to the ground by their own weight. The doorbells over the shop entrances gyrate noisily, the fabric banners shred, the whole city whistles, screeches and moans.ⓙ "The unfortunates who were obliged to go out had to struggle like sailors in a storm: pushed along willy-nilly with the wind behind them, they could hardly move at all into the wind. They were covered in black dust from head to foot, as if they'd been buried alive, and their red eyes ran with tears that dug furrows of mud as they flowed down their cheeks." But at the end of the day, the wind drops as night falls, spilling a form of lightness and serenity over the a city that still trembles, but is purified, cleaned and as if unified by a fine layer of yellow sand.

J——Dongsi pailou dajie (Avenue of the Four Porticos of the East), 1909 ?, Beijing. Jacques Gachet. © Albert Kahn Museum

Wang Jun, chronicler of the new Beijing

Amélie Manon

In October 2003 in China, the publishing house San Lian published a book that had a major impact, quickly becoming one of the bestsellers of 2004. Reissued several times in less than two years and the winner of multiple awards, this book *Chengji*—literally "record of the city", in this case Beijing, which could be translated *"Beijing Chronicle"*—retraces the architectural and urban development of the city from 1950 to the start of the 21st century. The first remarkable thing about this book is the profusion of references. Its author, Wang Jun, conducts a historical and political analysis of the debate on the choices for the urban development of the Chinese capital. The book is punctuated by the lives of the various major architects of the time, figures such as Liang Sicheng, Chen Zhanxiang or Hua Lanhong, known in France as Léon Hua. Their work, their visions of architecture and urban development, together with the multiple decisions at government and municipal level, are carefully recorded.

The history of a city

When he began his research, Wang Jun intended to write a biography of Liang Sicheng. "I was profoundly impressed by his commitment to preserving the old city. At the same time, I wanted to present him in opposition to the founders of the new China, but during the writing process, I realised that a book could not focus on just one subject. So I changed my perspective." In the course of writing, this project became a "biography of Beijing". Wang Jun emphasises Liang Sicheng's continuing efforts to save the old city and its architectural heritage, essentially the work of the last three dynasties: Mongol, Chinese and Manchu.

A native of Guizhou province, Wang Jun arrived in Beijing in 1987 to study journalism at the People's University (*Renmin daxue*). Graduating in 1991, he quickly joined the official New China agency (*Xinhua she*) as a journalist, covering urban development issues. "I had already been a student in Beijing for four years when I realised that I really knew very little about the old capital: I wasn't aware that the walls had stood for hundreds of years, but only that demolishing them had been a serious problem. I wanted to understand what had happened and it took ten years of research to satisfy my curiosity." In 1993, he began his investigations into the history of urban planning in Beijing, and into Liang Sicheng's writings and background. Wang Jun explains: "As a journalist, I had frequent contact with the city council and witnessed the many problems a city has to face in carrying out radical transformations that can prove dangerous and painful. These experiences made me think and prompted me to write a history of the process. Given this perspective, my academic research is, perhaps for that reason, different from other research. Problems that other researchers might find irrelevant can seem important to me."

This book, with its more than three hundred documents, press articles, memos of official decisions, numerous interviews, architects' notes, drawings, sketches, recent and contemporary photographs, all mostly unknown and hard to access, is an unusual genre in China. It is a good introduction for anyone interested in knowing the history of Beijing and understanding its current transformations. Wang Jun's writing maintains an objective tone. Although the book is not the work of a specialist, it is considered to be the first work to provide an accurate and comprehensive account of the development of Beijing since the 1950s. *Chengji* is now seen as being of significant historical value. "The main purpose of my book is to remind readers not to forget the past, otherwise history will repeat itself", explains Wang Jun.[1] It would seem that his gamble has paid off, as evidenced by the frequent reissues of the book and the many awards it has received, such as the literary prize for the national bestseller (*Quanguo youxiu chanxiao shujiang*). *Chengji* is currently being translated by an English publisher.

An early militant: Liang Sicheng

For Wang Jun, no study of Chinese architecture and urban planning can ignore the work of Liang Sicheng (1901, Tokyo – 1972, Beijing), the protagonist of *Chengji*. The son of Liang Qichao, who took refuge in Japan after the failure of the "One hundred day reform" in 1898, he had the advantage of a good education and an unusual degree of contact with foreign countries. And architectural graduate of the University of Pennsylvania in 1928, he is considered one of the most famous Chinese architectural theorists of the 20th century and the founding father of the teaching of architecture in China. Returning to China in the 1930s, he wrote numerous reference works on ancient architecture (*The History of Architecture in China*), conducting accurate surveys all across China, and became director of the Chinese Society for Architectural Research (*Zhongguo yingzao xuehui*). In 1948, he founded the architecture department at Tsinghua University in Beijing. In 1949,

1——Wang Jun writes regular articles on the city of Beijing in different periodicals, which can be accessed on his blog: http://blog.sina.com.cn/m/wangjun

he was appointed Deputy-Chairman of the Beijing Urban Planning Committee. Liang Sicheng worked for the preservation of the old city of Beijing. He is known for his opposition to the systematic destruction of traditional buildings, in particular the walls Ⓐ and gates Ⓑ of the old city, which he felt should be restored. In 1956, as Wang Jun mentions, he declared: "I feel the demolition of the watchtowers like cuts in my flesh, and the removal of bricks from the ramparts like being flayed alive."

In October 1949, Beijing once again became the capital of the People's Republic of China.[2] This decision brought about profound political upheavals which would have a powerful impact on the city's architectural and urban identity. Liang Sicheng became an emblematic figure for his desire to spare the city any destruction following the change of regime, and wanted Beijing to become a cultural and political centre that could be preserved in its entirety "as a museum of art and history". He envisaged the creation of a new administrative centre, to the west

of Beijing, which would be the seat of central government. In February 1950, he developed this idea in the famous text: "Proposal on the Location of the Central People's Government Administrative Center" (*Guanyu zhongyang renmin zhengfu xingzheng zhongxinqu weizhi de jianyi*) , written jointly with Chen Zhanxiang,[3] in which both authors explicitly talk about the preservation of Beijing.

A——The ramparts of the city, Beijing, 8 September 1966. © Solange Brand
B——The Eastern Gate, Beijing, 1966. © Solange Brand

2——The Nationalist government moved the capital from Beijing to Nanjing between 1928 and 1949. Beijing (Capital of the North) was then renamed Beiping (Peace of the North), becoming Beijing again on September 27, 1949, and being proclaimed capital by the new Communist government in October 1949.
3——The architect and urban planner Chen Zhanxiang (1916-2001), or Charlie Cheng, was a pupil of Sir Patrick Abercrombie. After studying in England, in 1949 Chen Zhanxiang was invited by Liang Sicheng to take up the position of director of the planning department of Beijing's municipal Urban Planning Committee.

In December 1949, the mayor of Beijing organised a meeting to discuss a development plan for the capital. At this meeting, Soviet specialists invited by the Party's Central Committee to help in the preparation of the master plan for Beijing, put forward their suggestions for the future development of the city. They insisted on the industrialisation of the capital and located the administrative centre at the heart of the old imperial city. Liang Sicheng and Chen Zhanxiang opposed this plan and an argument ensued. The Soviet specialists rejected the idea of keeping Beijing as a museum and were opposed to the development of the new urban zone to the west. The Beijing municipality's Bureau of Construction went along with the outside view and accepted the extension plan for Tiananmen Square.

In the first chapters of his book, Wang Jun records the chronology of the official decisions and the polemics they aroused. For him, it is important to understand the impact that this choice of location had on the future of the capital. Despite the best efforts of certain players, in particular Liang Sicheng, to protect the old city and its heritage, Beijing had to trade its historical monuments and its old districts for new monumental projects, embodiments of communist ideology, and then, more recently, for the buildings born of economic imperatives. Wang Jun's approach is historical. He describes the facts objectively and shows clearly how Beijing's current problems had already been stated 50 years ago. His aim is to provide the widest possible access to information about past choices and current transformations, considering both demolition and urban development.

Modernisation and preservation

In the 1950s, there was a clash between two opposing viewpoints. One was protective. The projects envisaged by Liang Sicheng reflect his wish to integrate traditional culture with urban modernity. He is very clear that Beijing's heritage does not lie only in its historical monuments, but that it is an urban unity which is embodied in the morphology and spatial organisation of the city, with its central axis, its walls, the arrangement of urban features defined by ritual rules. If Beijing was to be protected, this unity needed to be recognized. He was persuaded that Beijing could modernise and be preserved at the same time. He explains that the protection of heritage is intimately linked with urban planning.

The opposing viewpoint saw urban development as a functionalist process, in which all obstacles—in particular monuments and the existing fabric—are erased. Most of the leaders of the time felt that it was enough to keep the Forbidden City as a witness to the past, and that there was no need to preserve any other historical monuments. Liang Sicheng expressed himself as follows to Peng Zhen, mayor of Beijing, in 1951: "On these matters, I am forward-looking and you remain backward. In fifty years, history will show that you were wrong and I was right." Liang Sicheng hoped to reconcile these urban features with the new requirements of modernisation; for example, he recommended a protected perimeter around the *pailou*—arches or commemorative gateways—to deal with the problem of traffic whilst highlighting the monument, or else the creation of a hanging park along the 40 km of walls around the city.

Wang Jun draws on valuable personal accounts in retracing the destruction of the city: demolition of the walls and gates of the city to make way for the orbital road and subway; demolition of the *pailou* to improve traffic flow; development of the Beihai Bridge©, which was considered dangerous and replaced by a new, wider bridge; destruction of the twin pagodas dating from the Jin dynasty, to allow the widening of Chang'an Avenue [4]... From 1958 to 1960, Beijing underwent a first big phase of transformation, with the development of Chang'an Avenue, creating an east-west axis cutting across the traditional north-south axis, and the enlargement of Tiananmen Square to accommodate events for the glorification of the regime,© and the erection of ten emblematic buildings,[5] inaugurated for the 10th anniversary of the People's Republic of China.

4——These two pagodas (*Shuangta Qingshousi*) located on West Chang'an Avenue were built between 1190 and 1209, and had survived until this time. To preserve them, Liang Sicheng proposed the creation of a protected island in the middle of the avenue, which would highlight the pagodas and enhance the landscape.

5——During the Great Leap Forward, Beijing was given ten great buildings erected in less than 10 months to celebrate the 10th anniversary of the People's Republic of China. These ten great monuments (*shida jianzhu*) are: the Army Museum, the Palace of Agriculture, the Workers' Stadium, the State Guesthouse, the People's Assembly, the Museum of History and of the Revolution, the Culture Palace of the Nationalities and the Minorities Hotel, Beijing Station and the Overseas Chinese Hotel. The last six are located in the old town.

C——The Northern Lake and the Beihai Bridge, Beijing, 1966. © Solange Brand
D——Tiananmen, 1st October 1966: National Day Parade, Beijing. © Solange Brand

Finally, Wang Jun describes the second phase in the transformation of Beijing, in the 1990s, with the creation of major arteries within the urban fabric, inner-city real estate speculation and the Beijing master plans of 1973, 1983 and 1993, which reflect the decision to allow urban sprawl based on a model of radiating growth.

As Zhang Liang recalls in his work on Chinese heritage: Beijing did not have to deal with the problem of post-war reconstruction, but with the equally complex issue of modernisation. From the 1950s onward, the city's building heritage lost not only its hitherto preserved monuments but also its old neighbourhoods, the repository of successive layers of an urban history begun eight centuries earlier. Nevertheless, these terrible waves of destruction did raise awareness of the existence of an urban heritage.[6]

Wang Jun wishes to alert public opinion and, through an objective presentation, to informed citizens about the situation of their city.

At the moment, change in Beijing is happening at an ever faster pace. Published in 2003, after the decision to make Beijing the host city for the 2008 Olympic Games, this book has reignited debates already begun fifty years before.

Bibliography

Bobin, Frédéric, Wang Zhe, *Pékin en mouvement*, Autrement, col "Villes en mouvement", Paris, 2005.
Clément, Pierre, Clément-Charpentier Sophie, Goldblum, Charles (dir.), *Cités d'Asie*, Parenthèses, col. "Les Cahiers de la recherche architecturale", n°35/36, Marseille, 1995.
Darrobers, Roger, *Pékin. Au détour des rues et des ruelles*, Bleu de Chine, Paris, 2000.
Fresnais, Jocelyne, *La Protection du patrimoine en République populaire de Chine (1949-1999)*, CTHS, Paris, 2001.
Henriot, Christian (dir.), *Les Métropoles chinoises au XXe siècle*, Arguments, Paris, 1995.
Jonathan, Philippe, *Pékin*, Institut français d'Architecture, coll. "Portrait de ville", 1983.
Jonathan, Philippe, "Destruction du vieux Pékin et polycentralité" in *L'Information géographique*, n.1, march 2005, p. 5-16.

Liang Ssu-ch'eng, *Chinese Architecture: A Pictorial History*, Dover Publications, New York, 2005.
Loubere, Antoine (dir.), "Villes chinoises en mouvement", *Urbanisme*, n°341, march-april 2005.
Nussaume, Yann, Mosiniak, Michelle (dir.), *Construire en Chine*, Éditions du Moniteur, Paris, 2005.
Xu Pingfang, " La Structure urbaine du vieux Pékin et sa protection ", *Cahier* n°1, École Française d'Extrême-Orient, Pékin, juin 2002.
Xu Yong 徐勇, *Xiaofangjia hutong* 小方家胡同, China Photography Publishing House 中国摄影出版社, Pékin, 2003.
Wang Jun 王军, *Chengji*城记, Éd. San Lian三联书店, Beijing, 2003.

6—Zhang Liang, *La Naissance du concept de patrimoine en Chine (XIXe-XXe siècles)*, Recherches/Ipraus, coll. "Archithèses", Paris 2003, pp. 139-140.

Impact of the Olympic Games on the city of Beijing

Wang Jun

Since 2001, the year when Beijing was chosen to host the 2008 Olympic Games, more than thirty million square metres of buildings have been erected every year in the Chinese capital. Beijing has become a vast building site, a focus of attention in China and throughout the world, a place for many foreign architects to come and show their skills, notably with five major constructions: the National Centre for the Performing Arts,[1] the Olympic stadium and swimming pool, the CCTV (China Central Television) headquarters and the International airport's third terminal. This foreign role is an extremely new phenomenon.

During the period of entente between China and the USSR in the 1950s, the Chinese government invited Soviet architects to contribute to national projects such as the Army Museum, the Museum of the Chinese Revolution or the broadcasting headquarters. However, no building of any significance was commissioned from a western architect before the French architect Paul Andreu was chosen to design the National Centre for the Performing Arts in July 1999. This marked a turning point. Since then, and even more since 2001 when Beijing was chosen to host the Olympic Games and China entered the World Trade Organisation (WTO), the architecture market has opened up to foreign bidders.

This irreversible process of liberalisation is undoubtedly one of the first consequences of the city being awarded the Games, one which has had repercussions for the entire country. Preparing for the Games has brought China within the nexus of global economic flows, a fact that is not insignificant for humanity as a whole and more especially for the fourth of humanity that China represents. Against a backdrop of global economic uncertainty, China's insolent growth—a consequence of its new openness and the opportunities afforded by the Olympic Games—has attracted world-renowned architects to Beijing, with projects that have aroused heated debate.

The first act was played out in the National Centre for the Performing Arts. The architect Paul Andreu, designer of France's Roissy Charles-de-Gaulle airport, built an immense egg-shaped titanium shell, containing three auditoriums, placed in the middle of a lake with no visible access route other than a gallery running beneath the water. [2] Detractors draw attention to the purely formal aspect of the building and to the high operating costs and the waste of energy entailed in heating and cooling its internal structures. In addition, the titanium shell has a highly reflective surface, which generates light pollution in its immediate environment and is visible all the way from the Hall of Supreme Harmony, at the heart of the Forbidden City. For the project's defenders, on the other hand, the shape of the Grand Theatre, suggesting a pearl floating on the water, is a tremendous aesthetic achievement.

1—The National Centre for Performing Arts (国家大剧院 guójio dàjùyuàn), often known as Beijing Opera, is close to Tiananmen Square, on Chang'An Avenue, a building of 150,000 m².
2—The building has an opera hall (2,416 seats), a concert hall (2,017 seats) and a theatre (1,040 seats), all three covered by a single titanium and glass shell, set in a lake. Access to the building is via an underground gallery with its entrance on Chang'An Avenue.

The polemics around building shape and function reached their apogee with the Olympic Stadium, designed by the Swiss architects Herzog & De Meuron, and with the CCTV headquarters designed by the Dutch architect Rem Koolhaas and his firm OMA (Office for Metropolitan Architecture). The Stadium, which bears the now official nickname the "Bird's Nest", is a gigantic edifice made up of 42,000 tonnes of steel—more than the Eiffel Tower—in a structure 333 m long and 298 m wide.Ⓐ The 230 m high CCTV Tower resembles two twisted, vertically connected "Zs", with a 70 m section forming a horizontal overhang 180 m above ground.Ⓑ Like the Centre for Performing Arts, these two colossal structures are criticised for the primacy assigned to appearance, which required immense investment to achieve formal aesthetic and structural qualities that seem deliberately to challenge intuitions about stability. Those favourable to the project, on the other hand, celebrate the performance of these innovative architectures as a perfect fusion of art and technology.

Indeed, the debate arises out of the new possibilities that computer design techniques offer the architect, and their impact on construction. As international architects from Frank Gehry to Rem Koolhaas have acknowledged, the engineer has brought freedom to the architect—in fact their involvement has taken on a cultural dimension—since all sorts of architectural creations are now possible.

The controversy on whether primacy should be assigned to form or function has certainly been driven by the Olympic projects, but it can be considered from a wider perspective, in terms of the role of architecture in our societies. In fact, the question is not restricted to the architectural field alone: in this era of

A—The Olympic Stadium, 2008. © Aurélien Chen
B—The new China Central Television (CCTV) headquarters, 2008. © Aurélien Chen

globalisation, the quality and impact of the urban landscape are weapons wielded in the competition between cities. For certain urban leaders, the construction of prestigious buildings with the visual power to attract attention—by whatever means—becomes a sort of "function" of the building itself. In which case, is this a phenomenon of alienation or a sign of progress?

A second question has also aroused much debate: this ancient capital of Beijing, repository of more than 3000 years of history, inheritor of a remarkable legacy, including such splendours as the Forbidden City, the Temple of Heaven, the Great Wall..., possessed an extraordinary urban fabric. Did it really need structures of such disproportionate size to establish its architectural status? In recent years, the protection of Beijing's urban heritage has been a central preoccupation of many figures, both in China and abroad, concerned about the threat posed to the city by the transformations associated with the Olympic Games, even though the main sites are situated a dozen kilometres from the centre to the west and north.

After the award of the Games, the city immediately initiated and implemented a new urban masterplan for Beijing, based on a multipolar approach to development: apart from the historic centre, seen as a protected area, the emphasis is on the construction of new urban hubs which would spread the functions of the capital across several zones and regulate the development of real estate operations.

In fact, as long ago as February 1950, shortly after the foundation of the People's Republic of China, the architects Liang Sicheng (1901-1972) and Chen Zhanxiang (1916-2001) proposed that the city of Beijing should build a new administrative centre outside the walls of the capital city, reminiscent of the development of La Défense in Paris in 1958. Their proposal was rejected by the government, in favour of the approach backed by the Soviet experts. In the 1958 Beijing masterplan that was finally adopted, the city retained a single centre at the heart of the old imperial capital, which was restructured and developed outwards radio-concentrically through the construction of major radial axes and orbital highways. This form of urban expansion was maintained in the successive masterplans of 1983 and 1993, with the result that the ancient imperial capital was restructured three times, in 1958, 1990 and 2000. Numerous edifices were demolished one after another, beginning with the city walls, the pailou, commemorative arches or porticos situated on main roads, then whole neighbourhoods of *hutong*, whose plots and alleyways had been laid out under the 13th-century Mongol dynasty, and the many siheyuan, the typical Beijing courtyard houses,[C] all to be replaced by soulless high-rise blocks and buildings.[D]

This process of renovation in Beijing was purportedly inspired by the work of Baron Haussmann, who led the modernisation of Paris in the second half of the 19th century, and even more dangerously, by the theories of Le Corbusier, developed in the International Congress of Modern Architecture (CIAM).[3] University professors and senior officials cited the transformations of Paris to justify the demolition and renovation of Beijing. The Voisin Plan that Le Corbusier developed for Paris between 1922 and 1925, creating wide avenues and tower blocks at

the heart of the city, was not implemented in the French capital, but in certain respects became a reality in Beijing. The application of this conception of urban development wiped out a long and rich historic legacy, well-suited to a city where walking was the primary means of transport. Although the spirit of the Athens Charter and the CIAM has largely faded, and new, more balanced approaches to urban development emerged in the 1990s, the theories of urbanism applied in Beijing, as in many other Chinese cities, are based on dogmas that have been abandoned elsewhere, in recognition of their drastic human and social consequences.

The wish to develop road traffic is the guiding thread of the urban restructuring plan, together with the decision to keep the capital's administrative departments in the centre (5.76% of the urban area). However, the great majority of Beijing's population lives in the outskirts, which generates disproportionate traffic flows between the city and its suburbs, ever-growing congestion and atmospheric pollution that has brought the city to the verge of asphyxia.

These problems of congestion, lack of public transport and pollution are a major challenge that Beijing took on in its bid for the 2008 Olympic Games. Aware of the problems, the municipality of Beijing has tried to implement a new masterplan, which distinguishes between the old city and the new hubs of urban activity.

C——Junction Wangfujing dajie (Avenue of the Prince Residence Fountains) and Dingzijie (street in T-shaped), 25-28 January 1909, Beijing. Albert Dutertre, © Albert Kahn Museum.
D——Wangfujing Avenue, 2008. © Aurélien Chen

3——In Athens in 1934, Le Corbusier argued for a functionalist approach to urban development, with a specialisation of urban sectors according to function.

In response, the urban planner Zhao Yanjing, Deputy-Chairman of the China Academy of Urban Planning & Design, and other researchers, have once again suggested that administrative departments should be moved out of the centre, so that new neighbourhoods can be built to restore harmony to the urban fabric and promote balanced development across the capital. As with the earlier projects proposed by Liang Sicheng and Chen Zhanxiang, these suggestions have remained on the drawing board.

In fact, despite the masterplan being approved by the Council of State Affairs in January 2005, most of the capital's administrative and institutional activities are still located in the old city, where wide avenues punctuated with skyscrapers bearing the neutral signature of big international construction firms continue to occupy what was once a pedestrian paradise.(E) Although Beijing's current municipal authorities are attempting to change tack, the transformations undertaken under the previous mandate were implemented before the revision of the masterplan, making it very hard either to stop or adjust them.

(E)

E——Changían Avenue in the Centre of Beijing, 2008. © Aurélien Chen

The Olympic Games, like some kind of growth hormone, encourage urban development whilst boosting its pathologies. It is easy to see: since Beijing was awarded the Olympics, construction sites for monumental boulevards and a spaghetti of interchanges have mushroomed, together with new subway building projects, all at a phenomenal price. Every day, more than a thousand additional vehicles join the city's traffic streams, whilst the rail transportation network is set to grow from 142 km to 200 km before the opening of the Games, then to 228 km in 2009, and up to 561 km in 2015. Private vehicles and public transport proliferate together, at a headlong pace, reflecting Beijing's general situation but also the interactions between different conceptions of urban planning and architecture, representative of the multiple currents of the 21st century world. The Olympic Games have done no more than speed up the process.

Chronology

—Shang circa 1500-1046 BCE

—Zhou
—Western Zhou 1046-771 BCE
—Eastern Zhou 770-256 BCE.
    Spring and Autumn Period 722-481 BCE
    Warring States Period 403-221 BCE

—Qin 221-206 BCE

—Han
—Western Han 206 BCE. - 24 CE.
—Eastern Han 25-220

—Three Kingdoms
—Wei 220-265
—Shu 221-263
—Wu 222-280

—Western Jin 265-316
—Eastern Jin 317-420

—Southern and Northern Dynasties

—Southern Dynasty
    Song 420-479
    Qi 479-502
    Liang 502-557
    Chen 557-589

—Northern Dynasty
    Northern Wei 386-534
    Eastern Wei 534-550
    Western Wei 535-557
    Northern Qi 550-577
    Northern Zhou 557-581

—Sui 581-618
    Tang 618-907

—Five Dynasties
—Later Liang 907-923

—Later Tang 923-936
—Later Jin 936-946
—Later Han 947-950
—Later Zhou 951-960

—Ten Kingdoms
—Wu 902-937
—Wuyu 907-978
—Southern Han 907-971
—Chu 907-951
—Earlier Shu 908-925
—Min 909-944
—Nanping - Jingman 913-963
—Later Shu 934-965
—Southern Tang 937-975
—Northern Han 951-979

—Song
    Northern Song 960-1127
    Southern Song 1127-1279

—Liao 916-1125
    Western Xia 1023-1227
    Jin 1115-1234
    Yuan 1279-1368
    Ming 1368-1644
    Qing 1644-1911

—Republic of China 1912-1949
    1934-1935 The Long March
    1937 Japanese Invasion

—People's Republic of China 1949
    1958-1961 Great Leap Forward
    1966 Cultural Revolution
    1976 Death of Mao Zedong
    1978 Deng Xiaoping accedes to power,
    beginning of the reforms and opening up
    1979 Limitation of births to one child per
    household 2003 Hu Jintao comes to power

IN THE CHINESE CITY, PERSPECTIVES ON THE TRANSFORMATIONS OF AN EMPIRE

An exhibition designed and produced by the Cité de l'architecture & du patrimoine jointly with the Barcelona Centre for Contemporary Culture

Under the high patronage of the Ministry of Culture and Communication and the Ministry of Foreign Affairs and with the support of the cultural service of the French Embassy in China and the Chinese Embassy in France

In collaboration with Tongji University in Shanghai, the Beijing Municipal Institute of City Planning and Design (BICP)
With the support of the Hauts de Seine Department / Musée Albert Kahn

Cité de l'architecture & du patrimoine
François de Mazières, Chairman of Cité de l'architecture & du patrimoine
Anne-Marie Le Guével, Chief Executive, Cité
Francis Rambert, Director of the French Institute of Architecture (IFA)

Barcelona Centre for Contemporary Culture (CCCB)
Antoni Fogué Moya, Chairman
Jordi Hereu Boher, Deputy Chairman
Josep Ramoneda Molins, Chief Executive

Curators
Frédéric Edelmann
With the assistance of Françoise Ged,
head of the Observatory of Architecture in Contemporary China, Ifa

Assistant curators and iconography
Lucie Haguenauer-Caceres, Chung Chih-Chia, Amala Marx, Ifa
Yves Kirchner
In China: Jérémie Descamps (8th Ring Road Ltd.)
Alain Jullien for contemporary Chinese photography

Production and general coordination
Barcelona Centre for Contemporary Culture:
Jordi Balló, Exhibition Director
Susana García, Exhibition Coordinator
In China: Jérémie Descamps (8th Ring Road Ltd.)

French Institute of architecture
Myriam Feuchot, Chung Chih-Chia, Delphine Dollfus, Lucie Haguenauer-Caceres, Amala Marx, Marion Zirk, Ifa
Production Department
In China: Jérémie Descamps (8th Ring Road Ltd.)

Documentary research
Cité de l'architecture & du patrimoine
Élodie Brosseau, Ségolène Dubernet, Lucie Haguenauer-Caceres, Amala Marx, Ifa
Marielle Blanc, Jean-Marc Hofman, Aude Mathé, Museum of French Monuments
In China: Jérémie Descamps (8th Ring Road Ltd.)

Cartography
Serge Barto

Documentary and fiction films
Production, coordination and filmmaking:
Barcelona Centre for Contemporary Culture
Angela Martinez, head of the audiovisual and multimedia department
Adriana Todó assisted by Verónica Zerpa, documentary research
Coordination in China: Jérémie Descamps

CCCB Film
Garden, Encounters between writing space and urban space, Ephemeral calligraphic, Documentary on the Weidoagan Taoist temple, Views of Chongqing, Destruction, The Nanxun Cockerel
Shooting and framing: José Antonio Soria
Production and editing: Cristina Brossa, Toni Curcó and José Antonio Soria

Commissioned films
Lose yourself In the exhibition
Find your way around the exhibition
Mamut Films: Lluís Bartra, Jordi Marqués and Sergi Mussull in liaison with Chung Chih-Chia
Illustration of the work of Dr Tan Li-Hai
Script and scientific expert in neurology: Felipe Martín
Computer graphics: Diego Bravo
Production: Lope Serrano
Shooting: Marc del Moral
Water: river of death, river of life
Editing: Núria Aidelman, Gonzalo de Lucas
Sound: with the collaboration of Veronica Font
Symphony of transformations
Production and editing: Luis Cerveró
Music: Blas Oliva, David Rodríguez
The Beijing of Lao She 老舍 (1899 - 1966)
Production and editing: Mariona Omedes
Motion graphics: Carles Mora

"5 x 18" Collection **(creative films)**
Project manager: Jia Zhangke
Production: Xstream Pictures
Producers: Jordi Balló, CCCB
Directors: Chen Tao (Xian)
      Han Jie (Shanghai)
      Jia Zhangke (Suzhou)
      Li Hongqi (Guangzhou)
      Peng Tao (Chongqing)

Model of Beijing
Multimedia design and production: Clémentine Eurieult, head of web and multimedia projects, Cité

Translation
Chinese–French: Liu Ning, Emmanuelle Péchenart, Wang Wenyan and Discobole Serveis Lingüístics
French–English John Crisp

EXHIBITION PRODUCTION
Scenography
Enric Masip, EMBA_Estudi Massip-Bosch Arquitectes with
Inma Rodríguez Sánchez and Natàlia Valldeperas Belmonte
Graphic design
Mònica Mestanza, Estudi mm ! avec Gaëlle Alemany
and Alícia Sánchez

Control room
Eric Michaux, service Production Ifa

Exhibit control room
Lucie Haguenauer, Ifa
Hélène Perrel, Laetitia Antonini, Jérôme Meneret,
Museum of French Monuments

Exhibition materials
Construction: Pyrrhus Conception
Printing: Créations du Val-d'Oise (CVO)
Audiovisual: Cinéparts

Communication, Cité de l'architecture & du patrimoine
Jean-Marie Guinebert, Director of Communication
and Partnerships
Guillaume Lebigre, graphic designer
Agostina Pinon, press relations
Valérie Samuel and Arnaud Pain, press relations, Opus 64

**Development and sponsorship, Cité de l'architecture
& du patrimoine**
Guillaume de la Broïse, Director of Development

The exhibition benefited from a partnership with the firms
Alcan composites and ThyssenKrupp Cadillac Plastic

CATALOGUE PRODUCTION
A joint publication by Cité de l'architecture et du patrimoine,
Paris, Barcelona Centre for Contemporary Culture, Actar
publications, Barcelona/New York

Editor
Frédéric Edelmann

Scientific adviser
Françoise Ged, head of the Observatory
of the Architecture of Contemporary China

Editorial coordination
Yves Kirchner

Iconography
Chung Chih-Chia, Lucie Haguenauer-Caceres
and Amala Marx, Ifa

Contributors
Jordi Balló, Catherine Bourzat, Dora Chesnes,
Chiu Che Bing, Patrick Doan, Lily Eclimont,
Frédéric Edelmann, Danièle Elisseeff, Patrice Fava,
Christophe Gaudier, Pierre Haski, Geneviève Imbot-Bichet,
Yves Kirchner, Arnaud Laffage, Liu Yanjun, Amélie Manon,
Brice Pedroletti, Jean-Louis Rocca, Ruan Yisan,
Delphine Spicq, Wang Jun

Cartography
Serge Barto

Actar Publications www.actar.com
Ramon Prat, Director
Anna Tetas, Editorial Coordinator

Design
Ulises Chamorro
Reinhard Steger

Translation
John Crisp

Digital image processing
Oriol Rigat
Carmen Galán

Printing
Ingoprint SL

Distribution
Actar-D
Roca i Batlle 2
08023 Barcelona
Spain
Tel: +34 93 417 49 93
Fax: +34 93 418 67 07
office@actar-d.com
www.actar-d.com

Actar-D USA
158 Lafayette Street, 5th Fl.
New York
NY 10013
Tel: 212-966-2207
Fax: 212-966-2214
officeusa@actar-d.com
www.actar-d.com

ISBN: 978-84-96954-49-6
DL: B-30158-08

*The exhibition and catalogue received documentary
resources and contributions from the following people and
institutions*

Lenders
Association La Mémoire de la Chine – les amis de François
Dautresme/ Collection Dautresme
Private collections: François Pourcelet, Qiao Bianyun and
Patrick Doan; Frédéric Edelmann; Alain Jullien;
Jérémie Descamps; Patrice Fava
Conservatoire national des arts et métiers, Deutsches
Architekturmuseum, Fonds national d'art contemporain,
Institut des hautes études chinoises-Collège de France,
Musée Cernuschi, Musée national des arts asiatiques-
Guimet, musée d'Art et d'Histoire de Saint-Denis
In China: School of Architecture/University of Tianjin, Beijing
Municipal Institute of City Planning and Design (BICP), Soho
China, Studio Pei-Zhu, Dongnan University in Nankin, Tongji
University in Shanghai

Institutional photograph sources
Archives Mission 21: Basel Mission; Bibliothèque nationale de France; British Library; École française d'Extrême Orient; Fondren Library / Rice University, Houston; Harvard College Library, Cambridge; The Library of Congress, Washington DC; Musée départemental Albert Kahn; Musée national des arts asiatiques-Guimet; Musée national du Palais, Taipei; Réunion des musées nationaux; Yale Divinity School Library
In China: Suzhou municipal local annals compilation committee (Xu Gangyi), China remote Sensing Satellite Ground Station/ Academy of Sciences, Tianjin cat University Publishing House, Suzhou-Wenwuju City Bureau of Cultural Heritage

Chinese photographers
Da Shi, Geng Yunsheng, Hu Jie, Hu Yang, Jiang Zhenqing, Jin Yongquan, Liang Longxing, Lily Yang, Li Haibing, Li Lang, Li Zhensheng, Lü Guangwei, Luo Yongjin, Ren Xihai, Shao Yinong & Mu Chen, Tang Jianren, Tang Haowu, Wang Fan, Wang Jingsong, Wang Minxi, Wang Shilong, Wang Tianlong, Wang Wenlan, Wang Xiangrong, Wei Lai, Wei Dezhong, Wen Min, Weng Naiqiang, Xiao Zhuang, Xing Danwen, Xu Yong, Yan Changjiang, Yu Haibo, Yu Kongjian, Zhang Xinmin, Zhou Ming, Zhou Zhenhua, Zhu Xianmin

Other photograph sources
AREP (Didier Boy de la Tour, ImagineChina, Tristan Chapuis), Ifa's Observatory of Architecture in Contemporary China, Zhong Hoi-Yi (Vu agency), Rue des Archives, L'Illustration, AKG Images, Sipa Press, Corbis, Eyedea Presse, Artedia
Private collections: Paul Bady, Caroline Bodolec, Solange Brand, Aurélien Chen, Chiu Che Bing, Patrick Chavannes, Dominique Delaunay, Sandrine Aucante, Françoise Descamps, Bruno Fayolle-Lussac, Foster and Partners, Jim Gourley, Arnaud Laffage, Dominique Lelong, Alain Marinos, Laïla Nady, Benny Shadmy, Jose-Antonio Soria, Thinking Hands, Ruan Yisan, Caroline Venencie, Wang Hao, Wang Qiheng

Audiovisual sources
Album Archivo Fotográfico, Barcelona; AP Archive, London; French film archives, Bois-d'Arcy; British Film Institute, London; British Movietonews Ltd., Denham; CNRS Images, Meudon; Discovery Channel, Chicago; E.D. Distribution, Paris; eFootage Llc, Pasadena; Footage Farm Limited, London; Framepool Stock Footage, Munich; Gaia Films, Madrid; Gaumont Pathé Archives, Saint-Ouen; Global Image Works, Haworth; Harvard Yenching Library, Cambridge; ITN Source/Reuters, Paris; Marc Riboud; MrFootage Limited, Bristol; Musée départemental Albert-Kahn, Boulogne-Billancourt; RAI Trade, Rome; Taschen España, Madrid; The Library of Congress, Washington DC
In China: China Film Archive in Beijing; Liu Zenchen; Olivier Meys & Zhang Yaxuan; Yan Yu; Yifan Li

Frédéric Edelmann, la Cité de l'architecture & du patrimoine, the Barcelona Centre for Contemporary Culture and the Observatory of Architecture in Contemporary China would particularly like to thank the following

For their generous assistance with the exhibition:
The Herzog and de Meuron and
OMA (Rem Koolhas) architectural practices

For having facilitated access to works and documents:
Germany: Christina Gräwe; USA: Paul Rascoe, Richard Smith; Spain: Filmoteca de Catalunya;
France: Samanta Deruvo, Gilles Baud-Berthier, Gilles Beguin, Marianne Bujard, Jean-Paul Desroches, Marie-Pierre Duhamel-Muller, Luca Gabbiani, François Pourcelet, Delphine Spicq, Victoire Surio; United Kingdom: Susan Whitfield;
Japan: Kazuko Natsume; Taiwan: National Palace Museum (Taipei), Hsin-Yin Shih.

In China:
Chongqing: Chunlan and Liu Yanjun; Nanjing: Dong Wei, Chen Wei; Beijing: National Bureau of Cultural Heritage, Beijing Urban Planning Commission, Du Liqun, China Institute of Cultural Heritage, Beijing Institute of Urban Planning, Fu Hongxing, Fu Shuang, Li Na, Li Xiang, Liu Dong, Liu Xin, Lu Zhou, Olivier Meys & Zhang Yaxuan, Ministry of Construction, Shi Weiliang, SOHO China, Wang Jinghui, Zhang Lan, Zou Huan, Zhu Pei; Shanghai: Lu Wei, Ruan Yisan, Shao Yong, Zhou Jian; Suzhou: Chen Rong, Ruan Yongsan, Wang Hao, Yang Zhenpin; Shenzhen: Yao Zhiyan, Lily Yang; Tianjin: Wang Qiheng, Zhang Chunyan, Wu Cong

For their advice and presence:
Association Shadows, Marine Buissonière, Chiu Che Bing, Augustin Cornet, Catherine Despeux, Vera Dorofeeva-Lichtmann, Marc González, Romain Graziani, Jie Jun, Arnauld Laffage, Nathalie Monnet, Thinking Hands, Isabelle Thireau, Sophie Labrousse, Thomas Sauvin